A HISTORY OF
ANCIENT GREECE
IN FIFTY LIVES

A HISTORY
OF ANCIENT
GREECE IN
FIFTY LIVES

David Stuttard

78 illustrations, 48 in color

 Thames & Hudson

To my wife, Emily Jane

Note: All dates are BC unless otherwise stated.
All translations are by the author.

Frontispiece: The playwright and politician Sophocles,
his manuscripts at his feet, is shown as the epitome of
the intellectual Greek in this Roman copy of a fourth-
century Greek bronze.

A History of Ancient Greece in Fifty Lives © 2014
Thames & Hudson Ltd, London

Designed by Kate Slotover

David Stuttard has asserted his moral right to be
identified as the author of this work

First published in 2014 in hardcover in the United States
of America by Thames & Hudson Inc., 500 Fifth Avenue,
New York, New York 10110

thamesandhudsonusa.com

Library of Congress Catalog Card Number 2014932759

ISBN 978-0-500-25205-5

Printed and bound in China by Everbest Printing Co. Ltd

Contents

Introduction

History and Identity in the Ancient Greek World

What we now call 'the ancient Greek world' embraced three continents and many generations. At its greatest extent, it stretched from modern Spain in the west to India in the east, encompassing most of the countries between. Even after the rise of Rome, no one man or city ruled these lands in their entirety, though there were some who tried. Rather, what gave this sprawling, disparate Greek world its peculiar sense of identity was its shared language, through which its peoples could express their common beliefs and values.

Many of these values were encapsulated in two early works of literature, the *Iliad* and *Odyssey*, epic poems which imagined all Greece united in the face of a common foe as they never were in reality. Yet even in these poems tensions threatened to disrupt Greek unity as egocentric heroes vied 'always to be best'. Although their scenario was largely fictional, their characterization reflected reality: ancient Greek history, too, was dominated by powerful personalities, some striving for their own or their city's glory, others to push back the boundaries of knowledge and their understanding of the world, still others to record ideas which (in the words of the historian **Thucydides**) would be 'a possession for eternity'.

How individual Greeks lived their lives reveals much about their wider history and society. In this book we shall consider fifty such lives, encompassing over 600 years from a time just after the Greek alphabet was first adopted to the assimilation of the Greek world by the Roman empire. The chosen lives not only reflect the diversity of the Greek experience but are among some of the most influential in early western history. From rulers and generals like **Pericles** and **Alexander III** to philosophers like **Empedocles** and **Plato**, writers like **Herodotus** and **Sophocles**, artists like **Apelles** and scientists like **Archimedes**, many shaped the way in which later generations viewed the world and laid the foundations for the societies in which many of us live today.

Yet all were products of their times. The world of Archimedes was almost as alien to that of **Pythagoras** as it is to our own; political solutions posited by **Cleisthenes** could not have worked for **Ptolemy I**; and whereas **Leonidas** feared an existential threat to Greece from Persia, **Philopoemen** foresaw that it would come from Rome. Only by setting the lives of such people within the context of their age and society can we fully understand them or appreciate their impact on the world. So, rather than being simply a collection of fifty stand-alone biographies, this book seeks to show how those lives were woven into the texture of Greek history, and in turn to offer a new look at the history of Greece.

In ancient sources much of what passes for biographical truth is invention, spun to compensate for ignorance or elaborated for effect, like the lovelorn suicide of **Sappho**, Empedocles' diverse and transcendental deaths or Archimedes' casual murder as he solved a mathematical conundrum. Yet such inventions are not worthless. Blatant falsehoods can be revealing: their Greek authors expected Greek readers (at least partially) to believe them, otherwise they would never have recorded them. Often such mythologizing reveals hidden, wider truths and casts valuable light on otherwise forgotten corners of the ancient Greek experience. So, while noting their unreliability, this book unashamedly includes anecdotes and episodes of dubious provenance. Besides, many of them are highly entertaining.

Indeed, the reliability of almost all ancient literary sources is to some degree questionable. Whereas archaeological artefacts can be dated, collated and scientifically analysed to produce more or less objective evidence (albeit coloured by our own interpretation), written sources are intrinsically subjective, while the accident of their survival can sometimes make it doubly difficult to judge their real importance. That the histories of Herodotus and Thucydides (like the *Iliad* and *Odyssey*) were prized by subsequent generations, influencing their views of the past, does not guarantee their accuracy. Many other works now exist only in tantalizing fragments, devoid of their original context, making it even harder to assess their reliability. Often these appear as quotations in the works of later historians and commentators, whose judgement (and truthfulness) must be open to question. Even the evidence of inscriptions cannot be taken at face value. 'Spin' is not a modern phenomenon: a memorial may be propagandist, while private letters (whether originals preserved in the sands of Egypt or documents carefully hoarded and transmitted but ultimately of doubtful origin, such as the letters of Plato) reveal only such versions of personal truths as their authors wished known.

A Greek archer and hoplite (shown heroically, if inauthentically, nude) face a Persian horseman dressed in trousers (which Greeks considered a sign of barbarism), on a late fifth-century amphora.

A second- or third-century AD mosaic from Rome of Orestes and Iphigenia, children of the legendary Agamemnon, demonstrates the all-pervading influence of Greek mythology.

At the same time, it must always be remembered that Greek literature in the main tells only half of any possible story – the vast majority of it was written by men. Because of this, and because of the androcentric nature of Greek society as a whole, ancient Greek historiography and biography focused largely on male lives. Drawing heavily on literary sources, our selection of biographies cannot but reflect this. Indeed, of the two women featured (Sappho and **Aspasia**, though many other women's lives are woven through this history), our evidence is so biased that, stripped of invention or slander, what remains is like a sculptor's broken mould once the bronze is removed. We can trace the statue's corresponding outlines, but the solid form eludes us. To an extent this is true of every biography in the book.

In order to try and trace the history and illustrate the wide diversity of the culture of ancient Greece, the lives in this book are arranged roughly by generations. Each chapter begins with a 'headline' life, which includes most of the historical background needed to appreciate the context of the other, 'subsidiary' biographies. Read together, these headline lives provide an outline of Greek history from around 700 to 100 (a continuity reinforced in the timeline, where, as in the text, all dates are BC unless otherwise stated), with the other lives helping to flesh out details. Equally, lives can be read on their own and in no specific order. Inevitably, some events recur in several biographies (for example, the battles of Marathon or Ipsus), but whenever possible the book tries to avoid repetition, aiming rather to show why an event mattered to the subject of the life in question.

By focusing on these 'great lives' it becomes clear how interconnected many of them were. Take **Polycrates**, the sixth-century ruler of the east Aegean island of Samos, where he built a vast temple to Hera. Polycrates' physician Democedes (a bit-player in our wider narrative) married the daughter of **Milo**, an Olympic boxer from Croton in south Italy; while, through his friend the poet Anacreon, Polycrates was connected to Xanthippus, the father of Athens' statesman Pericles, who was the guardian of **Alcibiades**, whose fleet was defeated by the Spartan **Lysander**, who (at the beginning of the fourth century) was worshipped as a god on Samos, where the festival of Hera (celebrated at Polycrates' now venerable temple) was renamed the Lysandreia. Like it or not, the ancient world was shaped by its elite, and many such nexuses appear throughout the book.

The fifty lives are bookended by short chapters touching on periods not covered in the biographies. They also consider two important themes which are central to this book: the development of historiography and biography. The ancient Greeks pioneered both, and it would be only a slight exaggeration to suggest that a developing awareness of each contributed to the way in which many Greeks led their lives and shaped their history.

Of course, the subjects of this book did not live in a vacuum. Jostling them in streets and markets from Byzantium to Syracuse and Alexandria were countless voiceless others who fought as heavily armoured *hoplites* in the battle line, gave birth to children, haggled at quaysides, hauled in their dripping nets, grew flowers for garlands or laboured in mines, factories and fields to help shape the ancient Greek world. If we cannot trace the lives of each, we still should not forget them, for without them nothing that was could possibly have been.

Chapter 1

Of Gods
and Heroes

'Goddess, sing…': this marble figurine of a harp player from the Cyclades dates from around 2700, two millennia before the Homeric epics were first committed to writing.

At the battle of Marathon in 490, blood-spattered in the crush of shields and spears, Epizelus, an Athenian hoplite, experienced a miracle. He saw a towering figure, long-bearded, heavy-armoured, bearing down, about to strike. At the last moment the enemy's blade swerved and Epizelus was spared. But he was struck profoundly blind. For the giant he had seen was a demigod (or so he later claimed), and no one can look with impunity on the divine.

This glimpse into an otherwise unremembered life was recorded by **Herodotus,** whose account of the wars between Greece and Persia are considered to be the first works of western historiography. Writing in the middle of the fifth century, Herodotus, originally from Halicarnassus on the west coast of Asia Minor (modern Turkey), travelled widely, interviewing everyone from Egyptian priests and Ionian explorers to Athenian war veterans like Epizelus, as he conducted research (*historie*) into the origins and outcomes of Persia's invasions of mainland Greece in 490 and 480/79.

Herodotus' world view was rooted firmly in the belief systems of his age. Like Epizelus, he believed in divine intervention. It was not until the end of the fifth century that the Athenian **Thucydides**, in his rationalizing account of the Peloponnesian War, wrote a history that tried to make sense of a past and present stripped of the supernatural and played out on a purely human level. In doing so Thucydides was aware of attempting something revolutionary; as he commented, 'Most people accept traditions as they hear them, including those of their own country, without employing any critical evaluation.'

For the early, pre-literate societies of Greece two centuries before Epizelus' birth, those traditions, even if unexamined, provided rare links with what we (but not they) would call their history. Except when the past impinged on the present (in cases such as inheritance or landownership), there was little reason why people *should* employ critical evaluation or be overly concerned about the accuracy of stories remembered from preceding generations, especially when embroidery or fantasy might make an oral narrative more entertaining. Yet lack of verifiable material did not stop the Greeks from forming traditions of their past which stretched surprisingly far back into time, and based on which they built their cultural identity.

Today it is generally agreed that most people's sense of their own family history encompasses at most three (or possibly four) generations, based on stories heard from grandparents, whose details become more blurred the further they are in the past. For ancient Greeks, oral storytelling meant that these blurred memories extended for many centuries. So, by the time of Epizelus' birth in the second half of the sixth century, people were familiar with stories set in societies six centuries earlier, evidence for which can now be discovered through archaeology. The earliest such stories, populated by characters such as Heracles, Theseus and Jason, may be imagined as occurring in around the thirteenth century, while the Trojan War, which both Herodotus and Thucydides regarded as historical, was traditionally dated to the early twelfth century. The third-century polymath Eratosthenes placed the sack of Troy in 1184.

Oral poetry told how aristocratic Greek societies, commanded by King Agamemnon of Mycenae, united to retrieve the flighty Helen, who had abandoned her Spartan home for the lure of life with Troy's prince Paris. Today we recognize that much of the story belongs to mythology, but as recently as the 1870s AD the German archaeologist Heinrich Schliemann was driven to excavate at Troy and Mycenae by his passion to prove the legends true and his belief that the characters of epic once existed. Famously he attributed ownership of a cache of jewelry found at Troy to Helen herself and, unearthing a rich burial at Mycenae, Schliemann telegrammed the Greek king to report: 'I have gazed on the face of Agamemnon.'

In the late nineteenth and early twentieth centuries AD, other excavations at Late Bronze Age (c. 1600–1100) sites uncovered clay tablets containing records written in a proto-Greek language, in a script now called Linear B. Not deciphered until the 1950s AD, these tablets revealed a highly structured society obsessed with record-keeping and terrified of attacks by 'peoples from the sea'. Physical evidence showed the sudden collapse of Mycenaean civilization in the twelfth century, when many palaces were destroyed by fire. The identity of the Sea Peoples, and whether they were responsible, is still hotly debated. While ancient Greeks wrote of the Dorian Invasions (influxes of migrant warriors, ancestors of the Spartans and their kin), archaeology offers no evidence for new cultures arriving on mainland Greece. Instead, the social disintegration of the so-called

Dark Ages was gradually replaced by aristocratic and largely agricultural societies, which still predominated in the sixth century.

With the collapse of Mycenaean Greece, writing and record-keeping disappeared, but in the middle of the eighth century an alphabet, based on that of the Phoenicians, was adopted. Its impact was revolutionary. Now writing was used not just for record-keeping but to preserve and refine the oral poetry which enshrined the heightened memories of Greece's past. Soon literature was helping to fill in spaces left by forgotten ancestors and to forge a Greek identity, as the first epic poetry – attributed to Homer and Hesiod – attests.

Hesiod and Homer: The Birth of the Gods and the Ages of Man

Like most peoples, the Greeks sought an explanation for the present in the past. One commonly held view of their most distant origins appears in *Theogony* (Birth of the Gods), a late eighth-century 'didactic epic', just over a thousand lines long, attributed to the poet Hesiod. Nothing is known about the author other than from the texts themselves, but in *Works and Days*, an exploration of the rituals of civilization through the medium of agriculture, which also bears his name, he adopts the role of a Boeotian peasant farmer. As we shall discover, ancient 'biographers' regularly took such internal literary evidence at face value, and thanks to them Hesiod's lowly background is still commonly accepted. In fact, Hesiod was probably a highly sophisticated writer working in a near-eastern tradition of 'wisdom poetry' to produce in literary form verses recited by itinerant bards to educate, inform and entertain elite aristocratic audiences.

After describing the creation of the world from Chaos, *Theogony* traces the birth and generations of the gods, presenting mythical prehistory as a cycle of struggles, as sons succeed fathers in their lust for power, and first Ouranos, then Kronos and (lastly) Zeus seizes the Olympian throne. Later, *Theogony* describes how, when the earth was inhabited by outlandish beasts, barbaric giants tried to overthrow the civilized order of the gods. Ostensibly rooted more firmly in reality, *Works and Days* also imagines a perilous world, where gods and spirits lurk at every turn, and inadvertently leaving a ladle in a mixing bowl or wading across a river with unwashed hands can provoke divine punishment.

In a pre-scientific age (without the vocabulary or correlating conscious objectivity to express abstract thought) such stories provided ways of making sense of the world, but to what extent they were taken literally must have varied widely. Beginning *Theogony* with a warning not to believe everything he writes, Hesiod claims that, while shepherding his flocks on Mount Helicon, he met the Muses, who breathed into him 'a sacred voice with which to celebrate the past and

A late third- or second-century marble stela, possibly Alexandrian, shows the 'Apotheosis of Homer': worshippers approach the deified poet, seated bottom left; above, Zeus reclines with his thunderbolt, surrounded by the Muses.

future', and told him that they possess 'knowledge to invent convincing lies, and the skill, when so desired, to tell the truth'. Readers should suspend their disbelief at their own peril.

Works and Days presents history as a sequence of 'Ages', tracing a downward progression from a Golden Age free from disease, when the earth produced crops with no need for farming, through a squabbling Silver Age, a brutal Age of Bronze, a fourth, Heroic Age, to the present Age of Iron, when 'men work and weep continuously by day, while by night they wither and die'. Although for Hesiod the Heroic Age is distinct from his own, for many other writers stories that we consider myth, like those concerning the Trojan War, reflected real history, whose repercussions were still being felt in the fifth century and beyond. This was thanks in no small part to two epic poems, the *Iliad* and the *Odyssey*, thought by Greeks to be the work of one man, Homer.

More than any other literature, Homer's epics defined what it was to be Greek. Originally composed orally, they were written soon after the invention of the alphabet at the dawn of a great diaspora, when many Greek cities founded colonies and trading posts as far away as Byzantium by the Black Sea (*c.* 657), Naucratis in Egypt (late seventh century), Cyrene in Libya (*c.* 630) and Massalia (Marseilles) in France (*c.* 600). As the real world fragmented, the epics preserved in imagination a time when Greeks were briefly united in one common enterprise.

Like the poems of Hesiod, Homer's world is populated by both men and gods, and the Trojan War unfolds simultaneously in the human realm and the divine; sometimes the two overlap, as gods sabotage or aid mortal endeavour. Both epics show a deep concern for the lives of their central characters, and reveal much about how contemporary Greeks viewed their place within society and history and how they felt that stories (including their own) might be manipulated.

Homer and the Beginnings of Biography

The *Iliad*'s opening line ('Goddess, sing of the anger of Peleus' son, Achilles') proclaims that, like Hesiod's *Theogony*, this is a work of inspiration, not historical research. Yet, as the reader progresses, it becomes apparent that it is also a well-observed study in human psychology, a slice from the fictive biography of its hero, Achilles. Achilles, obsessed with how his life will be regarded both by contemporaries and by subsequent generations, views himself as part of a heroic continuum. Skulking with his companion Patroclus in his tent, nursing his wrath against the overbearing Agamemnon, Achilles consoles (or torments) himself by playing his lyre while singing, like an oral poet, about 'the famous deeds of men'.

Scenes from the Trojan War appear on the late first-century BC–early first-century AD Capitoline Iliac Tablet: the Greek fleet lies before the walls of Troy (left), while warriors fight from chariots, on foot, and by the ships (right).

To Achilles, as to many Classical and later Greek aristocrats, reputation is everything. His mother, the sea-nymph Thetis, has informed him that he can choose between two fates: either to enjoy a long but unremembered life, or to die young and have 'immortal fame'. Choosing the latter, Achilles becomes the inspiration for many an ambitious young man in centuries to come. As the Greek polymath Plutarch, writing in the late first or early second century AD, records, when **Alexander III** visited Troy, he was asked if he wanted to see the lyre belonging to Troy's prince Paris (himself also known as Alexander). Declaring that all Paris had ever sung were 'wanton ballads designed to seduce women's hearts', Alexander replied he would rather see Achilles' lyre 'to which he sang the famous deeds of men'.

The *Odyssey*'s hero, Odysseus, reveals another way in which a Greek might inhabit his own history. A man of 'many wiles', he is the antithesis of the early-dead Achilles. His greatest wish is to survive, return home and grow prosperously

Gold funerary mask from *c.* 1500, found at Mycenae. When the archaeologist Schliemann lifted a similar
mask, he claimed the face beneath remained briefly intact, prompting his famous telegram:
'I have gazed on the face of Agamemnon'.

old with his family. Yet Odysseus too has an eye for his reputation. Already, on his protracted voyage, his fame is sufficiently widespread that, arriving on the far-off mythical island of Scherie, he can hear a bard sing of his exploits at Troy. But interestingly each time Odysseus himself is invited to recount the story of his travels, he weaves a different narrative, sometimes a variation on the truth, sometimes a complete fabrication (he once pretends to be a Cretan prince), always carefully calculated to enthral his immediate audience.

Although Odysseus is a fictional character, his cavalier attitude to 'fact' carries over to many real-life Classical biographers, for biography had its roots in *encomium* (writings or speeches in praise of the dead). The earliest surviving biographies (written in the fourth century by Isocrates and **Xenophon**) both fall firmly into this camp, while Xenophon's pseudo-biographical *Education of Cyrus* contains more fantasy than fact. All strive to show their subjects in as glowing a light as possible, as do the largely fictional accounts of episodes from the life of **Socrates** which appeared shortly after his execution.

Although some form of biography was written from the fifth century onwards, most of what survives dates from imperial Roman times, when the prolific Plutarch used the genre to strengthen ties between the two cultures by comparing famous Greeks and Romans, both historical and mythological. To Plutarch (growing up when the Gospel writers were exploring the life of Christ) biographies were a vehicle for examining philosophical truths, their subjects chosen as the embodiments of vice or virtue, with episodes selected or anecdotes slanted to illustrate a moral point.

In the third century AD Diogenes Laertius used his *Lives of the Philosophers* more as pegs for fanciful anecdote (and excuses to publish his own very average poetry) than as rigorous explorations of lives within historical, social or philosophical contexts. Similarly the tenth-century AD Byzantine encyclopaedia, *Suda*, whose authors had access to a wider range of sources than we do, indiscriminately draws on anecdote, accepting even the most unlikely details if they furnish a good story. Sometimes (as with the lives of **Sappho** or **Empedocles**) the fictitious elements are relatively obvious, but sometimes it is harder to discover the truth (what was **Aspasia's** real status in Periclean Athens?). Even if they did not invoke the Muses for their inspiration, ancient biographers were no less creative than epic poets. We ignore this at our peril.

The Logographoi *and the Stirrings of Historiography*
Ancient Greeks loved embroidering remembered truths. The story of the Trojan War may have evolved out of a series of real but relatively minor conflicts (which

are attested by archaeology) into an epic ten-year siege (which is not), its details incorporating distant memories of social structures and physical objects as well as some real people. At the same time a particular myth or historical episode might exist in a multiplicity of often contradictory versions which flourished simultaneously across a geographically separated world. As long as all that people wanted was to be entertained, this was not a problem; but when it came to solid information and the development of what we would recognize as history, a fresh approach was needed.

One use to which the Greek alphabet was put was record-keeping and the publication of documents, including legislation – the laws of the political reformer Solon (a shadowy but essentially historical figure from the late seventh and early sixth century) were written on large wooden boards fixed to a revolving axis and exhibited in Athens' *Prytaneum* (town hall). Eventually, probably in the fifth century, these developed into full-scale archives. The extent to which such documents were used by classical historians is questionable, but in the sixth century, reflecting a wider scientific awareness, antiquarians (or *logographoi*) began to research and write prose chronicles ranging from collections of genealogies to the annals of cities. Although most were little more than dry records, they revolutionized the study of the past and man's relationship with it. Sadly only fragments survive today.

The most innovative logographos was Hecataeus of Miletus. Born around 550, he aimed to rationalize diverse versions of mythology and recent history to produce a scholarly, orderly compendium, declaring in his *Genealogies*, 'I write what I believe to be true, since I consider the tales of the Greeks to be both innumerable and stupid.' He may have been inspired by a research trip to Egypt, where (writes Herodotus) the priests at Thebes revealed evidence of a sacerdotal line stretching back 345 generations. Before his visit, Hecataeus believed that mankind had been created only sixteen generations earlier. Thanks to the Egyptians, he realized that his (and the Greeks') entire conception of the past was in need of major revision.

Even in Hecataeus' *Genealogies* the gods played a decisive role, while the 'scientifically informed' account of the creation of the world by his contemporary Acousilaus of Argos was little more than a prose version of Hesiod's *Theogony* – although Acousilaus claimed that his study of ancient bronze tablets, unearthed on his own estate, made it more accurate. Acousilaus was not the first to recognize the value of archaeological evidence. In the sixth century this fledgling discipline was already being used to connect the present to the past, though not always for scientific reasons. In 560 Sparta received an oracle that it would not defeat neighbouring Tegea until it discovered and reburied the bones of the hero Orestes. Fortunately, a Spartan visitor to Tegea learned of the recent unearthing and reburial of an ancient coffin containing a skeleton over 10 feet (3 m) long. Surely such heroic proportions could belong only to Orestes. The bones were re-excavated and repatriated, and Tegea was defeated. Today we consign Orestes to mythology, but lest we too readily accuse the Spartans of naivety, we should recall how relatively recently Schliemann claimed to have gazed on the face of Orestes' father Agamemnon at Mycenae.

The process of re-evaluating history led the Greeks in different and sometimes opposite directions. While men like Hecataeus (and, in a sense, the Spartan archaeologists at Tegea) tried to strip away centuries' worth of accreted invention to discover truths about essentially mythological events, others, frustrated by a lack of evidence, happily invented details to produce a more rounded, fuller, but in the end much falser view of their own history.

Nonetheless, from the sixth century onwards enough historical, archaeological and epigraphic evidence survives to let us reconstruct a life like that of **Peisistratus**, the subject of the first biography in this book. In fact, what makes Peisistratus especially interesting within the context of Greek history is that he was himself part of the process of reassessing the past, consciously and even cynically manipulating it to suit his political ends and those of his city, Athens. But as we consider his life, we should remember that in outlook he was so much closer to the world of Homer than to our own. To Peisistratus, as to the legendary Achilles (and blind Epizelus, proud of the encounter with a demigod which made him worthy of his name – it means 'Enviable'), there was still a real imperative to lead a life of 'undying fame', and so ensure that his achievements would become part of that greater continuum, 'the famous deeds of men'.

Chapter 2

The Age
of Tyrants

PEISISTRATUS (?C. 605–528)
Tyrannos of Athens

*Peisistratus was so convincing an actor that, by feigning virtues which were
alien to him, he won more acclaim than those who actually possessed them.*

Plutarch, *Life of Solon*, 29

Mid-sixth-century Athenian politics were dominated by three powerful families:
the Boutads, the Alcmaeonids and the Peisistratids. These Peisistratids were
wealthy landowners whose estates in eastern Attica stretched from the coastal
sanctuary of Brauron north to the plain of Marathon, where the hard sand of
the gently sloping beach offered ideal conditions for those most aristocratic of
pursuits, riding and racing chariots. The family felt entitled to its privilege and
wealth – it claimed to trace its roots back over five centuries not only to Codrus,
the last great king of Athens, but to Nestor, king of Pylos, a major character in the
stories of the Trojan War. The power of history (or myth) made heady propaganda.

But propaganda could work in many ways. Stories circulated of how one
Peisistratid, Hippocrates, received a troubling omen from the gods at the
Olympic Games of 608 or 604. While he was sacrificing, the cauldrons boiled and
overflowed though no fire was lit beneath them, a sign which rivals took to show
that Hippocrates must never have a son, and Hippocrates as readily ignored. Soon
afterwards his wife bore Peisistratus.

Little is known of Peisistratus' early life. Dazzlingly handsome, he was the
cousin (and perhaps lover) of the lawmaker Solon, and it was Solon who first
identified Peisistratus' lust for power. In the 560s Peisistratus led Athens to war
against neighbouring Megara. Then, his popularity swollen by victory, in 561 he
made a bid to become his city's *tyrannos* (or ruler). In doing so he came into

Aristocracies and Tyrannies

Up to the end of the sixth century all Greek city-states were ruled by powerful families. In the 'Heroic Age' of Homer and Hesiod power lay in the hands of kings (*basileis*); later, such autocrats were known as *tyrannoi*. The nature of their rule depended largely upon the character of each basileus or tyrannos, but probably necessitated cooperation with some kind of legislative council of elders. 'Tyrant' today has pejorative connotations, but many basileis and tyrannoi were comparatively beneficent and fair. Towards the beginning of Hesiod's *Theogony*, written for a predominantly aristocratic audience, we read how a good basileus governs: 'The People all look to him. His judgments are honest and lawful. With one convincing argument he puts an end to bitter quarrels by speaking gently with soft words.' Problems arose when opposing aristocratic families not infrequently tried to seize supreme power themselves. Those whose support base was widest naturally proved most successful. However, in their bid to woo the People, they surrendered more and more of their powers to an increasingly strong popular Assembly, which in turn contributed to the birth of democracy.

direct conflict with the leaders of the other two Athenian dynasties, the Boutad, Lycurgus, and the Alcmaeonid, Megacles. The way in which he overcame their opposition is revealing.

Deliberately wounding both himself and his mules, Peisistratus drove his blood-soaked chariot into the centre of Athens, where he gasped out the (false) news that he had narrowly escaped assassination at the hands of his political enemies. Solon accused Peisistratus of dissembling, but the Athenians were outraged. They assigned him a bodyguard and escorted him to the Acropolis, the rocky plateau which had for centuries been the seat of power, as their ruler. Peisistratus had achieved his purpose, yet he seemed either loath or unable to impose his will by force. Even staunch democrats would later admit, albeit grudgingly, that his rule was fair, lawful and good. Not that this impressed his enemies. In a rare display of solidarity, Lycurgus and Megacles buried their mutual animosities and joined forces. In 556 they overthrew Peisistratus and drove him from Athens. But their coalition, always precarious, collapsed, and the next year Megacles secretly negotiated with Peisistratus to secure his homecoming.

To unite the families in alliance, Megacles offered Peisistratus his daughter in marriage. Peisistratus accepted, divorced his existing wife and, enlisting the aid of Phya, a tall and strikingly beautiful woman from his estates, he plotted his return. If his first bid for power had been dramatic, his second was positively theatrical. For, as Peisistratus drove into Athens in his chariot, his agents fanned through the city, proclaiming excitedly that Athene herself was escorting him home. In fact, it was Phya, dressed in full armour and radiating divine authority, riding beside him, a perfect casting for the goddess. Whether the Athenians believed the ruse or (like later historians) thought it an absurd piece of flummery, the result was the same. For the second time, Peisistratus was tyrannos.

Still he was not secure. Soon Megacles was spreading slanders that Peisistratus was forcing his new wife to perform unnatural sex-acts. When gleeful gossip turned into ugly threats Peisistratus once more fled the city. But he vowed he would be back. Although an exile, he commanded both respect and fear, and, calling in old favours, he worked to consolidate his power. Thebes, Argos and the island of Naxos offered mercenaries or money and in 546, with his sons **Hippias** and Hipparchus at his side, Peisistratus returned to Attica at the head of a great army. Landing at Marathon, they were soon marching towards Athens through Peisistratus' old estates. Caught curiously unawares, Megacles and his men swaggered out to meet them, blissfully underestimating the threat they faced. As Megacles enjoyed a shaded siesta near a sanctuary of Athene, Peisistratus gave the order to attack. Megacles' troops were routed. Peisistratus was back, and for the next eighteen years, until his death peacefully in bed in 528, he ruled Athens as its undisputed tyrannos. Later generations remembered it as a golden age.

Thanks to his disarming ways, public works and care to cultivate the People (in Greek, the *demos*), Peisistratus was hailed as kind, compassionate and forgiving, more like a private citizen than a tyrannos. In a *polis* (city-state) so recently divided, he had clearly

Athene, patron goddess of Peisistratus' city, is resplendent on a metal sheet, *c.* 530. Peisistratus dressed a girl as the goddess to escort him into Athens as he returned from exile.

learned by experience the benefits of ruling by majority consent. So he wooed the People through legislation, public works and bribery. Realizing the importance of maintaining Athens' food supply, he agreed to a member of a rival dynasty, Miltiades the Elder, becoming tyrannos of a new colony in the Chersonese in return for his policing the grain convoys from the Black Sea. At the same time, he installed his own son, Hegesistratus, on the opposite side of the Dardanelles as tyrannos of Sigeum to keep a watchful eye both on the sea lanes and on Miltiades.

Peisistratus boosted Attica's agricultural economy through generous loans and appointed a board of peripatetic judges to ensure that farmers could enjoy the same rights as urban Athenians. Meanwhile, to enhance city life and stimulate employment, he inaugurated an ambitious building programme: an aqueduct to feed the dusty Agora, a *propylaea* (gateway) for the Acropolis and a temple of Olympian Zeus near Athens' River Ilissus. His motives were not entirely altruistic – keeping the city dwellers productive and the farmers busy in their fields gave them less time to foment trouble, while the 10 per cent tax he levied on their profits increased Peisistratus' own wealth. Nonetheless, he took great pains to be seen to uphold the law, employing a brigade of Scythian archers as a proto-police force, and submitting to a charge of manslaughter. He would have been tried, had not his prosecutor backed down at the last moment. Yet it was Peisistratus' wider vision that most transformed his city and set it on a course for greatness. To help mould its future, he redefined Athens' past. Most Greeks still relied for their knowledge of the past on oral traditions and epic poetry, where fact soon became embroidered and reality subsumed in myth. To endorse their status, many patrician families claimed links with heroes of these legendary tales. Now Peisistratus set out to do the same for Athens.

This vase, signed by the painter Nicias and originally containing olive oil, was presented to the victor of a foot race in one of the first Panathenaic Games, founded in 556.

Greek Poleis

During the period covered in this book the polis – usually translated as 'city-state' – was at the heart of Greek life. Physically the polis comprised a discrete tract of agricultural land, normally with a single, urban centre, for example the territory of Attica with its capital Athens. More importantly, however, the polis was the collective embodiment of its citizens (*polites*) – in the case of Attica, the Athenians. At the urban heart of the polis were public spaces, such as temples, outside which citizens could gather to perform sacrifices to their patron gods for the good of the community, *agoras* or marketplaces, where they met to conduct commercial activity, and (in democratic poleis) open areas where citizens could discuss politics: matters central to the life of the polis. As time went on many poleis built other venues for large-scale civic events, such as theatres and stadiums.

At its height the Greek world consisted of more than 1,000 poleis, some with little more than a hundred citizens, a handful with tens of thousands. Many were the result of colonization, but even when a colony was set up far away it still kept close ties with the *metropolis* ('mother city') which had founded it. Because each polis had its own distinctive character, and often its own system of government, rivalry was common. At best this manifested itself in the Olympic and other panhellenic games; at worst in the wars which frequently raged between Greek cities.

The most celebrated epic poems were the *Iliad* and the *Odyssey*. Originating in the eastern Aegean, they were at first transmitted orally (in widely differing forms) throughout the Greek world. Realizing that to control their content was in a sense to control the Greeks' vision of their shared past, Peisistratus commissioned a written 'authorized version', the basis for the texts we possess today. In doing so he turned the project to Athens' advantage: where possible, lines were added to enhance the city's profile and her international *kudos* (glory).

Peisistratus elevated Athens' standing in other ways, too. Recently, three new international festivals had been established to rival the Olympic Games: Delphi's Pythian and Corinth's Isthmian Games (both dated to 582) and the Nemean Games (perhaps inaugurated in 573). In 556 Peisistratus added the Greater Panathenaic (All-Athenian) Games, held every four years and open to competitors from across the Greek-speaking world. They evolved out of a yearly festival which traced its origins to the legendary King Erechtheus and included sporting contests, sacrifices, a procession and the presentation of a robe to an

The Mysteries of Eleusis

Thirteen miles (21 km) northwest of Athens on the Bay of Salamis, Eleusis was home to one of the most profoundly spiritual cults in ancient Greece. Legend told that here Persephone, abducted to the Underworld by its god Hades, had been restored to her mother, the earth goddess Demeter, an event marked each September with a procession to Eleusis from Athens and the performance of the Greater Mysteries. Admission required a series of initiations (*mystes* means 'initiate'), but as the penalty for revealing their nature was death, our evidence is not unsurprisingly sparse. Rare sources (including Christian Fathers) suggest that worshippers had to be Greeks free from blood guilt and that the ceremony culminated in the unveiling of an ear of corn, which, cut down in the previous harvest, contained the seed of future life. Thus the Mysteries celebrated the cycles of nature and offered hope of life after death. Given that their focal deities were Demeter and Dionysus, gods of bread and wine, some see in them a tantalizing forerunner of the Christian Eucharist. The Eleusinian Mysteries attracted worshippers from across the Greek world and later from the Roman empire, when the rules for eligibility were occasionally spectacularly waived: the emperor Nero was initiated despite having killed his mother. The shrine was eventually closed by the Christian emperor Theodosius in AD 392 and desecrated by Alaric the Goth four years later.

ancient olive-wood statue (or *xoanon*) of Athene, said to have fallen from heaven, the embodiment of Athens' soul. Imbued with pomp and ceremony, the games would play an important part in city life, though they never attained the cachet of the other four, perhaps because they were so chauvinistic.

Meanwhile, Peisistratus expanded Athens' territories. At Eleusis, he brought under Athenian control the Sacred Mysteries while in Athens itself he inaugurated a new festival to Dionysus. For generations, village celebrations had involved choral dancing to songs commemorating the deeds of ancestral heroes. Recently a performer called Thespis, quitting the chorus to assume the role of one of the song's characters, had become the first recorded actor: western drama was born. Peisistratus (who had once cast the lovely Phya as Athene) well understood its potential. In 534 he instituted the City Dionysia, part arts festival, part religious ceremony, part civic competition, where increasingly sophisticated dramas played an important role not only in shaping Athenian self-image but in projecting it to the wider world.

Still bearing traces of its original paint, this sculpture of a triple-bodied deity with a tail of coiling snakes adorned the pediment of the mid-sixth-century temple of Athene built by Peisistratus on the Acropolis.

In foreign policy, too, Peisistratus took pains to ensure good relations. In exile he had forged close ties with Argos, Thessaly, Macedon and the Euboean city of Eretria, while ensuring that he still remained on good terms with their enemies. Not that his was a policy of passivity. He fully sanctioned Miltiades the Elder's annexation of the Chersonese, led Athens to war with Megara and, seeing the long-term benefit of expanding Athenian influence in the Aegean, not only installed his ally Lygdamis as proxy tyrannos on Naxos, but exerted his influence on the island of Delos.

Citing an oracular command, Peisistratus undertook to purify the island by disinterring remains from a centuries-old graveyard close to the sanctuary and reburying them on the far side of the island. As an undertaking it was relatively simple; but its implications were profound. Delos was one of a small number of sites revered throughout the Greek diaspora, equal only to Delphi and Olympia on the mainland. By declaring himself the man chosen by the gods to cleanse the island, Peisistratus proclaimed his status and staked Athens' claim as a key player on the panhellenic stage.

Peisistratus knew his audience well. Sail east from Delos and a ship would reach the glittering cities of Ionia, with which the Athenian tyrannos was already cementing ties. Here, on the coastal strip of Asia Minor, the Greek colonies had become immensely wealthy thanks to their trade with Persia and beyond. These riches excited the ambitions of another tyrannos, Polycrates of Samos. While Peisistratus was consolidating power in mainland Greece, Polycrates was raising a new empire of his own, but his was based on the sea.

POLYCRATES (?–522)
Tyrannos of Samos

As long as my song endures, Polycrates, you shall enjoy undying fame for your beauty.

Ibycus, encomium of Polycrates (*Oxyrhynchus Papyri*, 1790)

In 546, as **Peisistratus** was establishing himself as tyrannos of Athens for the third and final time, events were unfolding in the heartlands of Asia Minor whose shockwaves would threaten to engulf the Greek world. The year before, Croesus, king of Lydia, had been defeated in battle by Cyrus the Great, and his territories incorporated into the Persian empire. Among them were the Greek cities of Ionia.

Separated from the mainland by barely a mile (1.6 km) of sea, the islanders of Samos, with its mountainous heartland and fertile plains lush with vineyards, watched in trepidation. Yet the feared invasion failed to materialize. Instead, revolution came from within. Around 540, at an annual festival of Hera, the tyrannos Aiakes' three sons staged a coup. Their fraternal loyalties soon proved as tenuous as their filial devotion when the elder brother, Polycrates, killed one of his siblings, drove the other into exile and proclaimed himself tyrannos of Samos.

With the support of Lygdamis, Peisistratus' puppet on Naxos, Polycrates set about expanding his regional influence. His ultimate goal, so it was rumoured, was not only to create a maritime empire but to rule Ionia as well. To help achieve this Polycrates made an alliance with Egypt's pharaoh Amasis, thanks to whose generosity he built and maintained a hundred vermillion-painted warships, each manned by fifty oarsmen and a unit of archers, at an annual cost of more than 7 tons of silver. Intended by Amasis as a bulwark against Persia, Polycrates' ships were before long conducting raids on neighbouring Greek islands, and Polycrates soon annexed Lesbos. Then in 530, in a dramatic switch, Polycrates abandoned Amasis in favour of Persia's new Great King, Cambyses. Perhaps Polycrates, never one to refuse gold, had received a handsome bribe. Perhaps, too, this had helped him to transform his navy. For, numbered among his fleet which now sailed south to Egypt, there were forty state-of-the-art new warships, *triremes* (named from

Once the largest of all Greek temples, Polycrates' temple of Hera, erected in the mid-sixth century on the site of his coup against his father, proclaimed both his piety and his power.

An illustration from the German journal *Then and Now* (1832) of Herodotus' tale: to escape divine envy Polycrates threw a ring in the sea, but a fisherman found it in a fish's belly and returned it to him.

their three banks of oars) – sleek, fast vessels equipped with a lethal 'ram', which would soon transform the face of naval warfare.

Sadly, Polycrates' plans backfired. With his defection to Persia and Amasis' subsequent defeat, the flow of Egyptian cash dried up. His opponents saw their chance. Like Athens, Samos seethed with rival aristocratic families, many of whose members (including the philosopher **Pythagoras**) had either fled or been exiled. In 525 they sent ambassadors to enlist help from mainland Greece. Sparta dispatched a substantial army in her first overseas campaign, but despite such formidable allies and a siege of forty days the rebels failed to capture Samos, and the insurrection crumbled.

Just three years later, turbulence within the Persian empire cast a fresh shadow over the Greek world. As the Great King Cambyses lay dying in Ecbatana, far to the west one of his regional governors, the *satrap* Oroetes, seized his chance to settle an old score. Polycrates had slighted him. Now, claiming terror of assassination, he made the tyrannos an offer he could not refuse: in return for safe haven, Oroetes would give him untold wealth – enough to make him king of Greece. With a large delegation Polycrates journeyed to the satrap's court. But there his luck ran out. Brutally murdered, his body was nailed to a stake to rot under the harsh sun and driving rains of Anatolia.

Cambyses scarcely survived him. In the struggle for the throne his appointed successor (backed by the priestly caste, the Magi) was stabbed to death by a cabal of seven conspirators. In a ceremony at sunrise on the Nisaean Plain, ringed by the jagged Zagros Mountains, the assassins chose as their new king a young man whose ambition would in time encompass Greece itself and threaten her fragile freedom: Darius I.

Shortly after Polycrates' death, Samos was taken by the Persians, but during his lifetime the island benefited greatly from his rule. Like Peisistratus in Athens he spent much of his vast wealth on public and religious works. Five miles (8 km) outside the city walls, where he once staged the coup against his father, Polycrates

Democedes of Croton

With medicine in its infancy, successful doctors were at a premium, and in the sixth century the best came from Croton in south Italy. Chief among them was Democedes. Driven from home by his father's temper, he practised in Aegina and Athens before being lured by high fees to Samos. After Polycrates' murder, he was imprisoned by Oroetes but later summoned to treat Darius, whose sprained foot was not responding to the ministrations of his Egyptian osteopaths. A successful treatment earned Democedes lavish rewards. His intervention spared the Egyptians from death by impaling, while he himself was granted the largest house in the Persian capital Susa, and regularly dined with Darius. Democedes, however, longed for home. Having successfully removed an abscess from Queen Atossa's breast, he was granted a ship and crew to reconnoitre mainland Greece prior to a Persian invasion. Somehow Democedes succeeded in including south Italy in his itinerary and, evading his shipmates at Taras, returned to Croton, whose citizens intervened when the Persians tried to abduct him from their agora. Democedes' pluck won the immediate approval of the Olympic wrestler Milo, who arranged for the physician to marry his daughter.

dedicated a colossal temple, the largest in the Greek world, to Hera. Meanwhile, seizing the island of Rhenea, he dedicated it to Apollo by linking it across the narrow strait to nearby Delos with a chain (an accepted method of transmitting divine 'energy' from one location to another).

Back on Samos, Polycrates commissioned two extraordinary works of engineering: a breakwater 120 feet (37 m) deep, stretching 400 yards (366 m) from the harbour mouth to protect shipping; and a tunnel 1,130 yards (1,036 m) long beneath Mount Castro to supply the city with fresh water. As tunnelling proceeded from both ends simultaneously, its designer, Eupalinus of Megara, staked everything on the precision of his calculations. They were staggeringly accurate. Although he was forced to create doglegs to compensate for a 6.5 foot (2 m) horizontal discrepancy that would have stopped the two ends meeting, on the vertical plane Eupalinus' computations were almost exact. The disparity between the tunnel mouths was just 1.5 inches (4 cm).

Like many tyrannoi, Polycrates was a generous patron of science and the arts. His court was populated by international celebrities including two Greeks from colonies in south Italy: Democedes of Croton, the most skilled physician of his generation, and the lyric poet Ibycus of Rhegium. His favourite, however, was Ibycus' colleague Anacreon of Teos, during one of whose performances Polycrates offended Oroetes by failing to greet the satrap properly. Such was Anacreon's reputation that, after Polycrates' death, Peisistratus' son Hipparchus sent a warship to Samos to convey him to safety in Athens. When a later traveller saw his statue on the Acropolis he recalled fondly that Anacreon was 'the first poet after Sappho of Lesbos to devote himself to love songs'.

SAPPHO (POST 630–c. 570)
Lyric Poet

We greet you, Sappho, wherever you might be, an equal of the gods: we still possess your songs, your immortal daughters.

Dioscorides, epigram on Sappho (*Greek Anthology*, 7.407)

Sappho, the first female voice in western literature, lived in an age before historiography, when chroniclers concerned themselves chiefly with the deeds of cities and powerful men. As a result, most of what is known of her comes from her own poetry. Since we cannot tell to what extent her verses were intended to be autobiographical, such evidence should be treated with caution. However,

The spirit of Greek lyric poetry is evoked in Sir Lawrence Alma-Tadema's romantic *Sappho and Alcaeus* (1881), in which Sappho, surrounded by her entourage, gazes wistfully at the poet who sang of her 'honeyed smile'.

both in antiquity and in more modern times this has not prevented would-be biographers from trying to reconstruct often divergent narratives of her life.

Sappho was born probably at Eresus on Lesbos in the late seventh century and spent much of her life in the island's capital, Mytilene. She belonged to a mercantile family which derived at least some of its wealth from exporting wine to the Greek colony of Naucratis in Egypt. (Sappho, writes **Herodotus**, strongly disapproved of her eldest brother Charaxus' involvement with Doricha, a Naucratian *hetaera* or courtesan.) In Lesbos, as elsewhere, the moneyed class was riven with bitter rivalry and in her youth and early adulthood Sappho experienced a series of coups that resulted in the establishment of the tyrannos Myrsilus, who consolidated his rule by banishing many of his enemies. It is not impossible that Sappho's family was among them or that, together with her brothers Charaxus, Erigyius and Larichus, she spent her exile far to the west in Sicily. Her statue would later be erected in Syracuse's prytaneum.

Early the next century, however, the political situation on Lesbos seems to have improved sufficiently for the exiles to return. Despite new laws aimed at curbing immorality and limiting private spending, Sappho's brother Larichus resumed his prestigious post as cup-bearer in Mytilene's prytaneum, and life on Lesbos became more settled. Sappho may have lived to see Lesbos' beneficent tyrannos Pittacus resign in 585, but (like many details of her life) even early accounts of her death are fanciful. They tell how, driven to suicide by her unrequited love for a fisherman Phaon, she leapt into the sea from the Shining Rock. However, since Phaon was the name of a legendary ferryman possessed of handsome looks who once conveyed Aphrodite in his barge (perhaps the subject of a lost Sapphic poem), and the Shining Rock appears in Homer's *Odyssey* as a landmark on the way to the Underworld, the story serves as a good example of how biographers mined Sappho's verses for even the most tenuous autobiographical detail. Together with the dubious tradition that she was married to Cerikles from Andros (loosely, 'Willy from the Isle of Man'), it shows too how later scholars, uncomfortable with the evidence from her own writing, tried hard to establish her heterosexuality, citing apparent references in her poems to a daughter, Cleïs, to show that Sappho's life was, in fact, that of a blameless matron.

Sappho's poetry, which now survives only in fragments, reveals a rare and remarkably intimate picture of the world of women in early antiquity and of the relationships between them. Many of her verses are melancholy, like the short poem: 'The moon has set, the Pleiades sunk low, midnights and long hours have passed; and I lie in bed alone.' Others are redolent with sensuous imagery: the heavy scent of frankincense; chervil, dew-spangled in the silver moonlight; a hyacinth sliced by a plough-share, leaching its sap into a hillside. All offer glimpses of well-educated and well-travelled women, some of whom were perhaps Sappho's students. The precise nature of their association is unknown, but, as well as being in part a 'wisdom poet' (like Hesiod), Sappho may have given instruction in composition, singing, playing the lyre and other feminine accomplishments. She may also have provided hymns and wedding songs to be performed within the context of the community as a whole.

Although much of Sappho's poetry is anchored firmly in the cloistered world of the women's quarters, it is by no means parochial. While describing a cosmopolitan society, where travel to Lydia is commonplace and luxury imports from Lydia's capital Sardis readily available, it weaves into its fabric easy echoes from Homer, adapting and subverting martial images to suit more domestic settings, and confidently lionizing Helen of Troy as a maverick free spirit wilfully abandoning the shackles of marriage and motherhood. Unfettered ingenuity characterizes Sappho's writing, from daring similes to the invention of new metres and modes of music. She even pioneered the *pectis* (a large, many-stringed lyre) and the plectrum.

Sappho's genius was quickly recognized. Her contemporary, Solon, is said to have insisted on learning one of her songs immediately, that he might die knowing it. Later, **Plato** called her the tenth Muse. But despite her pioneering poetry and acute observations of old age and relationships, it is for her sexuality that Sappho is most commonly remembered. The English words 'lesbian' and 'Sapphic' recall her, and many of her verses are imbued with longing for other women. One describes a girl whose voice is sweeter than any flute, her hair more golden than gold; another tells of garlanding a lover's neck with flowers and scenting her hair with myrrh before 'slaking desire' on a bed of soft sheets and plush cushions.

Within the women's quarters same-sex relationships may have been accepted, but Sappho's openness made many men uneasy. While her contemporary, the poet Alcaeus, who also came from Lesbos and whom some claimed was her lover, wrote of 'violet-haired, pure Sappho with the honeyed smile', at least one later commentator liked to imagine her as short, dark and physically repulsive. But it was **Polycrates'** favourite, Anacreon, who best summed up his fellow male Greeks' view of Sappho and her Lesbian circle:

Eros, golden-haired, throws his purple ball at me once more and calls me out to play with a girl in colourful sandals. But she mocks me for my grey hair; and besides, being from Lesbos, she's gazing at another girl.

Homosexuality in Ancient Greece

Homosexual relationships played an important role in Greek society. In Athens, it was expected that a young man (*eromenos*) should attach himself to an older male lover (*erastes*) who would help educate him and introduce him into society, while in the army of fourth-century Thebes a special regiment, the Sacred Band, was formed exclusively from pairs of homosexual lovers. Although homosexuality is absent from the Homeric epics and extant Athenian tragedy, it pervades other literary genres as well as philosophy and art, where some vase paintings are accompanied by the name of the artist's eromenos and others depict often graphic scenes of homosexual and lesbian love-making. Because of the androcentric nature of Greek literature, little is known about female homosexuality, almost the only literary sources being the poetry of Sappho and her older contemporary, the Spartan poet Alcman.

PYTHAGORAS (c. 570–c. 485)
Philosopher, Mystic and Mathematician

Pythagoras and his followers were the first to embrace mathematics, a discipline which they developed, and whose principles they zealously believed to be the foundations of all things.

Aristotle, *Metaphysics*, 1.685

During the political upheavals of the sixth century some Greeks turned their eyes towards further horizons, seeking to unravel mysteries more cosmic and eternal. Among them was Pythagoras, a philosopher, mystic and mathematician, whose influence on subsequent generations is matched only by the paucity of hard evidence for his life. Yet, however dubious the surviving biographical details, they nonetheless cast valuable light on how later Greeks perceived the man and his age.

Stories of Pythagoras' golden thigh, which he once exhibited at the Olympic Games, can be discarded. But the tradition that his father Mnesarchus was a Samian merchant who traded throughout the Mediterranean at least places him in the relatively high socio-economic bracket required to support the kind of education that Pythagoras must have received. Many celebrity teachers are credited with tutoring him, including the scientific philosopher Thales (who predicted a solar eclipse), the astronomer Anaximander (who first proposed a free-floating spherical globe) and the mystic Pherecydes (whose work explored the origins of the earth and the immortality of the soul). Pythagoras was said to have travelled widely around the eastern Mediterranean, acquiring knowledge from Chaldean astronomers, Egyptian priests and Persian Magi. Given that his father's mercantile activities would have involved foreign voyages, there is no reason why some of these traditions should not be based in fact. Equally, since we lack real evidence, they may be as fanciful as the later tradition that Pythagoras journeyed to the Underworld (and back).

Most accounts agree that in 530, perhaps prompted by international politics, Pythagoras went into exile in Italy to escape the burdens of political life on Samos. This was the year in which Polycrates betrayed Amasis to Persia, and tradition suggests that Polycrates had been instrumental in introducing

A first-century AD Roman copy of an original Greek bust imagines Pythagoras as a typically bearded Greek philosopher, but wearing an orientalizing turban.

Pythagoras to the Egyptian pharaoh. The uncertainties of imminent war and suspicions over where Polycrates' true loyalties lay may have been enough to force Pythagoras to seek sanctuary elsewhere.

In Croton, a Greek colony (founded *c.* 710), which later claimed him as the author of its constitution, Pythagoras plunged wholeheartedly into the life of his adopted city. The first man to call himself a *philosophos* (lover of wisdom), he quickly attracted as many as 300 followers who, unusually for the time but in common with the entourages of later radical thinkers, included women. With them he led a life of proto-monasticism and formed a school, 'the Society'. After a five-year period of initiation, members were divided between an inner circle of 'learners', noted for their rigorously abstinent lifestyle, and an outer circle of 'listeners'.

But Croton was not immune from the political upheavals convulsing the Greek world and some viewed Pythagoras and his followers as dangerous aristocrats. Led by Cylon (who perhaps resented not being admitted into the Society), a pro-democratic faction set fire to the Olympic wrestler **Milo's** house, where the Pythagoreans were meeting. Many lost their lives in the inferno, including (some said) Pythagoras himself, though others claimed he escaped to the nearby city of Metapontum, where he died of self-inflicted starvation in the temple of the Muses. Still others maintained he died in Sicily fighting for Acragas against Syracuse, though, as he was said to have lived until he was at least eighty (or even a hundred), this account stretches even the most vivid imagination.

Pythagoras is best known for the mathematical formula that, although not attributed to him until five centuries after his death, bears his name. To Pythagoras the importance of this theorem – that the square on the hypotenuse of a right-angled triangle is equal to the sum of the squares on the other two sides – which had been familiar to Babylonian mathematicians for over a millennium, lay in its apparent revelation of a sacred geometry underlying all creation. Pure mathematics, he believed, were the portal through which might be glimpsed a divine order, and to understand numbers was to understand the cosmos. Among Pythagoras' mathematical discoveries the *tetractys* (an equilateral triangle descending from one dot at its apex, through two and three to four dots at the base, the sum of the dots adding up to the perfect number, ten) was considered supremely significant; while in music he is credited with working out the ratio of the length of a lyre's string to its pitch.

Permeating Pythagoras' enquiries into the workings of the physical world was a deep interest in the spiritual and the divine. He believed in *metempsychosis* (the transmigration of the soul from one body to another after death), maintaining that he could trace his own past lives, including that of a fisherman, a courtesan and a hero of the Trojan War, back to Hermes' son, Aethalides, and claiming to recognize the voice of a reincarnated friend in the barking of a dog. His doctrine that rebirth continued until souls were purified through experience of corporeal life may have had parallels in the Eleusinian Mysteries, and, like much of Pythagoras' teaching, influenced subsequent philosophers such as **Socrates**, **Plato** and **Aristotle**. Plato is said to have bought three books supposedly written by Pythagoras, though many believe that Pythagoras in fact wrote nothing.

As befitted a sage or shaman, Pythagoras was said to have dressed in pure white robes, couched many of his teachings in deliberately obscure language and considered certain foods taboo. Perhaps it was his belief in reincarnation which led to his celebrated vegetarianism (though some claimed that his equally renowned avoidance of beans was prompted by their propensity to promote flatulence). Curiously, however, he appears to have waived these restrictions when it came to devising his special diets for athletes. He was the first to feed them specifically on red meat, for which his fellow townsman Milo was profoundly grateful.

MILO (*c.* 555–?)
Wrestler and General

Milo won seven victories at Olympia, and never once fell to his knees.

Simonides, epigram on Milo (Greek Anthology, 16.24)

In an age when physical prowess and political power were inexorably linked, and the boundaries between mythology and reality remained creatively blurred, Milo utilized his international reputation as an Olympic athlete to turn himself into one of the western world's first celebrities. He was a native of Croton in south Italy, a thriving Achaean colony which produced a disproportionate number both of Olympic victors and (perhaps from the need to treat athletic injuries) of physicians.

For twenty years Milo was unbeaten in the Olympics, winning his first crown in the boys' contest for wrestling (?540). Usually, boy victors found they had peaked too soon and few could repeat their triumphs as grown men. Milo was an exception. As champion adult wrestler he was crowned on five consecutive occasions (?536–?520). He did not triumph only at Olympia: he is recorded as having won seven times at the Pythian Games, nine times at the Nemean and ten at the Isthmian. At last he was beaten at Olympia, not because he had weakened with age, but because his opponent, who had devised a new technique, refused to come to close quarters. Yet despite Milo's defeat, his fellow citizens still celebrated. The new champion, Timasitheus, also came from Croton.

Though beaten, Milo remained unbowed. Now one of Croton's leading men, he was their clear choice as general when the neighbouring polis of Sybaris (a fellow Achaean colony) invaded their territory in 510. Like **Peisistratus** before him, Milo demonstrated his understanding of the power of theatre as propaganda. His army drawn up for battle, he paraded before them, his head festooned in his Olympic olive crowns, his body oiled, his muscles bulging, draped in a lion-skin and wielding a club – the embodiment of Heracles, the strongest of all Greek heroes. Famous for their foppish ways, the Sybarites were unnerved. Their phalanx collapsed and Sybaris was ransacked.

In the aftermath of victory, Croton was riven with political upheaval. Milo had become embroiled with the Pythagoreans, unashamed aristocrats who were wielding great power in Croton. In fact, Milo reportedly once saved **Pythagoras'** life: when they were dining together a column gave way, and Milo supported the roof until the philosopher could escape to safety. Incensed by the Pythagoreans' high-handed ways, a popular uprising targeted Milo's house, burned it to the

Two muscular wrestlers struggle to throw one another to the ground as stick-wielding judges watch attentively on this Attic amphora from around 520.

ground and killed many of those inside. Milo, however, escaped. Legend told how he finally met his death in heroic (if careless) circumstances. On a walk he came across a tree whose trunk was being held open with wedges to dry it out. Confident that he could split it apart, he thrust his hands inside it. But the wedges slipped, his hands were trapped and Milo was mauled to death by wolves, which roamed the countryside near Croton in large packs.

The hyperbole of Milo's death, a frontiersman savaged by marauding beasts in a dangerously unsettled and wild western colony, was matched by stories of his life. These included tales of how he carried his own statue single-handedly into the sanctuary at Olympia; how he tied a cord tightly round his head, held

The Olympic Games

Founded in 776, when they consisted of just one footrace covering a *stade* (approximately 200 yards or 183 m), the Olympic Games formed part of a four-yearly religious festival in honour of Olympian Zeus. Originally relatively parochial, the preserve of the polis of Elis, in time further contests were introduced and more cities took part until, by the sixth century, the games were truly international. Athletes and spectators alike had to be Greek-speaking males free from blood guilt (there were other, distinct games held at Olympia, sacred to Zeus' wife Hera, which included contests for girls and women). As crowds flocked to the festival the Olympic Games became one of a few truly panhellenic gatherings, an underpinning of Greek identity, where powerful men from across the Greek-speaking world could meet to conduct business, both political and commercial. Although other panhellenic games were introduced by the mid-sixth century to form a 'circuit', the Olympics remained supreme. While the only prize was an olive crown, on his return home a victorious athlete invariably won both kudos and great wealth.

his breath, and filled his veins with so much blood that the cord snapped; how he clasped a pomegranate in his fist so tightly that no one could prise it from him, though the pressure of his grip never damaged the fruit; how every day he ate 20 pounds (9 kg) each of meat and bread and drank 2 gallons (9 litres) of wine. Not all these stories can strictly be true, yet that they were (even in part) believed says much about the process of mythologizing a human hero, which Milo himself did much to aid.

In fact, Milo was more subtle than his propaganda might suggest, engineering successful alliances, marrying Pythagoras' daughter Myia and accepting money to betroth his own daughter to the physician Democedes, who had fled to Croton from the court of Persia's Great King Darius. Indeed, Milo's presence may have deterred Darius' agents from trying to recapture Democedes. Certainly the athlete would have felt some pride when Democedes taunted the retreating Persians, bidding them tell Darius of his forthcoming marriage, 'for the king had heard of Milo's reputation'.

Yet it was not only Milo whose reputation would vex Darius. Soon the name of Athens, too, would fan his anger, as Persia reeled from the repercussions of that city's tumultuous relationship with its last tyrannos, Hippias.

HIPPIAS (?–490)
Tyrannos of Athens

By nature, Hippias was politically skilled and clever.

Aristotle, *Athenian Constitution*, 18

After **Peisistratus'** death in 528 his son Hippias became tyrannos of Athens. With a reputation for being readily approachable, he ruled alongside his younger brother Hipparchus, continuing their father's policy of enlightened government and civic adornment. Near the River Ilissus work began on an ambitious new temple to Olympian Zeus to replace that raised by Peisistratus, its prodigious size intended to rival the two greatest buildings of the Greek world: **Polycrates'** temple of Hera on Samos and the Artemision (temple of Artemis) at Ephesus. Meanwhile, on the Acropolis he raised a new temple to Athene Polias (the protectress of the city) to house the goddess's sacred xoanon.

Politically, too, Hippias pursued Peisistratus' policies, seeking to increase Athens' influence abroad and maintain harmony at home. Thus he ensured that the position of *eponymous archon* (the leading magistrate, after whom the year was named) was shared between rival patrician families. However, even this proved insufficient to maintain stability in Athens, and in 514 tension erupted into violence.

Hippias' brother Hipparchus, a great patron of the arts, was piqued that a young aristocrat called Harmodius had shunned his sexual advances and so he publically insulted Harmodius' sister. With family honour at stake, Harmodius and his lover Aristogeiton attacked Hipparchus while the procession was mustering for the Panathenaic Festival and knifed him to death. The assassins were quickly found and executed, but the event had consequences disproportionate to its immediate significance. Future generations would glorify it as the first blow struck for Athenian democracy, celebrating the two killers as 'tyrannicides', praising them in song and honouring them with the only statues of mortals permitted in the Agora.

For Hippias, Hipparchus' murder marked a watershed. Increasingly paranoid, he now ruled with an iron fist. As his exiled enemies, led by the Alcmaeonids, courted the Delphic priests – by funding the rebuilding of the temple of Apollo – and through them won the support of Sparta, Hippias scrambled to cement alliances with the king of Thessaly. The showdown came in 510. A joint Spartan and Alcmaeonid attack on Athens by sea was beaten off, but when Sparta launched a land invasion Hippias fled to the Acropolis. He might have withstood a lengthy siege, but he was compelled to surrender when his children were captured as they were being smuggled out of Attica. Just five days later Hippias left Athens.

His exile took him east. Within months Hippias was greeted as an honoured guest of Persia and soon, with Darius' backing, he was looking forward to returning home. For the Spartans had quickly discovered that the relatively democratic regime they had helped install in Athens held views ideologically opposed to their own. In 508 they invaded Attica and seized the Acropolis. Although they were soon expelled, a major war seemed imminent. In preparation the Athenians approached potential allies. In Sardis they blithely agreed to ratify a treaty with the Persians by giving them a casket of Attic earth and an amphora of water. It was a spectacularly shortsighted move, for in Persia these were the tokens of a nation's submission. At a stroke Athens had become a part of Darius' growing empire (albeit an insignificant one), and the obvious candidate to govern it was Hippias.

Athens greeted the news with horror. Its citizens pretended that the terms had never been agreed. Then, politics took another unexpectedly dramatic turn. In 499 the Ionian Greeks, inflamed by a desire for greater democracy and chafing at Persian taxes, rose in rebellion. The next year, Athens and the Euboean polis of Eretria sent troops to help them. In a running battle through the burning streets of Sardis, in which the temple of Cybele was accidentally set alight, they defeated the Persian garrison. They sailed home satisfied that they had furthered the cause of Greek freedom. In fact, they had seriously jeopardized it.

Four years later the Ionian Revolt was mercilessly crushed. Determined to deny any future insurgents support from the Greek mainland, Darius (who had ordered an attendant to remind him three times a day to 'remember the Athenians') resolved finally to bring Greece into the Persian fold. In 492 his first campaign ended almost as soon as it had begun, shipwrecked in a storm off the rocky peninsula of Athos. But just two years later, a second Persian fleet was cutting a course towards Eretria and Athens. With it, eager to regain his throne, sailed Hippias. On their way, the Persians sacked Naxos, burning its shrines in revenge for the destruction of the temple of Cybele in Sardis, but they spared Delos, the island Hippias' father had once purified. Within days Eretria had fallen, its temples too ablaze, its citizens led off in chains, eventually to be resettled by the oil fields of Cissia (modern Basra).

At last Hippias was in Attica, the Persian army camped on his ancestral landholding at Marathon. Victory seemed assured. But Hippias, a peerless interpreter of oracles and omens, was unsettled by a dream, and even as the

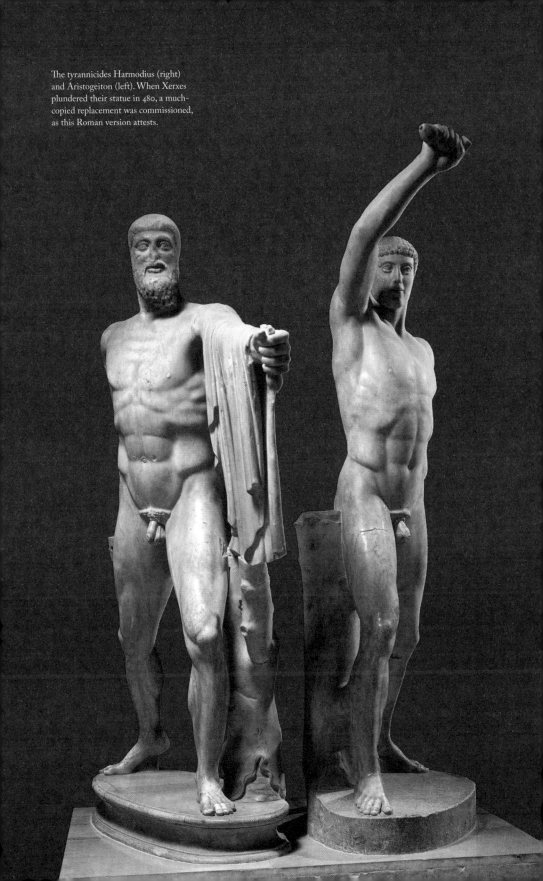

The tyrannicides Harmodius (right) and Aristogeiton (left). When Xerxes plundered their statue in 480, a much-copied replacement was commissioned, as this Roman version attests.

Persians were embarking for their voyage round Cape Sunium to Athens a Greek army, hopelessly outnumbered, launched a surprise attack. Despite their numerical superiority, the Persians were forced back, some to founder in the brackish marshes, others to be butchered in the bloody surf, and although most made it to the ships, none had the heart left for an assault on Athens. With autumn's squally seas approaching, they hugged the coast. At Lemnos, an island which Miltiades the Elder had once taken from the Persians in his name, Hippias, an old man, died. His hopes of once more ruling Athens had come to nothing.

Before they turned their ships for home, the Persians had coasted for a few hours near Piraeus, from where Hippias gazed for the last time on the Acropolis. The city skyline and the Attic hills were much as he remembered them; but, had he disembarked, he would have found that city life had changed beyond all recognition. For in the twenty years since Hippias' exile, his former fiefdom had experienced a revolution. Its mastermind was a man he had once appointed to high office: Cleisthenes.

CLEISTHENES (570–?507)
Democratic Reformer

Cleisthenes was the leader and the champion of the People.

Aristotle, *Athenian Constitution*, 20

Cleisthenes was an unlikely democrat. A leading member of the Alcmaeonids, he could trace his family's aristocratic ancestry back many generations and chart its chequered history. Thanks in part to the beneficence of Croesus, king of Lydia, the Alcmaeonids had accrued great wealth, but their role in resisting a tyrannical coup had won them an unshakeable reputation as a family accursed.

It was Cleisthenes' great-grandfather Megacles who was to blame. In 632, with most of Athens' great and good at the Olympic Games, a former Olympic champion who shared his name with Croton's firebrand, Cylon, occupied the Acropolis and declared himself tyrannos. As senior magistrate it fell to Megacles to oppose him. With great gusto he besieged the Acropolis where, in the August heat, conditions soon became unbearable. Somehow Cylon managed to escape and his followers, starving, dehydrated and crouching in supplication at Athene's altar, sued for peace. Megacles assured them they would not be harmed, but in an outrage against both religion and morality, as the insurgents made their way, dazed, down from the Acropolis, they were attacked and killed. Horrified, Athens broiled with rumour: ghosts stalked the streets; soothsayers proclaimed that sacrifices augured pollution and defilement; and in the end Megacles, together with his family and supporters, was driven into exile. Not even the Alcmaeonid dead were left in Attica. Their remains were disinterred and dumped beyond its borders.

In time unity was restored, thanks partly to the reforms of Solon, which reconciled competing factions while strengthening the hand of landowning aristocrats and simultaneously increasing the rights of the poor. But despite their banishment the Alcmaeonids still wielded influence, and in 594 they were allowed back home. By the middle of the century, however, their then paterfamilias, another Megacles, became embroiled in a power struggle with Peisistratus that in 546 culminated with their once again being forced into exile. By now, though, despite many setbacks, the Alcmaeonids had acquired even greater international prestige, thanks to Megacles' marriage to Agariste, daughter of the tyrannos of Sicyon, after whom he named his eldest son Cleisthenes.

Little is known of Cleisthenes' early life, but in the bleak aftermath of Hipparchus' killing, he rode with the 'liberating' army that swept into Attica in 510, and quickly emerged as one of the most powerful politicians in the aftermath of Hippias' overthrow. But the toppling of an increasingly totalitarian regime resulted in instability. Soon Cleisthenes found himself confronted by Isagoras, one of Hippias' allies still in Athens, and when his enemies cited the curse on the Alcmaeonids in order to enlist Spartan help, Cleisthenes and his supporters were forced into exile. But not for long. When Isagoras tried to legitimize his power by redrafting the constitution, the Athenians rose up against him, drove him and his Spartan allies from the city and recalled Cleisthenes. The People had demonstrated their ability to make or break their leaders. It was a message Cleisthenes could not ignore.

Despite his prolonged absence from Attica, Cleisthenes quickly showed how well he understood his city and had learned from the lessons of its past. Like Solon, whose reforms in his view had not gone far enough, he realized that for civil strife to be avoided the political structure of Athens – dominated as it was by powerful families – must be reorganized. He began by reshaping the identity of every Athenian.

Traditionally Athenians had belonged to one of four phylai (or tribes), each with strong family allegiances. Cleisthenes now broke down these ties by assigning citizens to one of ten new phylai, each subdivided geographically in

The temple of Apollo at Delphi, seat of an internationally respected oracle and one of the most sacred sites in the Greek world, was extravagantly rebuilt by the Athenian Alcmaeonid family in the sixth century.

such a way that, by including members from rural, coastal and city districts, they would give a political coherence to Attica, where previously agricultural, maritime and manufacturing interests had competed to the point of violence. To lend this controversial restructuring some legitimacy and root it in the heroic past, Cleisthenes named each of the phylai after an Athenian hero, sending a shortlist of 100 names to the oracle at Delphi so that Apollo could make the final choice. Like Peisistratus, Cleisthenes well understood the propagandist power of myth as history.

Meanwhile, he revised the constitution of Athens so that membership of its lawcourts and most of its legislative bodies was both extended to a wider range of social classes and decided by lot, with each of the phylai allocated an equal number of seats. Thus the legislative council (*Boule*), where motions were selected to be put before the Popular Assembly (*Ekklesia*), consisted of 500 members, fifty from each tribe. One annual appointment not left to chance was that of Athens' generals. Theirs was a high-profile role, and one in which an ambitious Athenian might also wield considerable political power. However, here too the impact of Cleisthenes' reforms was felt: each phyle elected one of the ten *strategoi* (generals), while a *polemarchos* (war leader) held supreme command. Because only the wealthiest were eligible to serve as generals the office remained the last bastion of aristocratic rivalry, but lest anyone become too powerful Cleisthenes introduced another potent deterrent: ostracism.

Nothing is heard of Cleisthenes after the period of his reforms. He may have died soon after or fallen into disgrace – perhaps he and the Alcmaeonids were suspected of complicity in Athens' decision to offer earth and water to the Persians in 507. Later, Cleisthenes was called the father of Athenian democracy ('rule of the People'), though tellingly the term that he himself used for his revised constitution was *isonomia* ('equality under the law'), an altogether more accurate description. For despite everything, the old dynasties still wielded disproportionate power, even if they now did so with more than a nod to the People – a stricture that Cleisthenes' great-nephew **Pericles** would take to heart.

Yet the perception that a city *could* be ruled by its People proved exhilarating, especially to citizens still struggling under the yoke of tyrannoi, whether home-grown or imposed by foreigners. So it was to Athens that the Ionian Greeks looked longingly as they contemplated their revolt against the Persians. Among its most active leaders was Histiaeus, tyrannos of one of the wealthiest of all Greek cities, Miletus.

HISTIAEUS (?–?494)
Tyrannos of Miletus

Histiaeus maintained that all of the [Ionian] cities would prefer democracy to tyranny.

Herodotus, *Histories*, 4.137

As the Persian empire spread west to the Aegean, it engulfed the prosperous Greek cities of the coast and nearby islands, requiring them to pay tribute, provide troops and submit to governors of Persia's choice. In the important entrepôt of Miletus – arguably the richest city in the Hellenic world – their proxy was Histiaeus.

Little is known of Histiaeus' early life. The tyrannos of Miletus, he first comes into focus in 513 by the banks of the Bosphorus as one of a detachment of Greeks guarding a bridge of great strategic importance linking Asia and Europe. Some years earlier the Persian empire had been harried by Scythians straying south from their ancestral lands beyond the Black Sea. Now in retaliation Darius the Great King had assembled a vast army, drawn from across his sprawling territories: 700,000 men (so it was rumoured) including cavalry. Each region was given its own responsibilities and to the Greeks of Ionia, Aeolia and the Dardanelles fell the task of building and protecting the vital pontoon bridge (masterminded by an engineer from Samos). Darius' trust in his Greeks must have been absolute, for without the bridge he and his army would be stranded north of the Black Sea in a hostile land, easy pickings for the Scythians when winter came. He nearly found his confidence misplaced.

Spurred on by Scythian envoys, the Greeks held a council of war. **Miltiades** (the Athenian sent out by **Hippias** to rule the Chersonese, whose lands had since been annexed by Persia) urged that the bridge should be destroyed, for with Darius stranded they could regain their independence. But Histiaeus urged caution. His argument was simple. Like him, the tyrannoi of Asia Minor owed their position to Darius, without whose support their citizens might rise up and depose them. Histiaeus' arguments won the day. To assuage the Scythians and encourage them to leave, the Greeks went through the motions of dismantling the northern part of the pontoon, but when Darius returned they quickly rebuilt it. They had proved their loyalty, or perhaps, faced with a potentially game-changing choice, they had simply suffered from a catastrophic loss of nerve.

With the Scythian campaign over, Darius rewarded Histiaeus with lands rich in silver mines and timber by the River Strymon in north Greece (near the future Amphipolis), on which to found a colony. But Histiaeus fell foul of the Persian general Megabazus, who had been charged with bringing Macedonia within the Persian fold, and in 510 Megabazus reported to Darius that Histiaeus was building a powerbase of his own from which to challenge the Great King. Darius acted swiftly. He ordered Histiaeus on the three-month journey east to Persia's capital, Susa, to be his personal advisor. There, like Democedes before him, Histiaeus chafed at his gilded captivity and for ten years he plotted his escape.

In 499 he hatched a plan. Believing that, if Ionia should revolt from Persia, he would be sent to troubleshoot, Histiaeus resolved to send an inflammatory message to Aristagoras, his son-in-law, the new ruler of Miletus. But Darius had spies everywhere. The message might be found. So, shaving the head of a trustworthy slave, Histiaeus tattooed the message on his scalp, waited for the hair to grow and sent him to Miletus. By chance, Aristagoras was thinking of rebelling anyway. An assault he had coordinated for the Persians on Naxos had been an abject failure and now Aristagoras, his position dependent on his overlords' approval, was anxious he might be deposed. With nothing left to lose, he abdicated as tyrannos, declared that thenceforth Miletus would embrace isonomia and energetically fomented insurrection throughout Ionia. His attempt to enlist Spartan support failed, but he persuaded the Athenians to help him and, in their

The Persian Great King receives tribute from his subject peoples, as Athene presents the personification of Greece to Zeus, on a fourth-century vase from southern Italy.

Built by Alexander III in the fourth century and restored by the Romans, the temple of Artemis at Sardis stands near the site of the temple of Cybele accidentally burned by the Greeks in 498.

attack on Sardis in 498, the city and its temples were torched. When Darius heard of this calamity, as predicted he sent Histiaeus west to help quell the revolt.

Somehow Histiaeus was found out. In fire-ravaged Sardis, the satrap Artaphernes accused him of complicity in the rebellion, charging him with 'stitching the shoe which Aristagoras then wore'. Against all hope he managed to escape and make his way to the island of Chios and the rebel camp. Even here he was not safe. The Chians seized and imprisoned him and it was only when he had convinced them of his hatred of Darius that he was freed. Desperately Histiaeus tried to impose his authority on the Ionians, inventing ever wilder claims about how he had thwarted Persian plans for a population exchange with Phoenicia and sending letters to allies in Sardis (which were intercepted and used as ammunition by Artaphernes). No longer welcome in Miletus and refused a fleet by Chios, in the end he managed to persuade the islanders of Lesbos to give him eight triremes, with which he sailed north to Byzantium to raid shipping sailing out from the Black Sea.

Here in 494 he heard grim news. The Persians had concentrated their efforts on Miletus, reckoning that if it fell the rest of Ionia would crumble. Between the low-lying island of Lade and the coast their two fleets had met in a one-sided battle. Faced by the grim stare of 600 Persian warships, many of the Ionians, ill disciplined and scared, set sail and fled. Blockaded and bombarded, its strong walls undermined, Miletus could not hold out for long. Its men were slaughtered, its women and children bound in chains to trudge the long road east to Susa, and its temples looted and then torched.

In a last futile gesture Histiaeus and his fleet swooped down on Chios (whose troops had fought courageously for the rebels at Lade) and unleashed wholesale slaughter on the islanders. But when he crossed to the mainland in search of food his men were intercepted by the Persians. Most were killed, but Histiaeus was captured and escorted to Sardis and the satrap Artaphernes. Still fearing his persuasive tongue and to prevent him from again outwitting the Great King, Artaphernes had Histiaeus crucified. His head, removed, embalmed and boxed, was sent to Susa where Darius, mourning his deceitful friend, had it ritually washed and buried. For he recalled with gratitude Histiaeus' loyalty at the bridge over the Bosphorus. But he remembered, too, the treachery planned by the Athenian Miltiades, little knowing that thanks to him the western tide of Persian expansion would soon for the first time be dramatically reversed.

MILTIADES (C. 554–489)
Tyrannos and General

Fighting in the front rank of battle for all Greece, the men of Athens destroyed the vigour of the gold-robed Persians at Marathon.

Simonides, *Epitaph on the Dead at Marathon*

Tracing its pedigree back to the hero Ajax, Miltiades' family, the Philaids, was unashamedly aristocratic and ostentatiously wealthy. Miltiades' father's penchant for entering winning chariots in the Olympic Games so excited the jealousy of **Hippias** and Hipparchus that they had him ambushed and killed. Yet realpolitik meant that personal vendetta could not always be allowed to interfere with statesmanship, and in the mid-550s **Peisistratus** entrusted Miltiades' uncle (and namesake) with expanding Athens' influence in the Chersonese. Here he earned a reputation for good government, and made strong international ties, including with Croesus, king of Lydia. When he died childless he was succeeded in 516 by his nephew, the subject of this life. Immediately he reached his new bailiwick the younger Miltiades set about imposing his authority. He imprisoned many of its leading men, enlisted an army of 500 mercenaries and arranged to marry Hegesipyle, the daughter of the Thracian king Olorus. However, his autonomy was not to last. Soon the seemingly inevitable expansion of Persia's empire forced Miltiades to become the Great King's vassal, and in 513 he was summoned to help guard the crossing of the Bosphorus while Darius campaigned against the Scythians. His belief (encouraged by the Scythians) that destruction of the bridge might lead to freedom for the subject Greeks speaks eloquently of his inexperience of his masters and his ignorance of the resources they commanded.

In what should have been a salutary lesson, not only was Miltiades' advice rebuffed, but in 510 the Scythians overran his territories and he was forced to flee. By 496, however, the Persians had repulsed the Scythians and Miltiades was back, but his situation was untenable. Darius had not forgotten his treachery on the Bosphorus, and now that the Ionian Revolt had been suppressed he was set on eliminating any last signs of Greek disloyalty. In 493, learning that Persian warships were dangerously close at the island of Tenedos, Miltiades filled five triremes with his family, wife and wealth and put to sea. The ships were detected by Persian lookouts, but after a tense pursuit, in which one trireme was captured, the remaining four set course for Athens and what Miltiades hoped would be a safe haven.

Once more, he had misjudged. Earlier that year the Athenians had wept over a tragedy showing the capture of Miletus by despotic Persians; now the arrival of a fugitive Persian lackey was greeted with suspicion. After all, one of the reasons democratic Athens had supported the Ionian Revolt was to rid the Greeks of tyrannoi like Miltiades. He was indicted on the capital charge of repressive government, but with a Persian attack on the Greek mainland imminent there was little appetite to condemn a man who had so famously stood up to the Great King. Not only was Miltiades acquitted, in August 490 he was elected one of Athens' ten strategoi.

His appointment came at a crucial moment. Soon Persia's fleet was beached at Marathon, and Athenian hoplites, backed by a thousand Plataeans, were marching out to meet them. The sight that met their eyes was chilling. The plain was thick with countless infantry – contemporary estimates suggest 200,000 – while on the beach, where the Peisistratids had raced their chariots, a thousand cavalrymen rehearsed manoeuvres. For the 10,000 Greeks, appallingly outnumbered, the situation seemed hopeless, but so passionately did Miltiades

On the inside of an Athenian wine cup from the 480s or 470s, a hoplite with the winged horse Pegasus resplendent on his shield prepares to administer a fatal sword blow to a fallen Persian warrior.

After the Greek victory at Marathon in 490, Miltiades
dedicated his helmet with his name proudly inscribed along
the bottom of its cheek guard to Zeus at Olympia.

persuade his colleagues to stay and fight that they waived the daily rotation of supreme command and placed themselves entirely in his hands.

After days of anxious waiting, the time came. The Persians were striking camp, ready to board ship and descend upon an undefended Athens. With the horses already embarked, the cavalry was out of action. Offering sacrifice for victory, Miltiades ordered the advance. As the hoplites ran towards the Persians, the enemy battle line, though hastily drawn up, held fast, forcing the centre of the Greek line back, but after heavy fighting their morale collapsed and the Persians fled for their ships. With many trapped in the marshland to their rear, over 6,000 Persians were killed. The bodies of the 192 Athenian dead were buried beneath a grave mound on the battlefield, their memory revered as the protectors of their city's freedom. But the danger had not passed. The remainder of the Persian fleet was bearing down on Athens (though claims that they were guided by signals flashed from Alcmaeonid shields were nothing but malicious slander). So, in a feat as heroic as the victory itself, Miltiades rallied his exhausted men and marched back the 26 miles (42 km) to Athens and its harbour at Phalerum. When the Persians saw them they set course for home.

In *The Funeral of Miltiades* (1872) by Jean-François-Pierre Peyron, the dead
hero is removed from his prison cell by attendants (one of whom carries
trophies from Marathon), while his son Cimon is chained in his place.

Despite his request for a victor's olive crown to mark his role at Marathon
being vetoed, Miltiades was feted as a saviour. Riding a tidal wave of acclamation,
he dedicated his helmet at Olympia and demanded an army and a fleet with
which to wage war – not on the Persians, but on Paros, an island towards which
he harboured a personal grudge. The campaign was disastrous. Not only did
Miltiades fail to take the island, but an injury to his knee soon turned gangrenous.
In Athens, jealous of Miltiades' success and hungry for revenge, the Alcmaeonid
Xanthippus brought him to trial on the charge of deceiving the People. Weakened
with disease and feverish, Miltiades lay on a couch while his friends tried to
defend him, but to no avail. Although the jury waived the death penalty, they
fined him 50 talents, more than the gross domestic product of many poleis,
enough to bankrupt him. For Miltiades, however, the sentence was academic.
Days later, he died of his wounds. The fine was inherited by his son Cimon,
and with it not just a hatred for the Alcmaeonids but a determination to restore
his family name and fortune. His chance came soon enough, for the Persians
regarded Marathon as nothing but a temporary setback. Within ten short years
they would return.

Chapter 3

Greece
in Peril

CIMON (c. 510–450)
Politician and General

I hoped that I might end my life a prosperous old man, my days spent feasting with divine Cimon, of all men the most generous, the best of all the Greeks. But already he has died and left me.

Cratinus, *Archilochi* (fragment 1)

Cimon was probably born in 510. It was a tumultuous year. In Athens, **Hippias** was overthrown and driven into exile; and in the Chersonese, Scythian incursions forced **Miltiades** to flee his fiefdom, probably for Thrace, where his father-in-law Olorus was king. Later, Cimon's enemies would sneer that, having never acquired an education in the humanities, he was devoid of 'the cleverness and eloquence that marks a true Athenian', a xenophobic charge which, like the reputation for womanizing and hard-drinking that would forever dog this charismatic, mop-haired politician, hints at his Thracian upbringing, on the borders of the 'civilized' Greek world.

In 493 Persia's growing power forced Miltiades to seek refuge in his native Athens, where his arrest for oppressing the Chersonese forced Cimon briefly to assume the role of family *kyrios* (head of the household). Miltiades' acquittal brought temporary relief, but Athens was under existential threat. In 490, in reprisal for Athens' support of the Ionian Revolt, the Persians invaded mainland Greece, but at the battle of Marathon Miltiades (a Persian 'expert') led the Athenians to victory. Months later, in a bitter twist, he was badly injured in a failed attempt to capture Paros, indicted for his part in the fiasco by his enemy Xanthippus and fined the crippling sum of 50 talents. When Miltiades died a few days later, Cimon inherited the fine.

Luckily Cimon had rich friends, among them Callias, a wealthy businessman. In return for paying off the debt Callias requested Cimon's sister Elpinice in marriage, a rare and controversial love match, which provoked outrage. Paying for a bride was unconventional – usually it was the bride who brought a dowry to her new husband – and, being unafraid to intervene in the male domain of politics, the intelligent Elpinice was an easy target for malicious gossip. Defamation of capable women for 'unfeminine' behaviour was rife in Classical Athens. Elpinice's misogynistic enemies gossiped freely of sibling incest and an affair with the artist Polygnotus, for whom she was accused of modelling. Cimon himself engineered a brilliant marriage to Isodice, whose great-uncle Xanthippus had so successfully prosecuted Cimon's father – a political alliance with the Alcmaeonids cannot but have stood him in good stead. Despite Cimon's adoration of women and many intense love-affairs, his marriage, which produced three sons, was characterized by deep mutual devotion and, on Isodice's death, he was inconsolable.

Meanwhile, an international crisis loomed. In 486 Darius died and, after a brief but bitter power struggle, his son Xerxes assumed the Persian throne. Cruel, caustic, mercurial and bent on revenge for Marathon, in 480 the thirty-six-year-old assembled a fleet and army so vast that even the mathematically brilliant Greeks could not compute its size. While his engineers constructed a pontoon bridge across the Dardanelles, he paid a symbolic visit to Troy, a site of numinous significance. For the Asiatic Xerxes, the sack of Troy, an Asian city, was like Marathon a Greek outrage that called for vengeance. Slaughtering a hundred white oxen on the altar of Athene, he swore he would deliver it. Within days his army crossed the bridge into Europe as if on dry land. Soon, by a canal cut through its low-lying neck, his navy sailed not round but *through* the promontory of Athos. The message was clear. Having been refused the gift of earth and water from certain Greek cities, Xerxes would seize them for himself.

The leaders of the free Greek poleis met to discuss their options. To delay the Persian advance south and buy time in which to assemble their main army they dispatched an advance force, including 300 Spartans under King **Leonidas**, to the narrow pass of Thermopylae, while the combined Greek fleet was sent to guard the approaches off Euboea. But the Spartans were massacred, and the fleet fled back to shelter in the Bay of Salamis. The Persians seemed unstoppable. In Athens opinion was divided. Some, buoyed by an oracle foretelling victory if they trusted their 'wooden walls', urged strengthening the palisade round the Acropolis; others, led by the populist **Themistocles**, who insisted that the oracle meant their newly strengthened navy, demanded they evacuate the city and fight at sea.

The intimidating sight of a phalanx of hoplites, armed with spears and protected by helmets, greaves on their shins, and large shields (each painted with a distinctive device), on a seventh-century Corinthian vase.

The stalemate was resolved by Cimon. An aristocrat more used to fighting on horseback than on a trireme, he rallied his blue-blooded companions and led them in a procession along the Sacred Way up onto the Acropolis, where he dedicated his horse's bridle in the temple of Athene Polias and prayed for victory. Then he walked down to the sea. Soon his fellow citizens were swarming the seafront at Piraeus, the women and children to be evacuated across the bay to safety, the men to crew the triremes. Within days Athens was overrun, its temples burned, its statues of the tyrannicides Harmodius and Aristogeiton crated up and shipped off to Susa; but at Salamis the Greek fleet won through and Cimon's bravery helped to cement his reputation. Hailed by the People, he was feted too by wily aristocrats who hoped that he would secure not only Athens' interests but their own.

The crushing of the Persian fleet at Salamis in 480 was followed the next year by overwhelming victory on land at Plataea, but although the Persians had been defeated and driven out of Greece, memorials to their invasion remained

A Greek hoplite (left) crouches over the body of a fallen enemy to face an attacking Persian horseman on the frieze of the late fifth-century temple of Athene Nike in Athens.

everywhere. Throughout Attica and Athens the temples had been deliberately burned, while at Delphi the priests claimed that only Apollo's intervention had protected the sanctuary from looting. (More plausibly, they had collaborated with the Persians.)

Determined to pre-empt future invasions and liberate the Ionian cities still in thrall to Xerxes, the Greek poleis, for once allied in the face of foreign aggression, now took the war to Persia. Pausanias, a Spartan, was placed in overall command, but his style of leadership was unsympathetic. Allegations of high-handed arrogance, treacherous negotiations with the Persians and a willingness to betray Greece in return for marriage to the Great King's daughter were enough to seal his fate. He was recalled to Sparta and later executed. In his place the allies (now minus Sparta) appointed Cimon. Soon, with his combination of charisma and strict discipline, he led his men to a series of important victories which, while won for allied Greece, did much to bolster Athens. Thus the expulsion of the Persians from Eion by the River Strymon in Thrace opened the mineral-rich region for new Athenian colonies like Amphipolis, while the defeat of Scyros (an island which in fact had not supported Persia) helped rid the waves of piracy and safeguard Athens' grain supplies from the Black Sea.

Occupying Scyros allowed Cimon to engineer another political coup. In 476, believing that the island was the resting place of Theseus, Athens' legendary king, he set out to find and repatriate the hero's bones. The search acquired an aura of mystique: when an eagle, tearing at the earth with its talons, showed Cimon's archaeologists where to dig they discovered a coffin containing the skeleton of a towering man buried with a bronze sword and spearhead. With ostentatious pageantry Cimon escorted the remains to Athens where he commissioned a new shrine to house them. This Theseum (temple of Theseus), its walls adorned with paintings by the greatest artists of the day, acquired extraordinary significance: in the very heart of Athens, enshrined in a reliquary linking heroic past to ambitious present, mythological history and legendary biography had become if not flesh then, at the very least, bone. It was a potent symbol of a new, ambitious age.

Rich from his campaigns, Cimon transformed his city. North of the Sacred Gate he landscaped the grove of the hero Academus with fountains, streams, a running track and leafy walks; in the busy Agora he planted shady plane trees; he enlarged the Acropolis with a strengthened southern bastion; and towards Piraeus he filled the swampy plain with rubble, foundations for long walls to link Athens securely with its port. Like **Peisistratus**, Cimon understood how public works brought not just civic benefits but personal kudos. So, flaunting his generosity, he fed the poor from his own kitchens, distributed clothes to needy citizens and removed fences from his vast estates so that anyone could help themselves to fruit. Meanwhile, artworks proclaimed the fame of Cimon's father. In a painting in the *Stoa Poikile* (Painted Stoa), one of the arcades which flanked the Agora in Athens, Miltiades was depicted leading the Greeks to victory at Marathon, while sculptures at Delphi showed him surrounded by gods and heroes. In time Cimon's own victory over the Persians at Eurymedon was celebrated on the Acropolis in a bronze statue of Athene Promachus (Athene 'who fights in the front line of battle'), 30 feet (9 m) tall, its glinting speartip visible for miles, a beacon for ships sailing in towards Piraeus, a reminder that the sea belonged to Athens.

For in 478, just one year after the battle of Plataea, on the sacred island of Delos the Greek allies had sworn to bind themselves to Athens in their common war on Persia. As members of this Delian League they promised to contribute ships and men according to their wealth, but from the start its constitution showed the primacy of Athens. Besides, as Cimon disarmingly encouraged fellow members to contribute money rather than materiel or men, Athens' resultant fleet grew stronger that that of any other polis. When Naxos tried to leave the League just six years later, Athenian triremes blockaded its harbour and the decision was hastily revoked. Already the signs were clear that, if not yet then certainly in time, what had begun as an alliance would transform into an empire.

Meanwhile, Persia remained a threat. Perhaps in 467 (though the date remains uncertain) Xerxes' fleet assembled for a renewed attack on Greece. Hastily, Cimon sailed east with 200 triremes. From friendly Cnidus he struck south into hostile waters. He found the Persians anchored at the mouth of the River Eurymedon awaiting Phoenician reinforcements. Time was of the essence. Most Greek naval battles were fought in open waters, but with the Persians huddled deep within the estuary and refusing to engage, Cimon was forced to attack. Caught in the shallows, the Persian ships floundered. As their crews struggled ashore Cimon led his hoplites at a run against the Persians on the beach. The fighting was fierce, the casualties high, but Cimon was victorious. Yet he could not rest. Embarking once again, he raced south to Syedra where the panic-stricken Phoenicians put up little resistance. It was a famous victory, and when Xerxes was murdered in a palace coup in 465 his successor, Artaxerxes, chose to consolidate rather than expand his empire. Formally or not, both for the mainland Greeks and for their Ionian and island cousins, the threat of Persian invasion was over.

Within Athens, however, power was still hotly contested. Returning in 463, triumphant from his conquests in Thrace and on the island of Thasos, Cimon was impeached for dereliction of duty. He should, his enemies sneered, have conquered Macedonia as well. The charge reeked of opportunism, but it exposed the fault lines fissuring Athenian politics. Cimon's prosecutor was the son of Xanthippus (the nemesis of his father Miltiades), a brilliant young man with a decisive legal and strategic brain: **Pericles**. Cimon was narrowly acquitted (thanks, perhaps, to his sister Elpinice's personal intercession), but the case did little to enhance his reputation. Two years later he was not so lucky.

Cimon had never hidden his admiration of Sparta, even naming one of his twin elder sons Lacedaemonius (the Spartan). So, in the aftermath of an earthquake which shook the Peloponnese in 464, he hurried south to help quell a prolonged Helot uprising. But other Athenians were less enthusiastic. Better, they urged, to seize the moment and crush their Spartan rivals. Nervous of such blatant hostility in the ranks of supposed allies, the Spartans sent Cimon's army home. His fellow citizens were furious. Accusing Cimon of humiliating them, they ostracized him in 461.

Soon, relations between Athens and Sparta soured further, and by 460 they were at war. In 457, when Spartan hoplites marched through friendly Boeotia towards Attica's borders, Athens responded quickly. At Tanagra near Thebes the armies met, but before the battle a horseman galloped into the Athenian camp. It was Cimon. Demonstrating his deep-seated patriotism, he begged, despite

Sparta and Her Helots

Living on some of the most fertile agricultural land in Greece, the Spartans should have enjoyed easy lives. Instead, they were suspicious of their Helot slaves, the original inhabitants of Laconia and Messenia, now Sparta's heartlands. As the Helots greatly outnumbered them, the Spartans evolved the most repressive regime in antiquity simply to keep them under control. Fearing an uprising, Sparta trained its men exclusively for battle, declared unending war on the Helots and subjected them to regular brutality from the youth movement known as the *krypteia* (loosely, 'secret service'). Paradoxically, while citizens underwent tough training, billeted in barracks and allowed only clandestine visits to their wives, Helots lived in relative luxury with their own families. Some Helots even fought alongside Sparta's army. In 424 the bravest were offered freedom. Two thousand were selected, garlanded and led round the temples rejoicing their good luck. Then each was led away and slaughtered. It had been a cruel ruse. In Spartan minds the bravest Helots were also those most likely to rebel. And they could take no chances.

his ostracism, to be allowed to fight alongside the Athenians. His request was rejected and Cimon dismissed; but to mark his loyalty a hundred of his staunchest supporters set up his armour where they were stationed and fought beside it to the death. The Athenians were routed, and although they soon avenged their loss it was not until Cimon's return from exile in 451 that a truce with Sparta was eventually ratified.

To divert Athens' aggressive energies away from Sparta, Cimon proposed an expedition against Persian-held Cyprus and Egypt, where in 454 an Athenian army sent to help the Libyan king Inarus shake off Persian rule had been disastrously defeated on the Nile. In 450, while conducting successful naval operations around Cyprus, Cimon sent a delegation to reconnoitre Egypt and journey far into the desert to the oracle of Zeus Ammon at Siwah. Here the priests announced that Cimon was with Zeus. Perplexed, the envoys returned to Cyprus where they learned of Cimon's death. Mortally wounded in the siege of Citium, he had forbidden his lieutenants to broadcast the news until his troops could be withdrawn to safety. His body was returned to Athens where a monument was raised to honour him. Subsequently, in Citium at a cenotaph where the townspeople made offerings in times of plague and famine, he was worshipped as a *hero*, a human being who had attained semi-divine status.

A Roman bust, copied from a mid-fifth-century original, of the bullish Themistocles, his characteristically close-cropped hair an outward sign that he identified not with well-coiffed aristocrats but with the Athenian People.

Greeks later recorded that in the year after Cimon's death a formal peace treaty was signed between the Delian League and Persia. Its chief negotiator was Cimon's brother-in-law and long-term ally, Callias. Confirming Persia's recognition of Athens' hard-won status as the leader of the Ionian Greeks, it was fitting tribute to Cimon's dedication, thirty years before, of his bridle to Athene and his life to Athens before he joined the triremes of Themistocles' new navy.

THEMISTOCLES (524–459)
Politician and General

Examine the facts impartially and carefully, and you will discover that the talents and achievements of Themistocles are more outstanding than those of any other man in history.

Diodorus, Library of History, 11.58

Themistocles was a bull of a man, thick necked and barrel-chested, his close-cropped head a sign that he identified not with the long-haired aristocrats of Athens but with the working People. His father Neocles was a self-made man; his mother was a foreigner; and while being 'mixed race' did not affect Themistocles' citizen rights it did bar him from many of the city's gymnasia, an inconvenience for an aspiring politician as these were crucial venues for networking. Being resourceful, he found a solution: he invited his well-born friends to *his* gymnasium instead. Barriers, Themistocles discovered, could be circumvented, problems ingeniously solved.

From an early age Themistocles was ambitious. As a child his favourite pastime was writing and rehearsing speeches, which caused his tutor to predict that for good or ill he would achieve extraordinary things. But in the twilight years of the Peisistratids, politics was a matter of life and death, and his father worried lest Themistocles' ambition lead to disappointment or worse. To teach his son a lesson, Neocles took him to Phalerum, at that time Athens' port, where decommissioned triremes were dragged onto the beach and left to rot. This, he explained, was how Athenians treated politicians: when no longer useful, they discarded them. The lecture fell on deaf ears, but seeing the triremes was to prove inspirational.

Themistocles hungrily embraced public life as a champion of Athens' poor. Such was his prodigious memory that he learned the name of every citizen he met, but inevitably his growing popularity brought him into conflict with the aristocrats and especially the Alcmaeonid puppet, Aristeides. In 493, barely in his thirties, Themistocles was elected to the powerful office of eponymous archon and set about the implementing plan he had been harbouring for many years: to transform Athens into a major maritime power. Greater access to the sea and foreign trade, he argued, would benefit not only Athens' landed classes but her artisans and businessmen, while manning triremes would provide employment for the urban poor. So work began at Piraeus on new port facilities to replace the docks at Phalerum, a public building programme on a scale to match that of the tyrannoi.

But in 490 the Persians came. Although Athens' victory at Marathon by yeoman hoplites seemed to confirm the city's close ties to the soil, Themistocles was undeterred. When a rich seam of silver was discovered at Laurium southeast of Athens in 483 he brought a radical proposal before the Assembly. Rejecting Aristeides' suggestion that the increased revenues from the mines be divided equally among the People, Themistocles argued that they should instead be spent on building a hundred new triremes with which to crush the nearby island of Aegina. To the aristocrats the prospect was alarming: the new fleet, together with the seventy triremes Athens already possessed, would require no less than 34,000 men to crew it. Previously wars had been waged on land by wealthy citizens, who could afford the expensive armour of the hoplite or cavalryman, but these ships would be manned by the urban poor, whose newfound fighting role might significantly threaten the political status quo (and increasingly over time by many of the city's *metics*, too, foreigners who lived and worked in Athens). Triumphantly the People ratified Themistocles' proposal, doubled the number of new ships to 200 and ostracized Aristeides.

Only three years later, in 480, Xerxes invaded mainland Greece. Responding to the threat, the Greeks sent their combined fleet – led by a Spartan admiral but advised by Themistocles – north to Euboea to try to delay the Persians. In a series of skirmishes off Artemision, they showed they had at least some hope of victory; but with King **Leonidas'** army defeated at Thermopylae the fleet was forced to retreat. Sailing south by night Themistocles ordered messages to be painted on the rocks, urging the Ionian Greek crews of Xerxes' ships to defect or sabotage the Persians' plans. Soon, with Athens taken, it was only Greece's triremes that could hope to ward off total disaster, yet half of them were Athenian, the ships barely built, their oarsmen woefully undertrained. Beached on the island of Salamis, the Greek commanders squabbled. Most advocated immediate retreat south to the Peloponnese; only Themistocles argued that they should stay and fight. Facing a

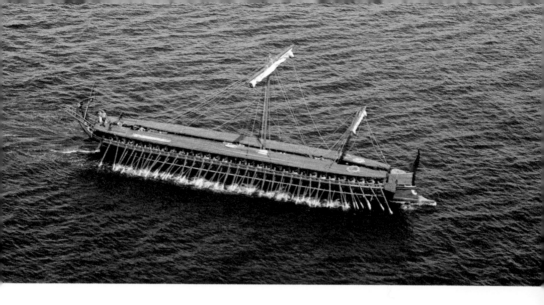

Like the modern replica *Olympias* (1987), ancient triremes were sleek, swift and bristling with oars, their prows equipped with a deadly bronze ram.

barrage of insults for being a man without a city, Themistocles retorted that the Athenian fleet was the greatest city in all Greece and that, if his allies voted not to fight, he would take Athens' ships to Italy and found a new colony there.

When it became apparent that he could not prevail by argument, Themistocles resorted to guile. He sent his sons' tutor, a Persian slave called Sicinnus, with a message for Xerxes: Themistocles had switched sides; the Greeks intended to slip away by night; the Persian fleet should be on full alert. Xerxes believed him. He ordered his ships to patrol the channels which led out from the Bay of Salamis, and in silence his crews waited for the Greeks. They never came. Instead, next morning, Themistocles briefed his colleagues: the Greek fleet was trapped. Flight was no longer an option. As the admirals accepted the inevitable and made sacrifice, three Persian prisoners, nephews of Xerxes, were brought to Themistocles in chains. Only by offering them as sacrifices to Dionysus Sarcophagus (Dionysus Flesh-Eater), the priest proclaimed, would Greek victory be secure. Themistocles, appalled but pious, did as he was instructed. Battle-ready, the Greeks launched their triremes, and in the narrows of the bay, with the breezes and a heavy swell behind them, they smashed the Persian fleet. Themistocles' gamble had paid off.

As Xerxes and his defeated fleet scudded home to Asia, Themistocles proposed preventing the Persian army's escape by destroying their bridge across the Dardanelles. Wiser heads prevailed. Better, advised the recalled exile Aristeides, to build a second bridge to let the Persians leave more quickly. It was not the only time the two men clashed over strategy. In private, when the Persians had departed and the Greek fleet was beached north of Euboea on the Gulf of Pagasae, Themistocles proposed that they could greatly benefit Athens by destroying their allies' ships; Aristeides was appalled at such dishonourable tactics and the plan was quietly shelved.

The fickle Athenians soon replaced Themistocles as admiral of Athens' fleet, but throughout the rest of Greece he was lionized. At the Olympic Games spectators rose as one to cheer his arrival in the stadium, while the Spartans awarded him a chariot. But if they hoped that he would favour them as a result, they were mistaken. In 479, with the Persians defeated at Plataea, Sparta tried to prevent the rebuilding of Athens' city walls, destroyed during the Persian occupation. Knowing that no stratagem discussed in the public Assembly could be kept secret, Themistocles won the backing of the smaller legislative council, the Boule, and journeyed to Sparta, supposedly to negotiate. In reality he was playing for time. Throughout his stay, work on the walls went on apace and, when the Spartans realized, it was too late. Once more Themistocles had protected Athens. But he had angered Sparta.

Back home, Themistocles celebrated by building further walls around Piraeus, while in rural Attica at Phlya (where the figurehead of the first Persian ship captured at Salamis was dedicated in the temple of Apollo) he funded the restoration of his family's *telesterion* (hall of initiation), in which were celebrated mysteries more ancient than those of Eleusis, with hymns said to have been written by the legendary Orpheus. Yet when he erected a temple to Artemis Aristoboule (Artemis of Good Counsel) near his house in Athens opinion turned against him. The epithet was considered self-aggrandizing, a crass reference to Themistocles' much-vaunted good advice to build a navy.

By 471, with scurrilous poems and drinking songs circulating throughout Athens, the People's goodwill haemorrhaging, and his aristocratic rivals, led by the pro-Spartan **Cimon**, constantly attacking him,

A potsherd, or ostracon, bearing the name 'Themistocles, son of Neocles', one of many votes cast in the ballot of 471, which saw Themistocles ostracized from Athens.

Themistocles was ostracized. At first he tried to weather exile among friends in Argos, but word came that his enemies were seeking to arraign him on an old charge of treason. Once before, Sparta had attempted to implicate him in the disgrace of its traitorous general Pausanias; but although letters had been produced in court as evidence Themistocles had been acquitted. Now these charges were resurfacing. Realizing that no jury would be able to withstand the pressure of his enemies and acquit him, Themistocles fled – first to Corcyra (Corfu), then to the mountains of Molossia, whose king, Admetus, granted him asylum. When Sparta threatened all-out war, Themistocles took flight once more. Declared a traitor in Athens and with all Greece now against him, he took his courage in both hands and sought sanctuary with his bitter enemies, the Persians.

As Themistocles escaped from Greece his ship was caught in high seas off Naxos. The captain raced for harbour, but the island was blockaded by Athenian triremes. Themistocles knew he would be recognized. He bribed the captain to ride out the storm and so came safe to Ephesus. From the rolling hills of nearby Aegae he was conveyed to Susa cowering in a covered carriage disguised as a Persian noblewoman. The chronology of the Classical accounts is confused, but they relate how Themistocles was then received into the court of Artaxerxes, who had attained the throne in 465, and how, through an interpreter, he convinced the Great King that despite his part in Persia's defeat he had rendered her great services – he even claimed to have prevented the destruction of the bridge across the Dardanelles to allow the Persians to retreat to safety. Sneering at the inherent weakness of the Greek poleis which had alienated such a great man, Artaxerxes granted him asylum, gave him a year to learn the Persian language and welcomed him as a valued advisor.

With his family and much of his wealth smuggled east from Athens, Themistocles lorded it at the Persian court, where he was initiated into the secrets of the Magi and joined Artaxerxes on his royal hunts. Appointed governor of Magnesia on the River Maeander, he lived lavishly on the wages of his treason. Yet he remained at heart an Athenian. When he died in 459 (perhaps at his own hand, reluctant to fulfil his duties to the Great King by assisting in a war against the Greeks), he requested that his body be transported home in secret for burial in Attica. Later, a cenotaph was raised at the entrance to the harbour at Piraeus and another in the agora at Magnesia.

Despite his treachery, later historians were generous to Themistocles, extolling him as one of the cleverest of all Greek politicians. Yet among his contemporaries his tarnished reputation cast a pall over his success at Salamis. No such opprobrium, however, would ever mar the memory of the hero of Thermopylae, Leonidas.

LEONIDAS (*c.* 540–480)
Spartan King

If you truly understood what is honourable in life, you would not desire what is not yours. It is better for me to die for Sparta than to rule the whole of Greece.

Leonidas, quoted in Plutarch, *Sayings of the Spartans*, 225

In antiquity as now, Leonidas was heralded as the archetypal Spartan warrior-king, the heroic fighter who, in the face of certain death, never flinched but willingly gave his life for his polis. So, to understand Leonidas, we must first know something of the unusual society which he represented.

Sparta was a uniquely militaristic society. Aged seven, boys from its ruling citizen class, the *homoioi* (equals), were removed from home to live in barracks and be schooled in the brutal *Agoge*, a system which trained them almost exclusively as fighters and must have produced many a paranoiac psychopath. For, vastly outnumbered, Sparta's 8,000 adult homoioi lived in fear of their Helot slaves, on whom each year (to sanction the Agoge's arbitrary atrocities against them) they ritually declared war. Meanwhile, Spartan girls were accorded greater freedoms than their counterparts elsewhere, enjoying better education and athletic training, in the belief that this would help them bear strong sons.

Sparta's constitution was unusual, too. Even in the sixth century homoioi aged thirty and above enjoyed equal voting rights in the *Apella* (Assembly), a 'democratic' system pre-dating that of Athens. At sixty, citizens could be elected to the *Gerousia* (Senate), a body of thirty elders with power to propose (and veto) motions in the Apella. In addition five *ephors* ('overseers') were elected annually whose diplomatic and judicial powers extended even over Sparta's kings. For, in another example of constitutional eccentricity, Sparta had not one king but two, heads of the ancient Eurypontid and Agiad families, who ruled simultaneously and whose primary role was to lead the army in war.

Leonidas was an Agiad. His father King Anaxandridas had been childless for many years but refused to divorce his wife, so the ephors, worried that he might die without an heir, allowed him concurrently to take a second wife, with whom he soon had a son, Cleomenes. Shortly afterwards, however, his first wife bore him two sons, Doreius and Leonidas. Heirs to the throne were educated apart from other Spartan children, but as Leonidas was thought unlikely ever to be king he was trained in the Agoge as a typical Spartan warrior.

When Anaxandridas died in *c.* 520, Cleomenes' succession fractured the family. Believing his claim was stronger, Doreius stormed out of Sparta intent on founding a new colony. He rampaged across the Mediterranean for ten years before fighting for Croton against Sybaris in 510 and falling in battle weeks later against the Carthaginians at Segesta in Sicily. The same year, Cleomenes helped expel **Hippias** from Athens; but in 506, when Sparta sent him with his colleague King Demaratus back to Attica to try to overthrow the new democratic government, they quarrelled. Their mission was aborted and thenceforth Spartan campaigns were led by one king alone.

Unsurprisingly, the two kings' hatred deepened. In 491 it erupted into all-out hostility, ending only when Demaratus was deposed and decamped in dudgeon to Persia. Two years later his supporters struck back. Declaring Cleomenes insane, they bound him in chains. Soon afterwards he was discovered dead, purportedly from shredding his own flesh, but in fact the victim of assassination.

With Sparta in crisis the Agiad throne passed to Leonidas. He had already proved his mettle on the battlefield, fighting against Argos at Sepeia in 494 and participating in the subsequent massacre when 6,000 Argive soldiers, corralled in a sacred grove, were burned alive. Now, to consolidate his power, Leonidas married Cleomenes' daughter, the dynamic and deeply

This early fifth-century statue of a smiling hoplite discovered on Sparta's acropolis is often claimed to be Leonidas himself.

intelligent Gorgo. Gorgo was no stranger to politics. In 499, when Aristagoras of Miletus, seeking support in the Ionian Revolt, offered Cleomenes a princely bribe, the eight- or nine-year-old Gorgo forestalled any agreement by warning, 'Father, if you don't leave now, your friend will corrupt you.' Later, in around 485, her wisdom again proved invaluable when Demaratus, now in exile at the Persian court, sent a bewilderingly blank wax tablet to Sparta. Only Gorgo knew what to do. She scraped off the wax and found Demaratus' message carved onto the wood underneath: the Persians were preparing for invasion.

Foreknowledge was one thing; resistance quite another. To play for time the allied Greeks resolved to try to hold back Xerxes' advancing army at Thermopylae, a narrow pass between the mountains and the sea, through which anyone making their way south from Thessaly to central Greece must travel. Although their Carneia festival in honour of Apollo (which had prevented them from fighting at Marathon a decade earlier) was imminent the pious Spartans were determined not to be found wanting. While most of the army stayed for the Carneia, Leonidas led 300 handpicked Spartans north to join the other Greek contingents. All had fathered sons. If they died, as they knew they would, their bloodline would continue and their sons would take their place among the homoioi. Leonidas' last words to Gorgo were, 'Marry well and bear good children.'

It was not only the Spartan troops which were depleted. Many other Greek cities were celebrating the Olympic Games. So at Thermopylae – the 'Hot Gates' – eerie with fumes from sulphurous springs, all that the outnumbered Greeks could do was build a wall across the pass and wait for the attack. As from afar the baffled Persians watched the Spartans grooming their long hair, only Demaratus, Xerxes' advisor, knew what their gesture meant: they were preparing to face death.

After five days Xerxes sent in the full force of his infantry. It was a tactical blunder. In the tight terrain the Greeks held the advantage; the Persians suffered heavy losses. Had it not been for a Greek traitor the impasse might have continued indefinitely. But when a local villager led a Persian unit over a mountain pass the Greeks were trapped in a pincer movement. On Leonidas' orders, his allies withdrew – all save the Thespians, who insisted on remaining, and the Thebans, whom, their loyalty suspect, he feared might sabotage the allied Greeks' retreat. Leonidas himself embraced his certain death, recalling a prophecy that Sparta would survive the war if one of her two kings died.

Again the Persians attacked. Crowded together, their overseers whipping on reluctant infantry, many slipped into the sea and drowned; others were trampled underfoot; and as the two sides met, spears snapping and swords drawn, Leonidas was cut down in the bloody combat. As the Thebans shamefully surrendered,

Leonidas' men dragged his body back to a small hill where they desperately held out until not one was left alive. When Xerxes toured the battlefield hours later he ordered that Leonidas' severed head be mounted on a stake for all to see.

Had Xerxes conquered Greece, Thermopylae might be remembered as an unimportant skirmish. As it was, the battle epitomized the spirit of Greek resistance and did much to enhance Sparta's renown. In time many sayings were attributed to Leonidas, typifying what the rest of Greece regarded as Sparta's laconic wit:

"When Xerxes told him to surrender his weapons, he replied, 'Come and get them.'"

"When someone remarked, 'The Persians are near us,' he said, 'Good, that means we're near *them*, too.'"

"He instructed his men to enjoy their breakfast in the expectation that they would take their evening meal in Hades."

Forty years later Leonidas' remains were reburied in Sparta, while at Thermopylae a stone lion was erected in his memory (the name Leonidas means 'Son of the Lion'). Near it was inscribed the epitaph written by Simonides, proclaiming: 'Stranger, give the Spartans this report: we lie here, obeying orders.' As Leonidas fell, not knowing how the war would end, he could not have conceived that Persia's invasion of mainland Greece was part of a greater pincer movement being played out on the panhellenic stage. For in Sicily the Carthaginians had launched a closely coordinated invasion of their own. On the same day as Thermopylae – or so history recorded – far to the west, at Himera, the Sicilian Greeks faced a fearsome threat of their own.

GELON (?–478)
Tyrannos of Syracuse

Like Peisistratus, Gelon and Hieron acquired power by bad means but used it for good. Though they came to the throne illegally, they became virtuous and beneficent.

Plutarch, *On God's Delayed Vengeance*, 6

By 500 Greek colonists had spread across much of grain-rich Sicily. With most of the native population forced back into the dangerous mountain interior, only the extreme west and northwest coast were not in Greek hands. Here, north Africa's Phoenician colony of Carthage, whose burgeoning empire founded on aggressive maritime trade already controlled much of the western Mediterranean, had settled cities of its own. With Carthaginians and Greeks both hungry to expand further into Sicily conflict was inevitable and in 480 tensions erupted into full-scale war. As Xerxes advanced on mainland Greece a Carthaginian fleet sailed north for Sicily, where the Greeks were mustering under Gelon.

Originally from the tiny island of Telos in the eastern Aegean, Gelon's family had settled in Gela (founded in 688) in south Sicily, becoming priests of Demeter and Persephone, enjoying respect and influence and weathering the political infighting which beset their city. While poleis in Ionia and mainland Greece embraced democracy, tyrannoi still ruled politically conservative Sicily and, when Hippocrates took power in Gela from his murdered brother, he chose as cavalry commander the battle-hardened Gelon, a general renowned for his good fortune. (As a boy, while chasing a fox which had purloined his writing tablet, he survived an earthquake which destroyed his school and everyone in it.) It was a wise appointment. Soon a succession of cities had fallen to Gela's growing empire. Only Syracuse held out.

But in 491 the balance of power shifted. Hippocrates was killed in battle, the Gelans staged a democratic uprising and in the ensuing confusion Gelon seized the throne. As soon as order was restored he turned his sights on Syracuse, whose landowning elite had sought his help against a rebel coalition of the urban poor and their slaves. At the head of a well-drilled army Gelon rode on Syracuse. When its people saw him from their city walls, they surrendered without a fight. It was a glittering prize, the jewel of Sicily, and Gelon made it his capital, leaving his brother **Hieron** to rule Gela. Once more Gelon showed his ruthless acumen. Determined to make Syracuse an economic powerhouse, in 483 he forcibly relocated all the citizens of Camarina, half the population of Gela and the entire aristocracy of Megara Hyblaea, whose poor – like those of Leontini – he sold as slaves. It was, he said, distasteful to have to live beside the demos.

In early summer 480 Greek envoys came to Syracuse entreating Gelon's aid against the Persians. Gelon was unsympathetic. Where had Greece been, he asked, when he was protecting Greek interests against the Carthaginians or avenging **Leonidas'** brother Doreius, killed at Segesta in 510? Still, he promised to help Greece on condition that it granted him overall military or naval command. The envoys refused and returned home to spread rumours that Gelon was pro-Persian. In fact, Gelon could not afford to take troops out of Sicily, for the Carthaginians were amassing an army of their own.

Recently, the tyrannos of Himera, on Sicily's north coast, whose lands abutted those of Phoenician Soleis, had been deposed. Escaping to Carthage, he had persuaded King Hamilcar to launch an armada against Sicily: 200 warships, 3,000 transport vessels and perhaps 300,000 men. The timing was perfect. Contemporaries were convinced that it was carefully coordinated to coincide with Xerxes' invasion of Greece. In a stormy crossing the ships transporting the chariots and horses all were sunk, but the rest reached shore safely and after an initial landfall at Phoenician Panormus they disembarked at Himera. Here they built a stockade around their beached ships and another round their camp and prepared for battle.

Learning of the landing, Gelon marched to Himera. His infantry were outnumbered six to one, but thanks to the storm the Carthaginians had no cavalry, and soon Gelon's 5,000 horsemen were harrying the invaders as they foraged for supplies. For days neither side risked battle, but when he learned that Hamilcar expected cavalry from Selinus to reach him on the same day he was planning to sacrifice to the Phoenician sea god Yam, Gelon knew this was a perfect alignment.

At dawn, as Hamilcar prepared for the ceremony, a squadron of cavalry trotted up to the Carthaginian naval stockade; the gates were opened and the horsemen clattered through. But they were not the expected Selinutes. They were Gelon's men, and as they butchered Hamilcar and set fire to his ships the

One of seven temples adorning the rocky ridge south of Acragas, the temple of Concord was built in the mid-fifth century in the aftermath of Gelon's victory over the Carthaginians at Himera in 480.

combined Greek armies of Sicily advanced. Taken by surprise, the Carthaginians poured out to face them and the two sides engaged. Only when they heard of Hamilcar's death and understood the meaning of the drifting tarry smoke did the Carthaginians break ranks. Then it became a rout. As many as 150,000 were massacred and many more enslaved. Plunged into mourning, Carthage sent envoys to Gelon with peace terms (including, it was later claimed, a promise to stop sacrificing children to Ba'al) and chests containing 200 talents of silver and a golden crown for Gelon's wife, Damarete (whose name, ironically given Gelon's elitist views, means 'the virtue of the demos'). For the next seventy years the Carthaginians left Sicily alone.

With booty won in battle and the money from the treaty, Sicilians celebrated – nowhere more so than in Acragas, which set prisoners of war to work building temples, sewers and the magnificent Kolumbethra. This was a circular pond 1,400 yards (1,280 m) in diameter and 30 feet (9 m) deep, which kept the city well stocked with fish and whose resident swans were much admired. As befitted a priest of Demeter and Persephone, Gelon himself built temples to the goddesses and sent a golden tripod overseas to Delphi. Hearing of the Greeks' victory at Salamis, he assembled his troops in full armour on the parade ground and appeared before them unarmed and naked except for a cloak. With swaggering confidence he listed all that he had done for Syracuse and invited any who would kill him to do so now. Instead, the army cheered him mightily and called him their saviour. It was the pinnacle of Gelon's triumphant life. Less than two years later he died peacefully in bed. Through bravery in battle and shrewd political manoeuvring Gelon had saved Greek Sicily and established Syracuse as its most powerful polis. Soon the city would become a spectacular hub of the Greek arts thanks to his successor, his brother Hieron.

HIERON (?–467)
Tyrannos of Syracuse

Hieron, you have revealed the enchanting flowers of your prosperity to all mankind. Silence is no jewel for such a lucky man. Rather, we should all remember his fine deeds and hymn his blessings with the honey-throated nightingale.

Bacchylides, *Epinicean Odes*, 3

In 478 Hieron's claim to succeed his brother **Gelon** was not uncontested. Gelon had left behind a young son: whoever was his guardian could claim to act as regent. So when another of Gelon's brothers, the popular Polyzelus, married his widow, Damarete, with indecent haste, Syracusan politics became unstable. To quash any potential uprising Hieron quickly enlisted a mercenary army and tried to send Polyzelus on an overseas campaign from which he intended his brother not to return. Instead, Polyzelus fled to Acragas, and with its tyrannos, Theron, prepared for a war. However, thanks to Hieron's goodwill gesture of delivering his own supporters, Theron's enemies in Himera, to Acragas for execution, peace was maintained, the warring brothers reconciled and Hieron's position within Syracuse and wider Sicily confirmed.

To consolidate his power, Hieron went far beyond the usual arranged political marriages. He forcibly relocated to Leontini the citizens of the nearby poleis of Naxos and Catana, replaced them with 5,000 Syracusans and 5,000 immigrants from Peloponnesian Greece, and refounded Catana under the new name of Aetna. To tighten his grip still further he established a network of secret police to spy on his own subjects, the first recorded use of such an agency in western history.

If he was resented at home, internationally Hieron was applauded. As early as 524 Euboea's colony of Cumae (founded in the eighth century) had defeated an alliance of Italians led by the Etruscans. Now, in 474, they were back. As the south Italian Greeks mobilized their hoplite armies, Hieron responded to an appeal from Cumae's tyrannos and launched his triremes. In the waters between the mountainous island of Ischia and Cumae's sandy beach they engaged the Etruscan fleet. It was a resounding victory. The Etruscan menace was destroyed, and with Hieron's navy now controlling the south Italian seas he was feted as a liberator. Hieron responded to his heroic role with gusto. At Olympia he dedicated the bronze helmet he had worn at Cumae. Lavish statues commemorated the victories of his horse Pherenicus at the Pythian Games in 482 and 478 and at Olympia in 476, and of his chariots at Delphi in 470 and Olympia in 468. Meanwhile, in Syracuse and Aetna, Hieron welcomed Greece's most pre-eminent writers and performers. Many of them were 'praise-singers', professional poets like **Pindar**, Simonides and his nephew Bacchylides, paid to eulogize victors in the panhellenic games. Pindar composed four *epinicean* (or victory) odes for Hieron; Bacchylides wrote three. One of Bacchylides' poems contains a memorable image, which could describe Hieron himself:

To commemorate his chariot victory at Delphi in 478 or 474, Hieron's brother Polyzelus erected a bronze statue of his horses and chariot as well as the winning charioteer, reins held in outstretched hands.

Lightning-fast on tawny wings the eagle, confident in its immeasurable strength, cleaves the vast unfathomable sky, the messenger of Zeus, the thunder god, whose rule is wide; and all the little birds, shrill-chattering, scatter in terror.

At Hieron's invitation Epicharmus, a pioneer of stage comedy, made his home in Syracuse, and in the newly built theatre, with stone seating for up to 24,000 spectators, the Athenian tragedian **Aeschylus** performed a revival of his *Persians*. At Aetna, in honour of the city so recently (and brutally) refounded, Aeschylus staged a specially written play, *Women of Aetna*. Hieron welcomed philosophers too, like the controversial Xenophanes, who taught that there was one universal and immortal god and scorned those who pictured deities in human form: 'If horses and cattle could paint or sculpt, horses would show their gods as horses and cattle as cattle.'

Hieron's last years were beset by illness and anxiety. When Theron of Acragas died in 472 his son, the cruel, impetuous Thrasydeus, raised an army with which to attack Syracuse, but he had misjudged his enemy. Before he could even march, Hieron was at his gates and in fierce fighting, in which 6,000 hoplites fell, Thrasydeus was beaten. He fled into exile, where he was tried and executed. While democratic coups erupted across Sicily, in Syracuse the secret police clamped down. But nothing could save Hieron. In severe pain from gall stones he died at Aetna in 467. Power passed to his brother Thrasybulus. Lacking either the charisma or the ruthlessness of Hieron and Gelon, he was overthrown within eleven months, and democracy came to Syracuse.

PINDAR (c. 522–c. 442)
Lyric Poet

Try to rival Pindar and you spiral on waxen wings, a halting hack, doomed to crash like Icarus into the sparkling sea. A torrent in flood, erupting down a mountain side, unstoppable, storm-swamped and seething, roaring thunder – such is the poetry of Pindar.

Horace, *Odes*, 4.2

Pindar's victory odes eulogize traditional values. Conservative and rooted in the heroic past, they appear oblivious to the political and religious revolutions sweeping the Greek world. As much of our evidence for his life comes from his poetry, it is not surprising that it can at times seem fanciful.

Born in Cynoscephalae, a village near Thebes, around 522 to a family which boasted descent from King Aegeus of Athens, Pindar (who blithely wrote of the 'turbulent masses') was staunchly aristocratic. Although we know little of his father, like many Classical Greek authors Pindar was part of a literary dynasty – his daughters Eumetis and Protomache were poets, too – though the Greeks attributed his 'honeyed voice' to a childhood bee sting on the mouth (a story told of several other writers).

As a young man, studying with Lasus of Hermione, a favourite poet of the exiled Peisistratids, Pindar's fame spread rapidly, perhaps thanks to demonstration performances to international audiences at the panhellenic games or lyric competitions, where poets displayed often bitter rivalry. Pindar's feuds with his contemporaries Simonides and Bacchylides were legendary. In 498, at the age of around twenty-four, Pindar was commissioned by the wealthy

Pindar, his head crowned with an olive wreath, raises his lyre in his right hand in
Jean-August-Dominique Ingres's *Pindar and Ictinus*, painted in the mid-nineteenth century.

Aleuadae of Thessaly to compose a victory ode for Hippocleas, winner of
the boys' *diaulos* (400 yards, 366 m) race at Delphi's Pythian Games. Already
these lyrics, written to be sung by a dancing chorus in a civic celebration in the
victor's polis, contained much that was characteristic of Pindar's later work: a
profound respect for aristocratic families; a wealth of striking imagery; and the
use of often oblique references to mythology designed to assimilate contemporary
triumphs into heroic and pseudo-historic tradition. The athlete's victory
may have been fleeting, but the epinicean ode was intended to bestow
immortal (and international) fame on him and kudos on the family which
commissioned it.

Pindar's music has not survived, but both it and its lyrics were so admired that the composer-poet was soon in great demand across the Greek world, commissioned by proud families from the mainland (Athens and Corinth) and east Aegean (Rhodes and Tenedos) to south Italy (Locris), Sicily (Syracuse, Aetna and Camarina) and north Africa (Cyrene). Unless he was required to train local choruses or perform himself, there was little reason why Pindar should travel as extensively as his poetry, but his verses hint at residences at the courts of **Hieron** of Syracuse and Theron of Acragas. In search of lucrative commissions he would certainly have been a regular visitor at the Olympic and other panhellenic games as well as more minor gatherings.

The Persian invasions of mainland Greece in 490 and 480/79 seem to have left Pindar largely untouched. Like Thebes, Aegina, his supposed refuge during Xerxes' attack, sided with Persia early in the conflict. But given Pindar's reliance on commissions from as wide a range of families as possible he needed to appear politically unbiased. Thus, embracing the games' idealistic spirit of panhellenism, he could praise the blessings of Sparta as easily as the beauty of Athens, 'garlanded with violets'. We do read, though, that Thebes fined him heavily for praising its arch-rival Athens – the Athenians responded by awarding Pindar double the amount and appointing him their *proxenos* (representative) in Thebes. Elsewhere, expanding on the ideal of the Greek-speaking world as one unified community, he used lyrics written for Hieron's chariot victory at the Pythian Games of 470 to celebrate Greek victories against not only Carthage and the Etruscans at Himera and Cumae but the Persians at Salamis and Plataea.

Although Pindar is best known for four books of epinicean odes (one for each of the panhellenic games), his output was diverse: later Alexandrian scholars compiled three additional books of 'maiden songs', two each of *hyporchemata* (dances to Apollo), *prosodia* (processional hymns) and *dithyrambs* (hymns to Dionysus), and single books of laments, general hymns and *paianes* (triumphal hymns to Apollo). Perhaps in recognition of these paianes, Pindar was appointed priest of Apollo at Delphi, where the second-century AD traveller Pausanias saw the iron chair on which Pindar sat to sing during the Theoxenia festival. Another, later writer tells how, when closing the sanctuary at night, Delphi's priests intoned, 'May Pindar dine well with the gods.' (He also records that the god Pan was once heard singing Pindar's songs on a nearby mountain.)

Tradition states that in around 442, at a festival in Argos, the eighty-year-old Pindar saw a vision of Persephone, goddess of the Underworld, for whom he had never composed a hymn, in which she reassured him that he could soon praise her in person. Ten days later he died, and his daughters took his ashes home to Thebes. Such was Pindar's fame that his lengthy ode commemorating Diagoras of Rhodes' Olympic boxing victory of 464 was later displayed in gold letters in the temple of Athene in the Rhodian city of Lindos; and when **Alexander III** of Macedon razed Thebes to the ground in 335 the one building he preserved was Pindar's house.

Like a Homeric hero, Pindar craved undying fame. In his verses he rails in deliberately heightened language, pitched to reflect the glory of the athlete's success: 'Ephemeral beings! What is someone? What is no one? Man is a dream of a shadow.' But then he proclaims that 'when a shining light, god-given, comes to men, the blaze of glory is within them and blessings in their lives'. For him, 'godlike words' paved the path to immortality, 'for, if a man expresses something well, his words, undying, spread, and over all the fertile earth, and over all the sea, the blaze of his fine deeds, unquenchable, shall shine forever'. Content to comment on rather than shape history, he was the antithesis of his contemporary Aeschylus, the dramatist whose actions on the field of battle helped save Athens.

AESCHYLUS (525/4–456/5)
Tragic Playwright

Go in peace Aeschylus. Save our city with your noble thoughts – and educate the ignorant, as well!

Aristophanes, Frogs, 1500–3

Aeschylus was born in the early years of **Hippias'** rule, probably at Eleusis, where his father Euphorion had his estates. As a young man, sleeping in a vineyard, Aeschylus is said to have been visited by Dionysus (god of the grape and drama), who bade him write tragedies. It was a tale which Aeschylus may well have encouraged, though in later years claims that he could write only when drunk were fuelled by his rival **Sophocles**, who quipped that even if Aeschylus used words well he did so unconsciously.

Aeschylus entered history in 490 when he and his brothers buckled on their armour and marched to Marathon. Here, in an act of desperate heroism, his brother Cynaegirus was cut down in the surf, his arm sliced off as he seized the stern of a Persian ship, an episode commemorated in Athens' Stoa Poikile in a painting showing Cynaegirus and Aeschylus fighting side by side. Ten years later, at Salamis, Aeschylus once more experienced the bedlam of war when he took his place on the Greek triremes as they smashed into Persia's fleet. Almost certainly he fought the next year at Plataea, too.

In 472 he commemorated Salamis in his first surviving tragedy, *Persians*. Financed by **Pericles**, the play imagined the impact of the defeat at Salamis on the Persian court at Susa. As the Great King returns broken to his lamenting mother Queen Atossa, the ghost of his father Darius berates Xerxes' *hubris* (transgressive arrogance) in bridging the Bosphorus and cutting a canal through Athos, concluding that 'Zeus is a stern judge and punishes excessive pride'.

With *Persians* (and the three lost plays staged with it) Aeschylus won first prize in the drama competition at the City Dionysia, the start of a run of victories which, between 484 and 458, saw him win thirteen times (with fifty-two out of

Aeschylus and Salamis

A tragedy by Phrynichus, *The Fall of Miletus* (493), which dramatized the crushing of the Ionian Revolt, resulted in its author facing a heavy fine. Thereafter tragedians were nervous about tackling current events, preferring instead to set their plays in the world of mythology, where observations on contemporary politics could be made more obliquely. The Persian Wars were an exception. In 476 Phrynichus himself dramatized them in his (lost) *Phoenician Women*, while four years later Aeschylus revisited the theme in *Persians*. As Aeschylus fought at Salamis, the play's messenger speech (though told from the Persian perspective) comes close to being an eyewitness account:

> Ship battered bronze beak into ship. First a Greek trireme swooped and sliced the stern from a Phoenician warship. Wave upon wave, each side closed. At first our fleet's sheer numbers favoured us, but soon our ships became constricted in the narrows: hundreds, helpless, and unable to go to one another's help, ramming each other with their bronze beaks, shattering each others' oars. The enemy surrounded us; attacked. Our ships capsized; the sea was covered, carpeted in corpses and in wrecks, and all the rocks and all the shores were bloated with our dead. Then all our ships broke ranks and fled, and as our shipwrecked sailors floundered in the sea, the Greeks snatched bits of wreckage, fractured oars, and sliced and stabbed at them as if they were a shoal of tuna or of fish trapped in a woven net. The sea was thick with screaming and the noise of death until night came and darkness blanketed our eyes. If I should speak for ten days and nights, I still could not tell everything. But know this: never before on one day have so many good men died.

Aeschylus' *Oresteia* perhaps inspired this fourth-century vase from south Italy, on which the matricide Orestes takes sanctuary from the Furies at an altar beneath Athene's sacred olive, as Apollo and Artemis protect him.

a total of between seventy and ninety plays, of which only seven attributed to him now survive complete). Many, exploring heroic themes ('slices of Homer' as Aeschylus called them), were profound studies of justice and retribution, whose tragedies traced the causes and effects of wrongdoing over many generations. Thus *Oresteia* (458) considers the consequences on his family of Agamemnon's sacrifice of his daughter Iphigenia, part of a spiral of vengeance whose roots lay embedded deep in the past, and which could be resolved only at the lawcourt on Athens' Areopagus hill. It was a startlingly contemporary ending to the drama. Only four years earlier, Athens' democrats had abolished the ancient aristocratic Council of the Areopagus, replacing it with a lawcourt exclusively to try cases of murder.

Politics were never far from Athenian drama. In 468 Aeschylus was the victim of partisan manoeuvring when **Cimon** and his fellow strategoi disrupted the normal process to award the first prize not to Aeschylus (the favourite of Cimon's arch-rival Pericles) but to Sophocles. They claimed their intervention was designed to prevent a riot, a barbed reference to an earlier production in which Aeschylus was almost assaulted on stage. Like many other tragedians, Aeschylus performed in his own plays – he is said to have played Clytemnestra in *Oresteia* – and once, having delivered a line which some thought revealed the secrets of the Eleusinian Mysteries, he was forced to take refuge at the theatre's altar of Dionysus. Only its sanctity prevented Aeschylus from being dragged off and killed. In his subsequent trial he was acquitted, thanks, it was said, to the memory of his bravery at Marathon.

Though written in a dense and archaizing style, Aeschylus' tragedies were rich in theatricality and stunningly innovative – the dramatic entrance of avenging Furies onto the stage in *Eumenides* (the third tragedy in *Oresteia*) shocked the audience and excited extreme consternation. He redefined the conventions of stagecraft in other ways, too. Theatre, in the autocratic age of the tyrannoi, had involved one solo performer interacting with a chorus. As befitted Athens' new democracy Aeschylus introduced a second actor, thereby transforming drama: now characters could enter into dialogue and truly debate the issues of the day.

In 456/5, Aeschylus returned to Sicily, an island he had first visited at **Hieron's** invitation two decades earlier. Approaching seventy, Aeschylus died at Gela, perhaps while supervising a production of *Oresteia*. According to legend he was dozing outside when an eagle dropped a tortoise from a great height, hoping to crack its shell. Disastrously for all concerned it had mistaken Aeschylus' bald head for a rock. (The story was told of others, too, and may have been allegorical: the eagle was the bird of Zeus and tortoiseshell the raw material for lyres.)

In an unprecedented decision Athens' Assembly voted to fund revivals of Aeschylus' plays at the Dionysia, a venue otherwise exclusively devoted to new writing. Meanwhile, Aeschylus' sons, Euphorion and Euaeon, and his nephew, Philocles, continued the dramatic line, winning victories over Sophocles and **Euripides**. In 405, with Athens close to defeat in the Peloponnesian War, the comic dramatist **Aristophanes** imagined Dionysus descending into Hades to bring Aeschylus back to life so that the wisdom of his verses might provide the salvation of his city. But it was not for his writing, but for fighting on behalf of Athens, that Aeschylus wished to be remembered. On his headstone in Sicily his self-composed epitaph read:

> *Beneath this marker lies Aeschylus, son of Euphorion, an Athenian who died in Gela, rich in wheat fields. The groves of Marathon tell of his courage, and the long-haired Persians know it well.*

Thanks to Hieron, Syracuse's theatre was one of the first to be built in stone. Aeschylus probably performed here during his first visit to Sicily in the 470s.

Chapter 4

The Age of
Pericles

Athens' first citizen Pericles, known as 'the Olympian', is shown as a helmeted strategos in this Roman copy of a fifth-century Greek original.

PERICLES (495–429)
Statesman and General

Thanks to his high standing, ability and celebrated honesty, Pericles could wield sovereign power over the People, and so lead them rather than be led by them.

Thucydides, History, 2.65

Athens in the second half of the fifth century embodied polar opposites. Domestically it paraded its democratic credentials, but its foreign policy was unashamedly imperialist, crushing dissent with increasing ferocity and using the revenues from its nominal allies to enhance its own prestige. For more than a generation the man who led his city and shaped its politics similarly personified two extremes, for while he drew his power from the People (relying on their support to turn proposals into policy), he was an Alcmaeonid aristocrat, seldom seen in public, who took great care never to betray his true emotions. Probably during his lifetime, and certainly immediately afterwards, he was considered so extraordinary that the period of history he dominated was named the Age of Pericles.

In 495, while pregnant with Pericles, his mother Agariste is said to have dreamt she was delivered of a lion cub. There were good reasons for her pride: a blue-blooded Alcmaeonid, she was the niece of **Cleisthenes**, while Xanthippus her husband was a rising star in Athens. Yet these were troubled times. Pericles was just one year old when the Ionian Revolt was crushed; five in the year of Marathon; and ten when Xanthippus, dangerously powerful following his conviction of **Miltiades**, was ostracized. It was a useful lesson. In adulthood Pericles took great pains to avoid the People's wrath.

Xanthippus' ostracism was cut short by war. In 480, as Xerxes bore down on Attica, he was recalled, to be appointed the next year as Admiral of the Fleet. At Mycale in Ionia, Xanthippus led his men to victory against the Persians (traditionally on the same day as the battle of Plataea). But the Spartans, who were still in overall command and loath to defend Asiatic Greeks who were ethnically related not to them but to the Athenians, proposed that the Ionians be evacuated to the mainland. Xanthippus vehemently disagreed and the scheme was dropped. Now no longer on the defensive, Xanthippus besieged Sestus on the Dardanelles, seat of Persia's governor, Artayctes. When Sestus fell months later Xanthippus crucified Artayctes on a hill overlooking the site of Xerxes' bridge and stoned to death the helpless Persian's son before his eyes.

Meanwhile, in Athens, Xanthippus' own son Pericles was enjoying a liberal education that would prepare him in adulthood to mix with some of the most progressive thinkers of his age. Among them were the mathematician-cum-philosopher Zeno, who perfected the *elenchic* method (later favoured by **Socrates**) of discovering truths through question and answer; the musician and musicologist Damon, who classified modes and metres and helped perfect Pericles' innate skills of rhetoric; and the cosmologist Anaxagoras, who revolutionized astronomy (discovering *inter alia* that the moon's light is a reflection of the sun's, thereby explaining lunar eclipses) and questioned conventional religious beliefs by proposing that the universe is governed by a pure, rational intelligence. Such opinions probably pleased Pericles – as a supposedly cursed Alcmaeonid he was well aware of the pernicious grip in which superstition held his fellow citizens. From Anaxagoras, too, Pericles was said to have acquired 'a mind imbued with abstract speculation, a dignity of spirit and a nobility of speech, free from the unprincipled, ridiculous vulgarity of the demagogue'.

Aristocratic by birth and inclination, Pericles was loath to enter politics. His uncanny resemblance to the now-disgraced **Peisistratus** hampered him, while his disproportionately large head, the butt of many jokes, led him to insist that every portrait showed him helmeted. When, finally, he did embark on a political career Pericles projected a carefully manipulated image of sobriety. Refusing invitations to social engagements he cultivated a reputation for aloofness which earned him (no doubt to his great satisfaction) the soubriquet 'Olympian'. Following Peisistratus' example he courted the People assiduously. In 472, while still in his early twenties, Pericles used his wealth to produce **Aeschylus'** *Persians*, a celebration of Athens' victory at Salamis, which had been won by the bravery of the common citizen and the wit of the staunchly democratic **Themistocles**. Yet in 471 Themistocles was ostracized. Deprived of his champion, Pericles lurked in the shadows for almost a decade. At last in 463 he re-emerged to prosecute the Alcmaeonids' bête noire **Cimon**, but the case collapsed – perhaps because Cimon's sister Elpinice's entreaties moved Pericles to (uncharacteristic) compassion.

In 461, on a wave of anti-aristocratic, anti-Spartan sentiment, Cimon was ostracized and the Assembly dominated by his populist opponents. Their leader was Ephialtes, the man credited with transferring to the People many of the powers of the Council of the Areopagus. But Ephialtes' reforming zeal cost him his life, his bloodied corpse left, gruesome, in an alleyway, his assassins never found. With the role of People's champion now vacant, Pericles' time had come. Such was his rhetorical power and personal charisma that Athens was soon his to command.

Much of the next decade bears Pericles' imprint. In 461/60 Athens' relationship with Sparta rapidly disintegrated as tensions erupted into war, the fruits of the deliberate policy spearheaded by Ephialtes of embracing Megara (when it broke from its alliance with Sparta), making treaties with Argos (Sparta's ancient enemy) and settling fugitive Helots in Naupactus on the Gulf of Corinth to create a useful naval base from which to conduct campaigns in the west. This First Peloponnesian War was bitterly contested. In 457, at Tanagra, Athens was badly defeated, and although she soon took revenge, it was clear by the time Cimon returned from exile in 451 that neither side could truly triumph. His five-year truce did not end all hostilities. In 448 Sparta's claims over Delphi led to the Sacred War and, as fighting flared again, Boeotia, Euboea and Megara renounced their alliance with Athens. When the Spartan king Pleistonax invaded Attica, it was rumoured that Pericles bribed him royally to withdraw. At last Athens retook Euboea, accepted the loss of Megara and Boeotia and in 446 signed the Thirty Years Peace with Sparta.

Abroad, Athens was still campaigning against Persia. Around 460, responding to an appeal from the Libyan king Inarus to help throw off the Persian yoke (and with an eye to fertile wheat fields), Athens and the Delian League sent a fleet to Egypt. Following a protracted campaign and some initial successes the Greeks eventually found themselves confined to an island in the Nile. At last in 454 the Persians diverted the river and attacked. In the ensuing massacre as many as 8,000 Athenians, possibly around a quarter of the citizen population, may have perished. Out of fear that Persia might seize the moment and invade Greece the contents of the League's treasury on Delos were hastily shipped under armed guard to Athens. The failure in 450 of Cimon's expedition against Persian Cyprus only further diminished the Athenian appetite for foreign wars, and they made peace with the Great King Artaxerxes. In 449 the Persian Wars were finally over.

To mark the peace, and to position Athens as leader of the Greeks, Pericles offered to host a panhellenic congress to discuss the future. Predictably Sparta declined to attend and the congress came to nothing. But it was a useful propaganda exercise, and when three years later Pericles responded to an appeal from the rootless peoples of Sybaris to help found a new colony at nearby Thurii, he announced that the polis should be considered not Athenian but panhellenic. The implications were clear: for Pericles the two terms were interchangeable. Yet his vision was not based on equality: as a sign of his polis' growing exclusivity, he had already imposed strict restrictions on Athenian citizenship.

In order to improve the lot of poorer Athenians, Pericles had introduced basic pay for state service on juries or as oarsmen in the fleet. Now he went even further in his efforts to redistribute Athens' wealth to citizens as diverse as hauliers and miners, carpenters and sculptors. Inspired by the Peisistratids a century before and disregarding the Oath of Plataea, he dazzlingly reconceptualized the very fabric of the city by announcing the most ambitious building programme Greece had ever seen: the reconstruction of the Athenian temples burned by Xerxes. At its heart, dominating the Athenian skyline on the Acropolis, was an exquisite Doric temple dedicated to Athene – the Parthenon. Deliberately designed to rival Ephesus' Artemision and Samos' temple of Hera, it was the most lavishly decorated temple on mainland Greece. With neither priests not altar, it had three main purposes: as home to an enormous, triumphalist gold and ivory statue of Athene by the renowned sculptor **Pheidias**; as treasury for the Delian League; and as a *trophy* or victory memorial commemorating the defeat of Persia.

As construction work commenced Pericles' political enemies saw their chance to undermine him. In 442, led by Thucydides, son of Melesias, they accused him of misappropriating the Delian League's funds to further his personal ambitions. In answer Pericles offered to pay for the Parthenon from his own purse – and to dedicate it not in Athens' name but in his own. The People, seduced by his audacity, applauded Pericles and ostracized Thucydides. From now on, as Thucydides' namesake the historian observed, with Pericles' enemies neutralized, Athens, nominally a democracy, was in fact ruled by its first citizen.

For the next decade Pericles, elected strategos every year and often on campaign, imposed his will on an increasingly imperialist Athens. In 440, when two League states, Miletus and Samos, became embroiled in hostilities, Athens sent a war fleet to the eastern Aegean. After a protracted siege Pericles crushed Samian resistance, executed the ringleaders, destroyed the city walls and imposed not just democracy but heavy fines. For the other subject states – once fellow allies in defence of Greek freedom – it was a salutary lesson.

Consecrated in 438, the Parthenon, the jewel in the crown of Pericles'
building programme, still dominates the Athenian skyline.

Meanwhile, in Athens intellectual life flourished. Next to the open-air theatre
where the plays of the City Dionysia were performed, Pericles built an enclosed
Odeon (its design inspired by the Persian royal tent abandoned at Plataea),
where musical contests were staged during the newly expanded Panathenaic
Festival. Foreign intellectuals were encouraged to settle in Athens, too, many
of whom shared Pericles' religious scepticism: **Protagoras**, a supreme rationalist
whose frustration with the limitations of anthropocentric observation caused
him to comment that 'man is the measure of all things'; **Empedocles**, a follower
of **Pythagoras**, who explained the universe in terms of the four elements, and
warned that our understanding is clouded by a lack of objective knowledge;
Aspasia, a witty and well-educated woman from Miletus, for whom Pericles
divorced his wife in 445 and by whom he had a son.

It was not only philosophers who flocked to Athens. Piraeus, now linked
to the city by impregnable Long Walls, had become a thriving commercial hub.
As Pericles boasted, 'Thanks to its greatness, every commodity from every land
pours into Athens, so we enjoy foreign products as easily as those we make or
grow ourselves.' They included oxhides from Cyrene, salt fish from the Bosphorus,
cheeses from Syracuse, papyrus from Egypt, frankincense from Syria, ivory
from Libya, carpets from Carthage, almonds from Paphlagonia and slaves from

Phrygia. In time such heightened economic activity brought Athens into conflict. In 432 Pericles responded to a dispute with Megara not by declaring war (which would have infringed the terms of the Thirty Years Peace with Sparta) but by banning the Megarians from all ports and agoras within Athens' empire. Megara's ally Corinth was outraged. Already the cities had clashed over Corinth's colony Corcyra; now they came to blows over control of Potidaea, a Corinthian colony in north Greece which was also a member of the Delian League.

Pericles counselled against facing the enemy on land. He advised instead that, given Athens' naval superiority and with the Long Walls ensuring access to Piraeus, the city should become a landlocked island and do battle at sea. So he persuaded Attica's country dwellers to abandon their homes, live in makeshift encampments within the city walls and hunker down for war. Some contemporaries believed that Pericles was trying to distract attention from his personal problems – in a recent flurry of litigation against his friends, Anaxagoras had been forced to flee the city, while Aspasia was prosecuted for immorality, a charge calculated to cause maximum distress (Pericles wept as he defended her). Even Pericles' eldest son Xanthippus attacked him, spreading slanders and dragging financial disagreements before the courts, a feud which was never reconciled.

War broke out in earnest in 431. Despite some resentment at Pericles' policy, at the end of the first year of hostilities he was chosen to deliver the traditional eulogy for the fallen. In a carefully crafted speech, a paean to democracy and the democratic spirit whose influence can still be felt today, Pericles not only reasserted his unashamed, if dangerous, nationalism, exhorting citizens to 'become Athens' lover' and describing Athens as an 'education to all Greece', but redefined the Greek concept of the hero, proclaiming that by laying down his life for Athens, every citizen could achieve heroic status.

Not everyone was convinced by Pericles' war strategy. In 430 he failed to be re-elected strategos. Then an unforeseen disaster struck. A virulent plague, which had originated in upper Egypt, reached Athens. With the urban population bloated by refugees from Attica, the effects were devastating. Soon the streets and sanctuaries were crawling with the dying and thick with the stench of death. In 429 Pericles – strategos once more – endured the bitter consequences of his policies. Both his legitimate sons fell ill and died. Burying the younger, Pericles again publicly broke down in tears. Soon he was himself infected. Facing death, the arch-rationalist hung a lucky charm about his neck. His last words, 'No Athenian ever put on mourning because of me', suggest that his mind was wandering.

Somehow life and war went on, but by the time the plague finally came to an end in 426 it had claimed a third of Athens' population. Pericles' successors abandoned his tactics – but not his strident nationalism – and the Peloponnesian War spiralled into brutal depravity. In *Agamemnon*, Aeschylus (the poet whom Pericles once championed) had written of a lion cub raised in the house, which when mature wreaked havoc. It could have been a metaphor for Pericles himself. Despite his disastrous bellicosity he was praised by the predominately aristocratic (anti-democratic) writers of his age. Yet curiously one close friend scarcely mentioned him, the writer who, even more than Pericles, helped to define the panhellenic spirit and shape our view of history: Herodotus.

HERODOTUS (c. 484–?420s)
Historian

In the writings of Herodotus, the Father of Greek History…we find almost as many fables as in the works of poets.

Cicero, *On the Laws*, 1.5

At the beginning of his *Histories* Herodotus proclaims his place of birth: the teeming port of Halicarnassus (modern Bodrum) on the Aegean coast of Asia Minor. Originally a Greek colony, it was annexed by Persia. Of Herodotus' life we have only sketchy, unreliable details, but these imply that he was wealthy, well-educated and connected to Panyasis, an author of epic poems on Heracles and Ionia. They suggest, too, that his family was driven into exile on Samos by the harsh rule of the tyrannos Lygdamis, but returned around 454 to depose him in an uprising which cost Panyasis his life. Meanwhile, Herodotus may already have begun researching the past, travelling widely to gather evidence in Egypt, Persia, Ionia and the Aegean. But it was Athens which most attracted him: in his opinion it was the best of cities, its radical democracy the most empowering of all constitutions.

Here he settled around 447, revelling in Athens' atmosphere of cosmopolitan enquiry and associating with many of its intellectuals and aristocrats. Marvelling that relatively barren Attica had become so prosperous, he concluded: 'Soft places produce soft people. One land cannot yield rich crops as well as brave and noble men.' Later in the 440s he probably enrolled as a citizen of Thurii, Athens' new colony in south Italy, an ideal location from which to explore and research the Greek west. By 431, however, he may have returned to Athens, perhaps to write about the Peloponnesian War, and possibly died there of the plague which devastated the city between 430 and 426 (though tombs of Herodotus were also seen at Thurii and Pella).

Herodotus' towering achievement, the *Histories*, helped to establish how Greeks and subsequent civilizations viewed their past. Beginning with a monumental exploration of the rise of Greece and Persia, it traced the causes of their conflict before presenting a narrative of the Persian invasions of Greece. Herodotus defined his intention in the first sentence:

> the publication [apodexis] of enquiries [historie], so that the accomplishments of men should not be forgotten through time, and the great and remarkable deeds of Greeks and barbarians together with the reasons for their conflict should not lack proper fame.

Although belonging to the tradition of recording 'the famous deeds of men', it was nothing short of revolutionary. Whereas earlier chroniclers such as Hecataeus had been mostly content to rationalize sometimes mythological accounts of an often distant past, Herodotus, true to the scientific spirit of his age, conducted an active investigation into events so recent that he could travel to the sites associated with them and interview many of their protagonists at first hand. He aimed to entertain as well as educate. 'Apodexis' means both 'publication' and 'performance'; and, like the Homeric epics, the *Histories* were originally intended for public recital. Herodotus is said to have declaimed extracts from the portico of Zeus' temple at Olympia, and his style – sometimes polemical, always entertaining – is reminiscent of fifth-century display lectures of the kind associated with sophists such as **Gorgias**.

In producing his innovative and sweeping prose narrative the only real model available to Herodotus was epic poetry. Indeed, the influence of Homer can be felt throughout the *Histories*, from the 'catalogue' of Xerxes' invasion forces (paralleling the *Iliad*'s 'catalogue' of Greek ships) to a sublime lack of racism or xenophobia: Greeks and barbarians (literally, those whose language sounds like a sheep's bleating, thus a non-Greek speaker) are both as capable of remarkable achievements as of committing atrocities. Yet Herodotus carefully distanced himself from Homer, stressing that his *Histories* were based on rational enquiry not divine inspiration.

If many of Herodotus' conclusions and accounts are flawed or questionable, this does not diminish his achievement. He was the first to define a new, evidence-based methodology with which to comprehend the past within the

Hippocrates of Cos

In the fifth century medicine, which had earlier relied heavily on magic, became more scientific. By the late 500s doctors such as Alcmaeon of Croton were conducting medical research, including dissection, and in the late 400s Hippocrates (c. 460–c. 370) founded a 'hospital' at the sanctuary of Asclepius on Cos. A shadowy figure, Hippocrates is credited with writing books on medicine and health, while the Hippocratic Oath, which dates from his lifetime, obliges doctors to work only for good, forbidding treatments likely to do harm, breaches of confidentiality and sexual relations with patients.

Hippocrates believed that diseases were not god-sent but the product of environmental, dietary or lifestyle imbalances, and that all had specific crisis points which, if treated correctly, could result in a cure. This holistic approach permeates the treatise *Airs, Waters, Places*, which meticulously records the location of patients' homes, their way of life and the progress and outcome of diseases. Hippocrates' teaching became widely accepted and authors as diverse as Herodotus and Euripides reveal how new medical knowledge influenced the Greeks' perception of their world.

context of the world as it was then understood. Painstakingly attempting to distinguish fact from hearsay, he used a vast range of sources: records and inscriptions, eyewitness reports, folk tales and poetry (including **Sappho** and **Pindar**), 'experts' like Egyptian priests, family and civic traditions. Like his contemporary, the celebrated doctor Hippocrates of Cos, Herodotus understood the importance of context, both historical and physical – his many 'digressions' on geography and anthropology are reminiscent of earlier *periplous* ('travel') literature, though he curiously rejects an apparently accurate record of the circumnavigation of Africa by Phoenician sailors.

Herodotus never questions the existence of the gods. Instead, he weaves divine intervention into his human narrative, believing that through both oracles and active interference the gods uphold a moral imperative that excess should be punished. This is well illustrated in his account of Solon's meeting with the boastful Lydian king Croesus. After displaying his overflowing treasuries, Croesus asks Solon 'Whom do you consider to be the world's happiest man?' Much to the king's annoyance Solon names first an obscure Athenian who fell fighting for his country, then a pair of humble brothers called Cleobis and Biton who died

Shown on an amphora that
pre-dates Herodotus' *Histories*,
Croesus' pyre is set alight.

piously pulling their mother in a wagon to Hera's shrine near Argos. Many years later, however, after misinterpreting an oracular warning, Croesus is defeated in battle, loses his kingdom and all his wealth, and faces execution on a pyre. Apparently too late, he realizes the truth of Solon's maxim, 'Consider no man happy until he is dead', and groans aloud – and to reward his newfound wisdom, Apollo extinguishes the flames in a deluge of rain. Herodotus probably knew that the story was fiction, but there are many kinds of reality. Solon and Croesus are exemplars, the one of honest Athens, the other of the opulent east. Speaking truth to power, Solon encapsulates the underlying morality of the *Histories*: power is transient, luxury debilitating and moral integrity superior to temporal wealth.

The *Histories* end with Xanthippus' crucifixion of the Persian governor of Sestus in 479. In the context of Herodotus' narrative of human excess and divine punishment it reads like a warning. By the 430s, thanks to Xanthippus' son **Pericles**, Athens had grown rich and powerful. Would this cause its empire to fall, too? Knowing that distressing the People could invite danger, Herodotus may have deliberately chosen to follow the example of tragedians like his friend Sophocles, who regularly dressed observations about the present in stories of past history or mythology.

SOPHOCLES (497/6–405)
Tragic Playwright and Politician

How blessed is Sophocles! He lived long, was accomplished and contented, and wrote many splendid tragedies; and in the end he died without experiencing disaster.

Phrynichus, Muses (fragment 31)

Sophocles was born in Colonus, a leafy village northeast of Athens. His father Sophilus was a wealthy arms manufacturer and landowner, able to hire the distinguished composer and performer Lamprus as his son's dance and music tutor. In 480, already a fine wrestler on the brink of adulthood, Sophocles flaunted his many talents when, 'oiled, naked and accompanying himself on the lyre', he led the chorus in the victory hymns after Salamis, a scene recorded in a later painting in the Stoa Poikile.

Sophocles' dramatic debut at the City Dionysia of 468 was controversial (the contest was judged not by a jury chosen by lot but by the ten strategoi), but his victory was just the first of many. In over thirty festivals (for which he wrote 123 plays, of which seven now survive) he was victorious eighteen times at the Dionysia and perhaps six at the Lenaea. He never came third. Initially, like all dramatists, Sophocles himself performed, playing the lyre in *Thamyris* and ball-games in *Nausicaa*, where he played the heroine, but later he stopped acting, blaming his weak voice.

Sophocles was a great innovator. Shortly after his first victory he began writing dramas which required not two but three actors. **Aeschylus** quickly followed suit, and soon playwrights were exploiting opportunities for greater realism and flexibility. Sophocles later increased the size of the chorus from twelve to fifteen, in order to compensate for their reduced dramatic role. He is also credited with introducing 'painted scenery', though what this means is arguable.

With theatrical success came public office. In 442 Sophocles was one of Athens' ten *Hellanotimai* ('Greek treasurers') overseeing the Delian League's annual tribute. In 441/40, as strategos, he accompanied **Pericles** on his expedition against Samos. Sent to raise reinforcements, Sophocles and his fleet were

Inside a mid-fifth-century Athenian wine cup, the hero of several of Sophocles' plays, Oedipus, is asked a riddle by the Sphinx: 'What walks first on four legs, then two, then three?' Correctly, he answered: 'Man.'

reportedly attacked and defeated, provoking Pericles to sneer that Sophocles was an excellent poet but a poor general. On another occasion, when Sophocles, insatiable in his pursuit of boys, praised a young man's beauty, Pericles snapped, 'Generals should have not just clean hands but clean eyes, too.'

Following victory at Samos, Pericles' own hands were sullied when he ordered the revolt's ringleaders be punished by *apotympanismos*: weak from crucifixion, they were clubbed to death, their corpses left unburied as a grim example to their followers. The episode perhaps inspired Sophocles' *Antigone* (*c.* 441), in which the heroine defies authority to bury her rebel brother, though later tradition recorded (perhaps wrongly) that the playwright owed his election as strategos in the first place to *Antigone*'s success. During the Peloponnesian War Sophocles may have again served as general twice in the 420s, while in 412/11 he was one of the ten *probouloi* (magistrates with emergency powers) charged with formulating strategy and bringing continuity to Athens' war effort.

Like many of his colleagues, Sophocles was offered lucrative employment by foreign kings and tyrannoi. He refused them all, citing his love for Athens, but hearing of the death of his fellow dramatist **Euripides** at the court of King Archelaus I of Macedon, Sophocles buried their rivalry and paraded his chorus in mourning robes. Later that same year, 405, Sophocles too died. The two traditions concerning the manner of his death may both be true – that he choked on a grape pip and that he suffered an attack while performing a speech from *Antigone* without stopping for breath. Until recently, reciting speeches with grapes in the mouth was part of an actor's vocal training.

At this time, as the Peloponnesian War was drawing to its bitter end, the Spartans were occupying Attica, but Dionysus is said to have appeared to their general **Lysander**, commanding him to grant Sophocles' funeral cortege safe passage to Colonus. Here, a grave, topped by a carved siren, would bear the words: 'I, Sophocles, am hidden in this tomb, who took first prize in tragic arts, the most revered of men.' But Sophocles still played a part in civic life. Several years before, when the Athenians had wished to introduce the worship of the healing god Asclepius from Epidaurus into the city, Sophocles had erected an altar to the deity and given him, in his guise as a serpent, temporary accommodation. After his death, in recognition of this piety, Sophocles received a hero-shrine on the west slope of the Acropolis, where he was worshipped as Dexion (Receiver).

Sophocles' surviving dramas reveal strong religious beliefs shot through with fatalism, exemplified in a chorus from *Antigone*. Announcing that 'there are many strange and terrifying things, and none more strange or terrifying than man', he catalogues human achievements – sailing, agriculture, hunting and domesticating animals,

> and speech and thought as swift as wind and sentiments that keep a city safe. Man taught himself all this.... And so he strides into the future. Nothing gives him pause. Yet there's one thing that he can't find a cure for: death.

These views resurface in *Oedipus Tyrannos*, an exploration of the powerlessness of man, condemned to suffer through no apparent fault save over-reliance on his own intellect – for **Aristotle**, it was the archetypal tragedy. First performed in 429, and set in a plague-ridden city, it has been interpreted as a commentary on Periclean Athens, a counterpoint to Pericles' own Funeral Oration delivered barely a year earlier. Even more intertwined with Sophocles' own life is *Oedipus at Colonus*. Written in 407/6 it is a reflection on old age.

Like Sophocles, the dying Oedipus will be worshipped as a hero – at Colonus, the poet's ancestral home, now in reality ravaged by the Spartans, but in the wistful world of poetry a haven, verdant with heavy foliage and resounding with the voice of nightingales, where 'drenched with dew, narcissi bloom by day … and saffron crocuses', while 'the bubbling springs of Cephisus' streams flow never-ending'.

Oedipus' quarrels with his sons, which drive the action of the play, may echo Sophocles' experience, too: his only son Iophon tried to have his aged father declared incompetent. In defence Sophocles read lines from *Oedipus at Colonus* and the case was dropped. Iophon too was a tragedian (he even competed against Sophocles at the Dionysia) as was his own son, also called Sophocles, who produced the first, posthumous performance of *Oedipus at Colonus* in 401. Sublimely mystical if religiously conservative, the play describes how Oedipus does not die but is transformed into pure spirit, a fate which (some said) had actually befallen the philosopher Empedocles a generation earlier.

EMPEDOCLES (*c.* 495–?)
Philosopher and Mystic

Satyrus writes that [Gorgias] used to tell of how he had witnessed Empedocles practising magic.

Diogenes Laertius, *Lives of the Philosophers*, 8.2.59

Although ancient accounts of Empedocles' life read more like fiction than biography, some factual details can be gleaned. His father Meton, one of a distinguished line of Olympic victors from Sicilian Acragas, owned an enviable stud of horses and helped overthrow the tyrannos Thrasydeus in 472. Empedocles' own views were said to be aggressively democratic. Rejecting the chance to become a tyrannos, he disbanded an oligarchic council and thwarted a potential despot by having him and his supporters tried and executed.

Empedocles is said to have travelled widely – to Athens, the Peloponnese and Persia, where he studied with the Magi – while in his native Sicily he reputedly stopped a plague at Selinus by diverting a nearby river. Other traditions suggested that he recited his works at Olympia, dressed in golden-belted purple robes, his feet shod in bronze sandals, his thick hair garlanded with laurel, and accompanied by a retinue of boys; and that he sacrificed a bull formed from either barley-meal and honey or myrrh, frankincense and other fragrant spices. For, being a vegetarian who believed in metempsychosis, he found it morally repugnant to sacrifice a living creature.

So far, so plausible. But Empedocles could reputedly quell the winds by trapping them in sacks sewn from asses' hides and, even more spectacularly, raise the dead: he kept the corpse of a woman, Panthea ('All Goddess'), in his house for a month, without any sign of decay, and then restored her to life. Still more remarkable was Empedocles' own death. A bewildering range of versions were recorded: that he died at the age of sixty; that he fell from a chariot at the age of seventy-seven; that he lived to 109; that he drowned at sea; that he jumped into the volcanic fires of Etna (which spat back one of his bronze-soled sandals); or that, like Oedipus at Colonus, he was transformed into a god:

When dawn came, Empedocles was nowhere to be seen. They asked his servants, and one said that he had heard a voice at midnight calling loudly for Empedocles. When he went to look, he saw a bright light in the sky but nothing else.

In fact, much of this 'biography' comes from misinterpretations of Empedocles' own writing, *On Nature* and *Purifications*. Composed in verse and surviving only in fragments, its rolling metres and well-judged similes were compared favourably in antiquity to Homer's. Its content, however, was pioneering. Following **Pythagoras**, Empedocles believed that nothing died. Rather, all matter consists of combinations of four immortal 'elements' (as **Plato** later called them): earth, air, fire and water. Ever-shifting, these combine in distinct patterns, causing living beings to form. Early creations were misshapen hybrids (like minotaurs or centaurs), but over time today's creatures evolved, and 'when elements are intermixed in human shape or as wild animals or plants or birds, we call it "birth"; when they separate, we call it "doleful death"'. Since nothing can be made from nothing, all elements of creation have always been in existence, as have the souls which inhabit the constantly forming and fragmenting bodies. Empedocles wrote that he himself had experienced many incarnations: 'I have been a boy, a girl, a plant, a bird and a voiceless fish in the sea.'

For Empedocles, the purpose behind metempsychosis is redemption. Mirroring Zoroastrian beliefs in the opposing deities Ahura Mazda (Lord of Light) and the destructive Angra Mainyu, Empedocles posited two governing principles, Love and Discord. In the struggle between them, played out over aeons, some souls succumb to sinfulness and are punished:

forced to wander for 3,000 years, reborn into a multitude of mortal forms:
the air pursues them into the sea; the sea, in turn, disgorges them onto the
earth; the earth into the hot rays of the sun; and the upper air into
the abyss.

Empedocles believed that sensation and understanding arise from
different elements contained within the body communicating with their
equivalents outside it, a constant exchange of *aporrhoiai* (effluences)
which are received and perceived through *poroi* (pores) in a reciprocal
transmission or 'transpiration'. Thus, vision results from light emitted
from the eyes coming into contact with light radiated from the object of
their observation. However, as perception depends on the observer's position
with regard to the object perceived, knowledge can be only partial and errors
are inevitable.

Empedocles would thus have understood how his own biography became
so fanciful – his bloodless bull at Olympia clearly derives from his description
of a time when:

Love was queen and men piously propitiated her with holy offerings:
representations of animals, sweet perfumed oils, pure myrrh and gifts of
aromatic incense, libations of honey dripping to the earth. The altar was not
drenched with the abominable slaughter of bulls, though men still practise this
iniquity to rob the creature of its life and eat its limbs.

Equally, Empedocles' reputation as arrogant and preening seems to be derived
from a passage now thought to describe the triumphant soul on its journey to
perfection:

I walk among you, an immortal god, mortal no more, honoured by all,
festooned with ribbons and fresh garlands. Men and women in their tens of
thousands follow me, longing for the true path, some seeking prophecy, others
protection against disease.

It is possible, however, that Classical authors who possessed Empedocles'
complete works and considered him a conceited shaman might just have
been right. As he himself observed, we are 'persuaded of only what each
has chanced upon', a sentiment with which his fellow thinker Protagoras
heartily agreed.

PROTAGORAS (490–420)
Philosopher

'We call Pheidias a sculptor and Homer a poet, but what do we call
Protagoras?' 'A sophist, I suppose.'

Plato, Protagoras, 311

Protagoras was born in Abdera, a thriving Thracian port at the mouth of the
River Nestus. It was founded in around 654 by Ionian Greeks from Clazomenae,
and its population swollen in 544 by refugees from the city of Teos fleeing the
advance of Persia. But in 513 the Persians defeated Abdera and, although the city
briefly regained independence, in 492 it was occupied again. In 480, when Xerxes
marched into Greece, its leading citizens were called upon to entertain him,
among them the family of Democritus, the philosopher credited with 'discovering'
Protagoras.

Lacking evidence, Classical biographers invented stories about Protagoras'
youth. **Aristotle** wrote that he designed a 'porter's pad'. Others described how
Protagoras, himself a porter, carried wood stacked so precisely that Democritus
recognized in him a natural geometer, offered him a home and taught him
philosophy. As Democritus was not born until around 460 this anecdote is
unlikely, inspired by the coincidence of the two men's birthplace, the similarity
of their philosophies and their roles as teachers.

Plato, who represents him in dialogue with Socrates, called Protagoras
the greatest philosopher of his age and the first of the sophists (sophistai),
professional teachers who travelled widely, tutoring rich young pupils for high
fees. His interest was in practicalities, especially how to be a good and useful
citizen, and (according to Plato) he taught that *arete* (meaning loosely 'virtue')
consists of running a household well and wielding political influence through
words and deeds. Because he claimed to teach this arete – so useful for ambitious
politicians – his lectures attracted wealthy students who could afford his 100-mina
fees (equal to fifty days' wages for an Athenian juryman).

Protagoras moved in heady circles. Plato represents him meeting Socrates
in Athens at the house of the wealthy Callias (the grandson of the peace-broker
with Persia) surrounded not only by his fellow philosophers Hippias of Elis
and Prodicus of Ceos, but by **Pericles'** sons Paralus and Xanthippus and ward
Alcibiades, for 'Protagoras entices men from every city that he visits, enchanting
them with his voice like Orpheus, so that, captivated, they follow him'. Perhaps
drawing on Protagoras' pamphlet *On the Origins of Things*, Plato imagines him

Democritus

Born around 460, Democritus is said to have travelled widely throughout Greece, Asia Minor, Egypt and Persia, studying with the Magi and recording his experiences in books such as *Concerning the Peoples of Meroe* and *On the Sacred Writings of Babylon*. He shared **Empedocles'** view that matter consists of infinite atoms of different forms, with similar atoms connecting to create physical beings or objects and eventually drifting apart to cause decay. For Democritus everything has a beginning and an end, including our own planet, which he believed was spherical and one of a number of worlds. Democritus praised education, considering it the noblest of callings and maintaining that through learning and experience the human race has evolved to live cooperatively. He taught, too, that, while observation-based knowledge is subjective, rigorous honing of the intellect can improve our objectivity, and that virtue can be acquired through practice. The titles of his many books betray the breadth of his interests. They include *On Homer*, *On the Planets*, *On Virtue*, *On Painting*, *On Fighting in Armour* and *On Coughing*.

employing a number of teaching methods, from the elenchic technique associated with Socrates to the use of parables. Exploring his own contention that primitive humans lacked moral and political wisdom, acquiring it only when they lived in cities, Protagoras playfully imagines Zeus instructing Hermes to plant justice into human hearts, concluding that since arete is not innate it must be cultivated with the help of teachers like himself.

Protagoras is said to have once spent a day with Pericles debating the accidental death of an athlete struck by a javelin: who or what was in the strictest sense responsible? The javelin? The man who threw it? Or the authorities supervising the games? Their discussion was more than theoretical: Pericles appointed Protagoras to write the constitution for the new Athenian colony at Thurii, where he probably spent some time. Tradition suggests that he died in the Greek west, perhaps in a shipwreck.

Protagoras is best known for two controversial dicta. Introducing his treatise *On Truth* he wrote: 'Man is the measure of all things: of those which are, that they are, and of those which are not, that they are not.' In other words, as moral observations are subjective and there is consequently no absolute or universal truth, conflicting observations should be given equal weight as long as their validity can be equally well argued. However, since not all conclusions drawn from such observations are of equal consequence (some might be beneficial, others damaging), it is the teacher's role to develop the capacity for discrimination. Protagoras stressed the importance, for achieving this, of correct use of language (regularly dissecting poetry to appreciate its author's meaning), and his linguistic expertise and rhetorical skills were widely recognized. However, his boast that he could make a weak argument seem more convincing than a strong one caused many to distrust him – in a democratic assembly such implied trickery could lead to chaos.

Even more contentiously he wrote in *On the Gods*: 'I cannot tell whether or not the gods exist or what they might be like, because the issue is opaque, and human life is short.' Such agnosticism threatened to undermine societies traditionally held together by state religion and rituals and it was perhaps to help avert any resultant anger that Protagoras let pupils either pay him a set fee or donate what they felt appropriate to a temple of their choice. His views, welcomed by fellow sceptics, were met with wider hostility. An unreliable tradition that he was exiled from Athens and his books burned in the Agora in the late 430s reflects hardening attitudes towards Pericles' circle of intellectuals and artists. Others, too, are said to have borne the brunt of this factional squabbling. Among them was Pheidias, whose renown as a sculptor matched Protagoras' reputation as a philosopher.

PHEIDIAS (c. 480–c. 430)
Sculptor

We admire the other six wonders of the world, but in front of Pheidias' Zeus we kneel in reverence – the skill of its workmanship is as remarkable as the statue itself is holy.

Philo of Byzantium, *On the Seven Wonders of the World*, 3

Pheidias' sculptures encapsulated the spirit of fifth-century triumphalism. Sited prominently at Delphi and Olympia or in the heart of Athens, they radiated confidence. Yet today all are lost, remembered only by their names (such as the Lemnian Athene at Athens; the Heavenly Aphrodite at Elis; the Warlike Athene at Plataea) and his life must be reconstructed from scattered and often contradictory references.

Born around 480, Pheidias (like his contemporaries Myron, creator of the Discobolus, or Discus Thrower, and Polycleitus, whose sculptures were informed by his theories of the ideal mathematical proportions of the human body) studied under Ageladas of Argos, whose work included celebrated statues of gods and Olympic victors. By the 460s Pheidias had attracted such attention in his native Athens that he received two high profile commissions, both designed to glorify not just the city but **Cimon** too. One was a group of sixteen bronze figures installed near the temple of Apollo at Delphi. Financed from the spoils of Marathon and commemorating the battle, it showed the gods and heroes of Athens clustered round one mortal: Cimon's father **Miltiades**, who had led the Athenians to victory. The second commission was the colossal bronze statue, 30 feet (9 m) tall, of Athene Promachus on the Athenian Acropolis, reputedly erected as a memorial to Cimon's victory at Eurymedon.

After Cimon's death **Pericles** appointed Pheidias to oversee his great building project on the Acropolis. His influence can best be seen in the Parthenon. Built on the site of two older temples, the Parthenon had a larger footprint than either as it needed to house Pheidias' radically innovative statue of Athene. Forty feet (12 m) high from floor to ceiling, it was the first colossal statue to be faced in ivory (for the flesh) and gold, and portrayed the goddess with characteristic helmet, shield and spear, and holding a winged Victory in her outstretched right hand. To create it Pheidias employed a team of specialist artists and artisans, some skilled in constructing the armature of cypress and citrus wood to which the outer 'shell' was fixed, others in treating elephant tusks to create a pliable thin ivory veneer, others in gem cutting or glass blowing or moulding gold sheets round the statue's helmet, shield, spear, dress and sandals. Forty talents (2,280 lbs or 1,034 kg) of gold went into its construction, all of which could be removed and melted down in times of economic crisis, provided that it was subsequently replaced to equal or greater value.

Unprecedentedly, Pheidias ensured that his statue and the decorative scheme on the exterior of the Parthenon were thematically unified, although it is unlikely that he sculpted any of the pediments (triangular gables), *metopes* (carved panels) or frieze himself. Thus, for example, on both the inside of the statue's shield and the east metopes sculptures showed gods fighting giants; on the outside of the shield and the west metopes, Greeks fighting Amazons; and on the statue's sandals and the south metopes Greeks fighting centaurs – all celebrating the triumph of civilization over barbarism and (by extension) of Athens over Persia.

Pheidias' close relationship with Pericles laid him open to political attack. One lawsuit, for allegedly misappropriating gold, was resolved when the statue's

A second-century AD marble copy
of Pheidias' gold and ivory statue of
Athene once housed in the Parthenon
(though the pillar was absent in
the original).

In Sir Lawrence Alma-Tadema's evocative painting, *Phidias Showing the Frieze of the Parthenon to His Friends* (1868), Pericles, Aspasia and Alcibiades stand on scaffolding to inspect the work in progress.

gold facings were removed and weighed. Another, for blasphemously representing himself and Pericles on a religious sculpture (the outside of Athene's shield), where only gods or heroes might be shown, resulted according to one tradition in his execution, according to another in his exile. Certainly in 438, once the Parthenon had been consecrated, Pheidias quickly left Athens for his next commission: the statue of Zeus at Olympia.

Here, in a specially built studio, its alignment and proportions exactly matching the temple's *cella* (central sanctuary), Pheidias and his workforce created his masterpiece. Like the Parthenon's Athene, the statue was 40 feet (12 m) tall, held a winged Victory in its outstretched hand and was veneered in gold and so much ivory that some marvelled that it was for this that nature had invented elephants. It showed Zeus enthroned, his head garlanded with olive leaves like an Olympic victor's, and Pheidias himself claimed that its majestic expression was inspired by Homer's description in the *Iliad*: 'Zeus the son of Kronos spoke and, as he inclined his head with its dark brows, the mighty king's hair, anointed with ambrosial oil, fell forward from his immortal head, and great Olympus trembled.' It was later considered a misfortune to die without ever having seen the statue, and in the second century it was listed as one of the seven wonders of the world.

Once again we hear that Pheidias, who had engraved his lover's name, 'handsome Pantarces', on Zeus' little finger, fell foul of the authorities and that, in exile from Athens for blasphemy, he was executed by the authorities at Elis, under whose jurisdiction Olympia fell. Before dismissing such stories, it is worth recalling that in 422, less than a decade after Pheidias' death, **Aristophanes** satirically observed that Pericles had instigated the Peloponnesian War as a distraction, terrified that he would share the sculptor's fate – though what that fate was he omits to tell us.

Personal attacks like these were characteristic of Athenian democracy, and as accusations were levelled against members of Pericles' inner circle Pheidias' was not the only reputation impugned by comic poets. In 425 Aristophanes had parodied **Herodotus'** *Histories* to trace the war's origins to another cause: an Athenian abduction of a Megarian courtesan, for which the Megarians 'stole two of Aspasia's young ladies in revenge'. Knockabout comedy it may have been, but it did little to enhance the reputation of Pericles' widow, Aspasia.

ASPASIA (c. 470–c. 400)
Intellectual

Let us consider Aspasia's abilities, her political acumen, her brilliant mind and her penetration, and so transfer it all to our own account of her as truthfully as possible.

Lucian, *Images*, 17

Aspasia was arguably the most influential woman in fifth-century Athens, yet her life remains shadowy, thanks to the extreme bias of our sources. Comedians and enemies excoriate her; philosophers praise her; and, as all are male, the comments of even the most sympathetic are tinged with the chauvinist prejudices of the age.

Aspasia came from Miletus, where research suggests that she was the daughter of a local grandee, Axiochus, and that she was brought to Athens in 450 as part of the household of **Pericles'** relative Alcibiades the Elder, who had been ostracized ten years earlier and had married Aspasia's sister during his exile in the Ionian city. When both Alcibiades the Elder and his son Clinias died Pericles, as head of the family, became Aspasia's kyrios or guardian in 447. He may even have married her. Certainly he divorced his former wife and soon Aspasia bore him a son, also called Pericles. Partly as a result Pericles' eldest son, Xanthippus, became bitterly estranged. When both he and his brother Paralus died in the plague of

429 the Athenians voted to waive Pericles' own legislation of 450 requiring both parents to be of citizen stock, and enrolled the younger Pericles into their number.

When Pericles also died in 429 Aspasia, accepting that respectable women should be married, became the wife of Lysicles, an emerging politician, but he was killed fighting in Caria in 428. As for Aspasia, she may have lived to see her son elected as strategos in 406, only to be executed with his colleagues for failing to collect the bodies of the dead after the sea-battle at Arginusae. Perhaps she witnessed, too, Athens' fall in 404.

Even if her life was as conventional as this reconstruction suggests, there was much that set Aspasia apart for, highly educated, she was one of the most brilliant women of her age. As a member of Pericles' household Aspasia mixed freely with the leading intellectuals of Athens. Possessed of a rare political insight and skilled in rhetoric (which **Plato** says she taught to **Socrates**), she was even rumoured to be the author of Pericles' Funeral Oration of 430, though as one of many jibes directed against Athens' 'first couple' this was probably intended as a slur on Pericles, his manliness and his abilities.

There was nothing most Athenian men hated as much as a clever, independent woman. Slandering Aspasia, they called her Pericles' *pallake* (concubine), a hetaera or, worse, a *porne* (common prostitute). Comedians named her a 'shameless bitch', a 'dog-eyed whore', a brothel-keeping madam whose house (and by extension Pericles' house, too) was filled with 'working girls'. Likening her to the mythical sirens Omphale and Deianaera, they accused Aspasia of emasculating Pericles so much that she planned his expedition against Samos of 440 and even the Peloponnesian War. Meanwhile, gossip suggested that Pericles was squandering his wealth on her and, even worse, that he kissed her every morning when he left the house and every night when he returned – an intimate glimpse of domestic harmony which to an Athenian smacked of shameful uxoriousness. By the late 430s, during a spate of lawsuits against Pericles' associates, Aspasia was charged with 'procuring freeborn Athenian women and bringing them home for him'. It was a vulgar, hurtful, trumped-up allegation, and Pericles wept as he spoke in Aspasia's defence. She was acquitted.

It was Aspasia's misfortune to be a clever woman in a male-dominated world. Even Pericles knew that there was little he could do to counter the status quo. In his Funeral Oration of 430 he observed that a woman's greatest glory lay in not being spoken of for good or ill. It was a sentiment with which, even in the wake of her trial, Aspasia may not have wholeheartedly agreed. As for Pericles' ward Alcibiades, he cared little what people said of him – as long as it was about him that they were speaking. Soon he would be the talk of Greece.

A Roman copy, possibly of a fifth-
century Greek original, this bust of
Aspasia shows her as a respectable
Athenian matron, her head covered,
her hair tightly styled.

Chapter 5

World
War

ALCIBIADES (450–404)
Politician and General

He could change faster than a chameleon. In fact, they say that a chameleon cannot make itself appear white, but Alcibiades could adapt himself with equal facility to whomever he was with, either good or bad, and assume the appearance of both vice and virtue.

Plutarch, *Life of Alcibiades*, 5

The death of **Pericles** in 429, so early in the Peloponnesian War, left a political vacuum in Athens. For the first time in over a generation there was no single statesman whose will the People seemed prepared to follow consistently. Instead, a series of firebrand demagogues emerged, each clamouring for attention and proposing disparate policies that destabilized the city and undermined Pericles' military strategy against Sparta. After ten years of fighting and heavy losses on both sides, hostilities were at last suspended under terms that essentially restored the status quo. However, not everyone embraced the prospect of peace. Aspiring, ego-driven young Athenians needed war to make their mark, and the most ambitious of them all was Alcibiades.

A fabulously rich Alcmaeonid, Alcibiades was orphaned in 447 at the age of three when his father Clinias fell fighting against Boeotia at the battle of Coronea. As a result Alcibiades found himself inheriting a fortune and growing up as the ward of Pericles, his mother's cousin, in the most powerful house in Athens. Intensely charismatic and with smouldering good looks, he would have been the talk of Athens anyway, but through his own calculated endeavours he ensured that his name was constantly on everybody's lips. Rumours swirled throughout the streets: how he bit an opponent at wrestling and, accused of fighting like a woman, replied, 'Not like a woman, like a lion'; how he lopped off the tail of his expensive hunting dog; how he swaggered through the Agora dressed in sumptuous robes (silk has in fact been discovered in his family tomb) which he ostentatiously allowed to trail on the ground until they were completely ruined. Warned by friends that all Athens was outraged at such behaviour he retorted, 'Good. If they're talking about *this*, they won't have time to speak of anything worse which I might do.'

In democratic Athens public recognition may have been key to gaining power, but individual patronage was crucial too. One way to achieve it was through forming homoerotic relationships with older men, one of the rites of passage to adulthood of most young Athenian males. Courted by some of the most influential citizens of Athens, the young Alcibiades chose his lovers well, calculating how best to manipulate each to further his career. Only **Socrates** resisted him, although the two enjoyed a close friendship. Indeed, Socrates was reported to have saved the eighteen-year-old Alcibiades' life while on campaign at Potidaea in 432, remaining by his side when he was wounded and guarding him from danger.

In other ways, too, Alcibiades was careful to consolidate his powerbase, although his impetuous nature could all too readily prove an impediment. An arranged marriage to Hipparete, daughter of Hipponicus, reputedly the richest Greek alive, should have opened many doors. Not only was her name attractive to a young aristocrat (it meant 'equine virtue'), the fact that she was an heiress made her irresistible. Yet despite giving Alcibiades a son (also called Alcibiades) and a daughter (whose name we do not know), hers was not a happy marriage. Irritated by her husband's many public affairs and indiscretions, Hipparete tried to divorce him. Proceedings were halted when Alcibiades dragged her forcibly from the courts. She died soon after.

Alcibiades is curiously absent from the records of the first part of the Peloponnesian War, but when peace was made in 421 he was swift to make his presence felt. Relishing the opportunities that only war could bring, he did his best to sabotage the treaty. As proxenos for Sparta, it was his responsibility to represent Spartan interests in Athens. Instead, he undermined them, earning popular acclaim by humiliating their ambassadors in front of the Assembly. Not for the last time Alcibiades allowed personal ambition to eclipse the national interest, and as a short-term strategy it worked beautifully – the People appointed

A tousle-haired Alcibiades stares out from a late fourth-century AD Roman mosaic laid down at Sparta, where he not only betrayed his own polis but seduced the queen.

him one of the strategoi. So, although direct hostilities between Sparta and Athens were suspended for almost six years, thanks to Alcibiades' disruptive efforts there was constant skirmishing between their allies. Wherever battle was, there too was Alcibiades. At the head of an alliance of Peloponnesian states united in their opposition to Sparta, he harried the enemy and won some minor victories. Then in 418 at Mantinea the Athenians were defeated, and his star seemed in danger of being eclipsed.

But not for long. At the Olympic Games of 416 he staged a spectacular comeback, parading not just his riches but a new nexus of powerful Ionian backers – Ephesus, Chios and Lesbos – all of which hoped to bathe in his reflected glory. For he was bent on victory, no matter the cost. In an unprecedented show of wealth Alcibiades entered seven chariots, coming first, second and third (or, according to some grudging enemies, fourth). Moreover, thanks to the largesse of his east Aegean sponsors, he entertained the entire Olympic audience to a banquet served from Athenian state silverware 'borrowed' for the occasion, a display of opulence calculated not just to enhance his fame but to intimidate. For he was already contemplating a new campaign: first against Sicily and then, so rumour had it, on to Carthage. Should he be successful the rewards would be incalculable. Hence the support of the Ionians.

Alcibiades still needed the People's backing. In the last recorded use of the mechanism his rivals tried to ostracize him. They failed. Claiming that he had won his Olympic victory purely to gain kudos for Athens, Alcibiades first formed an unlikely alliance with Nicias (who owed his riches, like Callias before him, to leasing slaves to work the mines at Laurium), then in the Assembly outmanoeuvred him in the debate over Sicily. To Nicias' horror he, Alcibiades and the veteran soldier Lamachus were appointed to lead the campaign, which almost certainly would not only reignite the Peloponnesian War but plunge the whole of the Greek world into conflict. But in 415, on the eve of the expedition's departure, most of the city's *herms* (statues of Hermes which Athenians believed protected their homes) were discovered inexplicably smashed, an act of gross impiety that Alcibiades' enemies were quick to lay at his door – quite literally, as his was one of the only houses whose herm had not been broken. Alcibiades was allowed to sail for Sicily, but on reaching Catana he found himself recalled to Athens to face indictment not only on this count but on the capital charge of profaning the Eleusinian Mysteries by staging a grotesque parody that revealed their secrets to non-initiates.

Rather than return to face trial Alcibiades evaded his guards at Thurii and disappeared. In his absence an Athenian jury condemned him to death, while priests cast a curse on him, its text permanently displayed for all to see. Not that Alcibiades cared. He had already found safe haven – in Sparta. In return for his protection he exchanged crucial military advice with his city's old enemy. In Alcibiades' absence Athens' fleet and army were defeated in Sicily, while in Attica itself – since, as predicted, the Sicilian expedition rekindled the war with Sparta – the Spartans seized and permanently fortified the strategic site of Decelea. The impact, both militarily and economically, was profound. Attica had no respite from Spartan raids, while production at its silver mines at Laurium, which funded much of the Athenian war effort, slowed to a halt.

In exile Alcibiades sloughed off his reputation for luxury. When he was a child, Alcibiades had been assigned a Spartan nanny by Pericles in the forlorn hope that she might instil some discipline. Only now did he demonstrate how well she had taught him. He led a life as 'spartan' as his hosts, living off their infamous black broth and swimming daily in the often icy River Eurotas. But not every Spartan relished his presence. When King Agis II grew suspicious that his wife, Timaea, was secretly referring to her new-born baby Leotychidas as 'Alcibiades' and calculated that he had not enjoyed conjugal relations since an earthquake ten months earlier, the extent to which his guest had integrated himself into Spartan high society was revealed. The honeymoon was over. While touring Ionia in 412 to incite poleis including his Olympic backers, Ephesus and Chios, to switch sides from Athens to Sparta, Alcibiades learned of Agis' plot to kill him. His options increasingly limited, he once again defected – to virtually the only state that he had not yet offended: Persia. Once more he traded military advice, urging the satrap Tissaphernes, until now a supporter of Sparta, to play the warring Greeks off against each other until they were so weak that Persia could defeat them all.

Even in Persia Alcibiades could not resist playing a double game. Athens had been hard hit by her defeat in Sicily and, with an oligarchic coup appearing increasingly inevitable, Alcibiades entered into discussions with its potential leaders about the possibility of his return. In 411, however, Athenian troops on campaign in Ionia, unhappy with the progress of the war and believing that Alcibiades could bring Persia in on their side, hailed him as their general. The prodigal had returned, albeit not yet to Athens itself. When he did set foot on his native soil, Alcibiades was determined it should be in style and with a string of victories to his name. For almost four years he remained in the east, raising money, leading campaign after campaign against the Spartans and playing a dangerous game of cat and mouse with Persia. The triumph of his destruction of much of Sparta's fleet at Cyzicus in 410 was made sweeter by the interception of a desperate message home from the rump of the Spartan army. Couched in suitably laconic terms, it read: 'Ships lost. Admiral dead. Men starving. What to do?' Only two years before, Athens had been on its knees. Bullish now, it rejected Spartan peace proposals out of hand.

In early 407, having regained much of Ionia, the Chersonese and the Dardanelles, Alcibiades sailed back triumphantly to Athens. He disastrously miscalculated his timing. The day he returned to Piraeus, Athens was marking the festival of the Plynteria, when the temple of Athene Polias was ritually closed and the ancient olive wood statue of Athene was covered, to protect its modesty, while its robes were washed in the sea. It was a time of ill omen not just for Alcibiades but for the city, a day on which no Athenian would begin any important new undertaking. However, it did not seem to matter to the ecstatic citizens. At Piraeus the quayside was crowded with cheering well-wishers waving crowns of gold and bronze. Overcome by emotion, the forty-three-year-old Alcibiades wept as he stepped ashore.

For more than a year Alcibiades enjoyed extraordinary power. All charges laid against him back in 415 were dropped, his confiscated property was returned and the inscription recording the curse against him was hastily removed and flung into the sea. He was appointed to the new and unprecedented post of Supreme Commander. If Alcibiades had ever harboured dreams of being tyrannos of Athens and leader of its empire this was the closest he would ever come to seeing them realized. He reached the pinnacle of his ambitions; but soon the kaleidoscope would twist once more and its pattern break unrecognizably. Thanks in no small part to Alcibiades' earlier intrigues Ephesus had defected to the Spartans. Now in 406 Alcibiades was determined to win it back. But his plans were thwarted. In his absence on a mission of his own and in contravention of all orders his helmsman, Antiochus, whom he had left in charge of Athens' fleet, joined battle with the Spartans at Ephesus. He was roundly defeated. Innocent for once of any wrongdoing, Alcibiades nevertheless was blamed for the debacle and summoned home. Of course, he did not go. Once again Alcibiades was on the run.

During his years of campaigning Alcibiades had built a powerbase of his own in the Chersonese. Now at the top of everyone's 'most wanted' list, he took refuge there on his estates, a middle-aged warlord ruling his small empire and watching as, without him, Athens' fortunes once again unravelled. But in 405 news came which he could not ignore. Athens' fleet was in the Dardanelles. So were the Spartans. But the Athenians had chosen a disastrous position for their base by the sluggish creek of Aegospotamoi ('Goat Rivers'). Foreseeing dire consequences, Alcibiades rode into their camp and sought out their generals. Desperately he tried to persuade them to move to a better location, but they ignored him. When they subsequently joined battle, they were comprehensively defeated and all but a handful of Athens' 180 triremes were lost. Without a navy, and with the Black Sea corn route now in Spartan hands, Athens could not survive for long. In 404 the starving city finally surrendered. It was in no position to make terms: twelve years before, egged on by Alcibiades, an arrogant Athenian Assembly had voted to slaughter the male citizens of captured Melos and to enslave the island's women and children. Now Athens awaited the same fate. But it did not come. Instead, the Spartans dismantled the city walls and the Long Walls to the sea, installed the oligarchic government of the Thirty Tyrannoi and spared the population. In victory the fiercest fighting force in Greece had shown a tender (if tempered) clemency.

But there was one man whom the Spartans could not forgive. In the months after Athens' fall, with the aid of a small band of local vigilantes – vengeful brothers of a girl whom (they claimed) he had seduced – they tracked down Alcibiades to a village in Phrygia. Silently they surrounded the house in which the two were sleeping. Then they set it alight. As Alcibiades ran out, a sword in his right hand, a blanket wrapped round his left arm as a shield, he was shot down in a hail of javelins and arrows. As a hoplite, his shield had been emblazoned with an image of Eros, the archer god of lust. Now, thanks to Eros, Sparta's arrows had found him. He died as he lived, loved and hated in equal measure – but ultimately alone.

The glamour of his flamboyant personality can make him seem exceptional, but Alcibiades was not the first (or last) politician for whom private ambition outweighed civic interest. Already at the beginning of the Peloponnesian War (if not before) the thin line between statesmanship and demagoguery was being blurred, but the politician most often credited with first crossing it was Cleon.

CLEON (?–422)
Politician and General

Through his attacks, Cleon more than anyone else corrupted the Athenians. He was the first to shout during a speech in the Assembly, use abusive language while addressing the People and hitch up his tunic.

Aristotle, *Athenian Constitution*, 28

Little apart from gossip is known of Cleon's early life. The date of his birth remains uncertain, and the fact that our two main sources, **Aristophanes** and **Thucydides,** each had good personal reasons to loathe him does little to strengthen our confidence in their objectivity. Born into a family which owed its undoubted wealth to the leather trade, the nouveau-riche Cleon was the antithesis of aristocratic **Pericles**, and in his politics and style he was determined to oppose the elder statesman at every turn. With the outbreak of the Peloponnesian War in 431 came his opportunity. Capitalizing on the bitter unpopularity of Pericles' strategy of passively allowing the Spartans to devastate Attica, Cleon relished his rival's brief deposition from office on charges of financial irregularity, and after Pericles' permanent removal by the plague in 429 he proposed a more aggressive military policy.

In 427 Athens eventually reconquered Lesbos, which had annulled its alliance with Athens four years earlier. Cleon used the occasion to vaunt his uncompromising patriotism. Urging zero tolerance against wavering allies, and proposing to make an example of the islanders, he persuaded the Assembly to dispatch a trireme with orders to kill every adult male and sell the women and children into slavery. Next day, however, less draconian councils prevailed; the

Assembly recanted. Straining desperately at the oars, the crew of a second trireme managed to arrive at Mytilene shortly before the sentence could be carried out. Nevertheless 1,000 citizens, perhaps a tenth of the entire adult male population, were executed, condemned en masse for their disloyalty. The People's compassion was not unqualified.

It was not only foreign enemies who endured Cleon's rage. In 426, after Aristophanes lampooned him in his lost *Babylonians* at the City Dionysia, whose audience included non-Athenians, Cleon accused the playwright of unpatriotic behaviour and took him to court. The verdict is unrecorded, but, although for many years afterwards Aristophanes performed only before the domestic audiences of the Lenaea, the satirist's voice was not silenced. It was mainly thanks to him – and especially to his *Knights*, which parodied Cleon as an unscrupulous foreign slave, cynically corrupting the Athenian democracy – that the politician's reputation became so tarnished in the eyes of later generations.

In fact, by the time *Knights* was performed in 424, Cleon's star was at its zenith. The previous year the Athenian general Demosthenes had captured the strategic promontory of Pylos in Messenia, from where Spartan territory could be readily attacked. Sparta had responded by installing a force of hoplites on the nearby island of Sphacteria. Stalemate ensued. With autumn and the end of the campaigning season nearing, Cleon heaped scorn on Demosthenes, suggesting to the Assembly that given an army and a mere twenty days he could either kill the Spartans or capture them alive. It may have been bluster, but the Assembly took him at his word; unconstitutionally it appointed him strategos on the spot. Before the allocated time had passed, Sphacteria was in his hands and 120 Spartan homoioi had been shipped in chains to Athens, prisoners of war and valuable hostages – the first time any Spartan soldier had willingly surrendered.

Nonetheless, the cost of war was weighing heavily on Athens, and Cleon followed his triumphs at Lesbos and Pylos by raising the annual tribute of the city's 'allies' by 300 per cent. Domestically it was a clever move. By ensuring that the money went towards not only the war effort but increasing jury pay by 50 per cent so that it constituted a living wage, Cleon improved the lot of many of the poorer citizens on whose support his power depended. But Sparta was unbowed. In 424 their general Brasidas, who had been defeated at Pylos, retaliated by leading his troops north against Athens' colony of Amphipolis in Thrace. The Athenian strategos in the region failed to respond in time. Amphipolis was captured, and Cleon saw to it that the strategos was convicted of treason and exiled. Yet again, though, victory in the

A scene on a mid-sixth-century amphora perhaps illustrates a scene from comedy: 'knights' on horseback are accompanied by a performer on the double aulos.

lawcourts may have dented Cleon's subsequent reputation. The unfortunate strategos was Thucydides, who in his *History* did his best to blacken Cleon's name.

Meanwhile, Brasidas continued to harry Athens' northern territories. With the region in danger of being lost, Cleon was again appointed strategos. Confidently he won back city after city (restoring their tribute to Athens' coffers) and formed alliances with local kings and warlords. In 422, with the Spartans now in effect besieged at Amphipolis, it seemed that victory was Cleon's for the taking. Yet Brasidas wanted to avoid a repeat of Pylos. While Cleon was returning from reconnaissance, he flung open the city gates and charged with his hoplites against him. Surrounded by vengeful Spartans, Cleon was cut down. Thucydides' slur that he was running away is probably nothing but posthumous revenge. Brasidas too fell at Amphipolis, and with their cities' most hawkish leaders dead, Athens and Sparta, exhausted by the war, made peace. Thanks to the treaty's terms neither had achieved anything in ten years of fighting.

Because of their respect for Thucydides and Aristophanes many historians have tended to pour scorn on Cleon, yet both authors had personal and social reasons for disliking him. For Athens was intensely class riven. Despite their dependence on the People to endorse their policies, aristocrats were deeply suspicious of overt populists. Staunchly conservative and jealous of the latter's powers, they distrusted anyone who threatened to disturb the status quo. As a result even the most apparently objective contemporary accounts of Cleon, because they were written by members of the upper class, must be regarded with some scepticism – and none more so than the *History* of Thucydides.

THUCYDIDES (c. 455–c. 395)
General and Historian

I have written this account to be a possession for eternity, not as a competition showpiece aimed at winning favour with a specific audience.

Thucydides, *History*, 1.22

Born into an age of reason, Thucydides sought to apply rationality to the study of his fellow men in his record of the Peloponnesian War. Luckily, he could observe many of the protagonists at close hand – a wealthy Athenian, he owned a gold mine opposite Thasos on the coast of Thrace (where he 'had great influence on the region's leading men'), and moved in the rarefied circles of the international elite. Indeed, he was probably related through his father Olorus to **Cimon** as well as to another of **Pericles'** rivals, his namesake, Thucydides, son of Melesias. However, it is perhaps a sign of his independence of thought that the young mining mogul quickly overcame his family's aversion to Pericles to emerge as one of that politician's greatest literary champions.

In Athens for the outbreak of the Peloponnesian War in 431, Thucydides almost died two years later when he contracted but survived the plague. His first-hand experience allowed him not only to document the plague's debilitating social effects but to record its symptoms and progress in a scientific detail which owes much to Hippocrates of Cos, but which was not sufficiently clear to enable later doctors to attempt a diagnosis. Only when archaeologists examined its victims' bones was the plague discovered to be typhoid fever. Nothing is known of Thucydides' personal involvement in the first years of the war, but his status was such that in 424 he was elected strategos, with particular responsibility for the north Aegean, a region which, given his business interests, he knew well. However, when the Spartan Brasidas attacked the Athenian colony of Amphipolis, Thucydides arrived too late from his base at Thasos to prevent the city's capture and as a result was exiled, a personal disaster, but a blessing for historiography, for:

> Because of my exile I could find out what was happening on both sides, especially the Peloponnesians', and the time I had at my disposal allowed me to acquire a better understanding of events.

Thucydides had probably already resolved to write a history of the war, 'beginning at its very outset, as I believed that it was going to be a mighty conflict and more worthy of being written about than any that had taken place before' (an early jibe at his predecessor **Herodotus**). In the spirit of the age his work would be revolutionary, shorn of divine interventions, though not ignoring the part that people's belief in omens and oracles could have on the course of history. It would be as rigorous as possible, too, informed by Thucydides' personal experience of politics and warfare: 'I lived through the entire war, being old enough to appreciate what was going on, and I applied my mind to what happened in order to observe it accurately.' Accuracy had its limits, though. Setting out his methodology, Thucydides admits that he could not recall every word even of those speeches which he had heard, 'so my procedure has been to have the speakers say what, in my opinion, the situation suggested, while adhering as closely as possible to the general sense of what they actually said'.

Thucydides may have intended his *History* to be the antithesis of Herodotus' work, but he nonetheless allows a philosophical strand to run through his work as he seeks to show how the war eroded previously accepted norms of decency. Thus as well as highlighting isolated acts of wanton violence like the massacre of schoolboys at Mycalessus by Athens' Thracian allies in 413, Thucydides devotes longer passages to serious reflection. Writing of Corcyra's civil war of 427 he observes how morality and even the meaning of words changed to suit the moment, what was once called 'thoughtless violence' now being praised as 'patriotic courage'. For Thucydides this was part of a broader picture:

> In peacetime, when they prosper, cities and private individuals adopt higher principles, because they are not forced to suffer grim necessity. But war, which deprives men of the easy means to satisfy their daily needs, is a stern teacher, which matches men's behaviour to their circumstances.

The Greek tradition of storytelling, however, was too ingrained to allow Thucydides to resist creating a compelling chronicle. In his account of the negotiations in 416 between Athenian envoys and the islanders of Melos over their surrender, where he chillingly records that Athens' chief argument was that might is right, he abandons his usual narrative structure in favour of a series of short speeches in the style of a Greek drama. Elsewhere he describes the final sea-battle of Athens' ill-starred expedition to Sicily in similarly theatrical terms, picturing the land army watching for the outcome from the shoreline 'swaying back and forwards, their bodies showing the fear with which their minds were gripped, agonized, as they thought themselves forever on the verge of salvation, forever on the brink of disaster'.

Tantalizingly, Thucydides writes of recording 'the course of events down to the time when the Spartans occupied the Long Walls and Piraeus' in 404, a clear indication that he was still writing some time after the defeat of Athens; indeed, the abrupt end of his *History*'s narrative (in the desperate days of the suspension of democracy in 411) suggests its author's sudden and unexpected death. According to tradition he was murdered in Thrace in 395 and his body

The Sicilian Expedition

In 415, thanks mainly to Alcibiades' enthusiasm and the misjudgment of the more cautious Nicias, Athens sent 100 ships and 5,000 hoplites to Sicily, ostensibly to protect Segesta against Syracuse, but in fact with an eye to annexing the island. When Alcibiades was almost immediately recalled to face the charges of impiety – but, instead of facing them, defected to the Spartans – the other two generals, Nicias and Lamachus, were left without a clear strategy. After Lamachus was killed, the seriously ill Nicias begged to be replaced. Instead, Athens sent a further 5,000 hoplites and seventy-three ships. By now Sparta, responding to a plea for help, had sent a small force under Gylippus to aid Syracuse. In 413, in a series of battles, including several in Syracuse's Great Harbour, Athens' fleet was crippled. Unable to sail home, the army attempted a dangerous overland retreat. Thousands were killed, the strategoi captured and executed, and the rest imprisoned in Syracuse's quarries where they were left to die in appalling conditions. The heavy losses left Athens desperately vulnerable, but surprisingly Sparta failed to exploit the situation and the Peloponnesian War continued for another nine years.

ΘΟΥ ΚΥ   ΔΙΔΗϹ

Thucydides and his *History* were widely honoured long after his lifetime. This third-century AD mosaic showing the author comes from the Roman city of Jerash in modern Jordan.

brought back to Athens for burial close to the tomb of his close relative, Cimon's sister Elpinice.

Unfinished though Thucydides' life-work was, it had a profound effect on historiography. For, despite being written so soon after the events he was describing, there is something in Thucydides' style which suggests mature consideration. As he himself declared, his was to be a universal (and eternal) readership. But the Peloponnesian War and its consequences affected literature aimed at more immediate audiences, too, as the white-hot passion of the biting comedies of Aristophanes makes clear.

ARISTOPHANES (c. 446–c. 386)
Comic Playwright

Even comedy recognizes Justice. So what I say may be strange (and even terrifying), but it will be Just.

Aristophanes, Acharnians, 500–1

The entrance of the comic playwright Aristophanes onto the Athenian theatrical and political scene was dramatic, assured and early. A precocious 'angry young man', his first play, *Banqueters*, was produced in 427 when he was barely nineteen. With the Peloponnesian War raging across much of Greece, **Pericles** only recently dead and the plague still ravaging Attica, the atmosphere within the city was febrile, and already the youthful Aristophanes (having no doubt recently experienced his first fighting) seemed bent on unleashing his acerbic wit on the personalities and policies of the populist politicians of the day.

The next year, Aristophanes' second play, *Babylonians*, won first prize at the City Dionysia – only to attract the demagogue **Cleon's** wrath, undoubtedly because he was the butt of satire, but ostensibly because of the comedy's unpatriotic sentiments. Whatever the outcome of the subsequent lawsuit, Aristophanes' wings remained unclipped. He continued to lambast Cleon until the politician's death in 422, most notably in *Knights* (424), where despite his recent victory at Pylos, Cleon appears in the guise of a seditious Paphlagonian slave who flatters his master Demos ('the People') to achieve his own ends. As the war dragged on Aristophanes offered bold criticisms of strategy and dire warnings of failure. In *Lysistrata* (411), with Persia beginning to take a predatory interest in Greek affairs thanks partly to **Alcibiades'** recent intervention at the court of Tissaphernes, he mercilessly ridiculed the newly appointed probouloi and urged Greece's poleis to shelve their differences, while in *Frogs* (405, for which the Assembly awarded him a sacred olive crown) he argued for a return to more old-fashioned values, embodied by the tragedian **Aeschylus** (and, by association, Pericles). With the defeat of Athens, and perhaps chastened by experiencing the rule of the Thirty Tyrannoi and the execution of **Socrates**, Aristophanes refocused his satire to take aim at social mores rather than at individuals. But by now his youthful bite was gone, and in his final dramas, including *Plutus* (Wealth, 388), he experimented with a new genre of situation comedy. The last play that we hear of is the (lost) *Kolakos* (386). He may have died soon after writing it.

Many of Aristophanes' best works are characterized by a feeling of intense frustration at the handling of the Peloponnesian War and centre on attempts by

On a late fifth-century vase, two performers in bird costume dance excitedly
to the music of a double aulos in a scene reminiscent of Aristophanes' *Birds*.

their otherwise disempowered protagonists (with names like Dicaeopolis, or 'Just
City') to make personal peace treaties in the face of state opposition. The scenarios
of his comedies may have been democratic, but Aristophanes was at heart an
aristocrat who seems to have had little ideological quarrel with Sparta, and,
despite having to tread (relatively) carefully lest he offend his audience and judges,
he was not afraid to proffer unpopular advice. Often this was cloaked in a mantle
of absurdity. He positively embraced the 'fantastical element' which **Thucydides**
renounced, and many of his comedies involve wildly unbelievable and anarchic
scenarios: men flying to heaven on the back of a giant dung beetle, talking birds,
singing frogs, women being sufficiently liberated (not to mention intelligent and
abstemious) to put an end to war by means of a sex strike. Nor were politicians
the only butt of his humour. Jurors and sophists too bore the brunt of his wit in
Wasps (422) and *Clouds* (419, revised 416) respectively.

Arguably much of Aristophanes' humour was specific to his day. As well
as topical jokes aimed at 'celebrities' sitting in the audience, comedies such as
Lysistrata and its sister play *Assembly Women* (?392), depended for much of their
effect on contemporary male preconceptions about the inferiority of women

and so may seem uncomfortably misogynistic to modern audiences. Elsewhere, for example in *Acharnians* (425), which portrays a Persian ambassador speaking barbarian gibberish, the humour is unashamedly xenophobic. Scatology and obscenity are prevalent too, which meant that sections of Aristophanes' plays remained unpublished in English translation until the mid-twentieth century AD.

Aristophanes' writing shows remarkable linguistic dexterity. He could jump from the colloquial to the poetic and back again in one short sentence and loved to create new words by compounding old ones – his '*nephelokokkygia*' (from *Birds*, 414) is familiar today as Cloud Cuckoo Land. Yet Aristophanes earned an (unfair) reputation for having contributed to the execution in 399 of the philosopher Socrates, whom he had satirized in *Clouds* as an unscrupulous and subversive sophist. It was a reputation that Plato sought to repudiate in his *Symposium*, which shows Aristophanes and Socrates at banquet enjoying each other's company (as well as that of Alcibiades). A hiccupping Aristophanes explains sexual attraction by imagining that the earth was once populated by primitive humans, either male, female or hermaphrodite, each with four arms, four legs and two heads. After Zeus sliced them in half to prevent them becoming too strong, they were bereft, and since then each has looked for its 'other half' to make it feel complete.

Despite his topicality Aristophanes probably had very little impact on the political life of Athens. Cleon was appointed strategos shortly after being satirized in *Knights*; Aristophanes' appeals to end the Peloponnesian War fell on deaf ears; and Socrates had ruffled sufficient feathers on his own account to cause the jury at his trial to condemn him. Ironically, the work of a tragedian whom Aristophanes had lampooned in both *Thesmophoriazusae* (411) and *Frogs* had a deeper impact on the fortunes of his city and its citizens, for it was to Euripides that, at key moments in the war, both owed their continuing existence.

EURIPIDES (c. 485–406)
Tragic Playwright

Sophocles said that he represented human beings as they ought to be, whereas Euripides represented them as they really are.

Aristotle, *Poetics*, 25

Euripides was the son of a wealthy family which owned land in the east of Attica, where it held the ancestral priesthood of Apollo Zosterios (Armoured Apollo), as well as on the island of Salamis. He was probably born in the years between the

Persian invasions, although one Classical tradition dated his birth to the very day of Greece's victory at Salamis. Of his youth and early manhood we know nothing. He was thirty when, in 455, a year after **Aeschylus'** death, his first tetralogy was staged, but he had to wait another fourteen years before he won first prize at the Dionysia, one of only three times he did so. Perhaps his relative unpopularity stemmed in part from his bold innovations – when his first surviving play, *Alcestis*, was produced in 438, it took the place of the satyr play, or comic pastiche which traditionally followed a tragic trilogy. *Alcestis* already reveals Euripides' ability to enter the psyche of his female characters, as well as introducing the first in a line of weak, selfish men who permeate his tragedies. In *Medea*, performed in 431 weeks before the Peloponnesian War began, he gives his heroine, abandoned by her husband Jason, a speech exploring the status of women in society, in which she proclaims: 'I'd rather stand my ground three times in battle, in the shield-line, than endure the agonies of child-birth once.'

Most of Euripides' nineteen surviving plays come from the period of the Peloponnesian War, and many council caution. Thus *Medea* can be read as a warning of the unforeseen consequences of blindly embracing conflict. Again, in *Trojan Women*, part of a trilogy staged in 415 only months before the Athenian expedition set sail for Sicily, Euripides explored the ruinous effects of war upon morality. Despite his relative lack of success at home, such was the playwright's international popularity that, when the Sicilian campaign ended in disaster and Athens' troops were incarcerated in the Syracusan quarries, their captors are said to have freed those who could sing the latest songs of Euripides.

Towards the end of his life Euripides' tragedies became ever more experimental, blurring the boundaries between tragedy and comedy to produce 'escapist' dramas with happy endings, such as *Iphigenia at Tauris* (*c.* 414) and *Helen* (*c.* 412). At the same time, prompted undoubtedly by personal observations of the effects of war on his fellow citizens, he increasingly explored the nature of psychopathy. In *Orestes* (408) he shockingly distorted received versions of the myth (such as those of Aeschylus' *Oresteia*) to portray a character tipped into madness by acts of violence which he himself has perpetrated. Later that year, at the age of seventy-seven, Euripides left war-torn Athens for the safer haven of the court of King Archelaus I of Macedon. It was here he wrote his last plays, including most famously *Bacchae*, the study of the destructive power of the capricious Dionysus, which he would not live to see performed. Tradition tells how in 406 Euripides died, torn apart by the Macedonian royal hunting dogs while he enjoyed a siesta in the pine woods, a dramatic ending too close to the scenario of *Bacchae* to be believed.

At Athens, where news of Euripides' death coincided with the *proagon* (at which dramatists announced their forthcoming plays), his rival **Sophocles** dressed his chorus in mourning; and when his last plays were performed posthumously the next year they won first prize. At the same time **Aristophanes** (who had mocked Euripides for dressing his characters in rags, accusing him of misogyny and his wife of infidelity, and taunting him that his mother had sold herbs in the Agora) paid Euripides a touching compliment. In his comedy *Frogs*, Aristophanes imagined Dionysus descending to Hades to bring Euripides back to life so that he could save Athens (although, in the end, Dionysus revitalizes Aeschylus instead).

In fact, Euripides did save his city. After Athens' defeat its enemies were minded to mete out the same punishment that it had inflicted on Melos in 416, killing its men and selling its women and children into slavery. The council of war relented only when one of its members stood up and sang a haunting melody which reminded them of Athens' artistic greatness. It was a lament from Euripides' *Electra* (*c.* 416).

As a man Euripides was said to be excessively serious and addicted to books, preferring contemplation to conversation or social interaction. His religious views were unconventional too, and his choice of friends not always calculated to endear him to the People. He associated not only with politicians like **Alcibiades**, in

Archelaus I and the Hellenizing of Macedon

In the fifth century, most Greeks considered Macedonia to be barbaric. Many of its kings, on the other hand, embraced Hellenism. By proclaiming his descent from Heracles, Alexander I (r. 498–454) was allowed to take part in the Olympic Games and offered patronage to the poets **Pindar** and Bacchylides. An unwilling ally of the Persians during Xerxes' invasion, he passed information to the Greeks before the battle of Plataea. Towards the end of the century his grandson Archelaus I (r. 413–399), inheriting Alexander's aspirations, attracted to his new capital Pella some of the most innovative artists of his age, including Euripides and the painter **Zeuxis**. In the fourth century Philip II (r. 359–336), desiring to rule all Greece, engaged **Aristotle**, himself educated at the Macedonian court, as tutor for his son **Alexander III**.

honour of whose triumph in the chariot race at Olympia in 416 he composed a victory ode, but with philosophers who questioned the accepted beliefs about the gods. Among them were Anaxagoras, **Socrates** and **Protagoras**, whose agnostic tract *On the Gods* was said to have been read aloud at Euripides' house. Scepticism creeps into Euripides' own writing too. In *Hekabe* (425) the heroine remarks: 'The gods are strong, but our belief in them is stronger. It is that belief which makes us think the gods exist.' But Euripides earned most disapprobation for a line in *Hippolytus* (428) in which the central character recants an oath, exclaiming, 'My tongue swore, my mind remains unsworn!' Such sophistries were deemed extremely dangerous.

After his death Euripides was acknowledged to be one of Athens' three greatest tragedians, along with Aeschylus and Sophocles. His influence on subsequent drama was immense. Although Aristotle called him 'the most tragic of poets', he brought the art form into a more human realm, creating characters moulded by the kind of keen observation championed by his famous contemporary, the doctor Hippocrates of Cos. Indeed, in *Hippolytus* the protagonists' behaviour is explained as much by genetics as by divine influence. However, Euripides was not unique in such intense, scientific observation of the world around him. In the visual arts the champion of this approach was his colleague at the court of King Archelaus, the painter Zeuxis.

ZEUXIS (?460–?)
Artist

After he had established his artistic supremacy, the great Zeuxis seldom painted common popular subjects like heroes, gods and battles. Rather, he was always intent on novelty.

Lucian, Zeuxis or Antiochus, 3

Born in Heraclea on the instep of Italy, Zeuxis worked and travelled extensively throughout the Greek world. Receiving his initial training in the Sicilian studios of Demophilus of Himera, he became first a proponent then the leader of a new wave of painting which valued naturalism. He relished realism, embracing chiaroscuro (extreme light and shade), the illusion of three-dimensionality and trompe l'oeil. In doing so, as the Roman polymath Pliny the Elder (whose *Natural History* contains a history of classical art) enthusiastically records, 'he led the all-daring paintbrush to great glory'.

In this painting by Pietro Michis (*c.* 1890), Zeuxis studies five girls from Acragas for his depiction of Helen 'to make a composite of the most admirable aspects of the bodies of each'.

As the fifth century progressed, painting took on ever greater realism thanks to further developments, in shading and in a broader range of pigments. For an innovator such as Zeuxis (whose experiments included monochromes in white and grey) the opportunities were boundless – in the words of his rival Apollodorus (known as 'Skiagraphos', the Shadow Painter), he 'stole techniques from others and made them his own'. Determined to make art pay, he recognized the need for self-promotion. At the Olympic Games he sported robes onto which his name was stitched in golden letters, while elsewhere he enhanced his reputation by donating paintings gratis to prospective (or existing) patrons, claiming that no one could possibly afford the price that they deserved. He gave a painting of Alcmena, the mother of Heracles, to the city of Acragas and one of the god Pan to King Archelaus I of Macedon. His marketing ploys paid off. Acragas subsequently commissioned a study of Helen of Troy and Archelaus employed Zeuxis to decorate his new palace at Pella, the first private building in mainland Greece to be so adorned with wall paintings. By now Zeuxis' reputation was such that he could command ever higher fees. In the end a rich, elderly and sadly ill-favoured woman is said to have paid him to paint her in the guise of the goddess Aphrodite. When the work was complete the artist died of laughter as he gazed on it.

In antiquity Zeuxis' works were held in the highest esteem. Pliny singled out a painting of Penelope 'in which her character shines through'. He described as 'magnificent' another work, showing Zeus enthroned amid the rest of the Olympian gods, as well as one depicting the baby Heracles strangling a pair of snakes while his mother Alcmena and her husband Amphitryon looked on in terror. Pliny also records an incident in which Zeuxis and another artist, Parrhasius, competed to see which of the two could achieve greater realism. The grapes which Zeuxis painted were so true to life that birds flew down to try to peck at them. Elated, Zeuxis demanded that Parrhasius draw aside the curtain which concealed his painting, only to discover that there was no curtain – he had mistaken Parrhasius' trompe l'oeil for the real thing.

Most of Zeuxis' paintings took as their subjects characters or scenes from mythology. His methodology in preparing for his famous study of Helen reveals much about the artist in the context of his time. Having searched for models throughout Acragas, for whose temple of Hera the work was destined, he resolved to employ not one young woman but five, 'in order to make a composite of the most admirable aspects of the bodies of each of them'. By striving to capture the essence of his subject while recognizing that any one physical embodiment of beauty was merely a facet of the abstract concept of 'beauty', Zeuxis was unconsciously espousing the notion which would later become known as the Platonic ideal. In fact, it could be argued that by using his own close observation of the world as the starting point for a consideration of the metaphysical he was cast in the same mould as philosophers like **Socrates** and Zeuxis' fellow western Greek, Gorgias of Leontini.

GORGIAS (485–380)
Philosopher and Rhetorician

Speech persuades the soul, and forces the soul which it persuades not only to obey but to approve what is said.

Gorgias, *Encomium of Helen*, 10

Born in 485 in Leontini in west Sicily, Gorgias was perhaps the greatest rhetorician of his age. His brother, Herodicus, was a doctor (**Plato** suggests that Gorgias was in the habit of accompanying him on his rounds), while his sister was sufficiently rich and influential to dedicate a statue at Delphi in his honour (one of several which were set up in his lifetime). As a young man Gorgias may well have been an associate of the Sicilian philosopher **Empedocles**, who originated the concept of the four natural elements (earth, air, fire and water); certainly both men were brilliant orators and were not so unworldly that they remained aloof from political life.

The first major episode involving Gorgias took place when he was fifty-eight. In 427, with Leontini under threat from her near neighbour Syracuse, Gorgias was chosen to head a delegation to seek military help from Athens, itself already embroiled in the Peloponnesian War. Here 'he amazed his audience, Athenians who were themselves natural orators and aficionados of the art, with his novel style of speech'. Leontini's request was successful. Athens did send a task force to Sicily, where she became involved in a more wide-ranging conflict than was initially anticipated, a precursor to her disastrous expedition to the island in 415.

As for Gorgias, with his reputation in Athens secure he settled in the city as a teacher. Here he wrote handbooks on rhetoric, which detailed for the first time many figures of speech (called by some ancient commentators 'Gorgian Figures'), charged high fees and attracted many of Athens' most pre-eminent citizens as his pupils. According to one source they included **Alcibiades** and **Thucydides**. For in a city which was not only becoming increasingly litigious but where a politician relied on his powers of oratory to convince the Assembly, skills such as those which Gorgias could impart were at a premium. As a result he found himself in the vanguard of a new breed of teachers plying their lucrative trade who became known as sophists.

Sophists

In fifth-century Athens the term 'sophists' (from *sophos*, 'wisdom') was applied loosely to intellectuals, many from abroad, who taught a wide range of subjects, but chiefly rhetoric, in return for high fees. Some, like the rationalist **Protagoras** (perhaps the first sophist), argued against accepted religious beliefs; others, like Gorgias, revelling in the power of language, were accused of valuing style over content; all were viewed with general suspicion by most conservative Athenians. Curiously, when **Aristophanes** ridiculed sophists in his *Clouds* he chose as his butt **Socrates**, portraying him as the charlatan head of a Thinking Factory (*phrontisterion*), growing rich on the fees of thrusting young men whose heads he filled with seditious nonsense – a very different picture of the philosopher from that proposed by his admirers Plato and **Xenophon.**

So electrifying and celebrated were Gorgias' lectures that among his devotees the days on which they were held became known as 'feast days', and he won an enviable reputation for his ability to speak on any subject, often impromptu, and to answer any question posed by his audience. Nor did he lecture in Athens alone, regularly visiting Delphi and Olympia, where, like other writers, philosophers and artists, he publicized his skills and attracted pupils. At the Olympic Games of 408, when the Peloponnesian War had exacted a heavy toll, he echoed Aristophanes' arguments (in *Lysistrata*) and urged Greeks not to fight among themselves but to unite against the common enemy Persia. According to at least one of his audience, harmony was the last subject on which Gorgias was qualified to speak as his own household was riven with discord stemming from his passion for a servant girl and his wife's resultant jealousy. But despite his domestic difficulties, and thanks to his professional success, Gorgias accrued great wealth and led a comfortable life. He died at Larissa in Thessaly aged 105.

Of Gorgias' works perhaps the most famous is *On the Nonexistent*, which survives only in later paraphrases, and which earned him the soubriquet 'the Nihilist'. In it he posited three arguments: that nothing exists; that, even if something did exist, it could not be properly known; and that, even if it could be properly known, it could not be communicated through language. The paradox of this last argument may suggest that what Gorgias was really exploring here was the nature and function of rhetoric, a fascination with the power of speech which is borne out in his other more-or-less surviving tracts: the *Defence of Palamedes*, a well reasoned argument aimed at acquitting a wrongly and maliciously accused Greek hero of the Trojan War; the *Epitaphios* (Funeral Oration), a virtuosic version of a public funeral oration for the war dead; and his *Encomium of Helen*, a short but brilliant exhibition speech, which he tellingly ends with the confession: 'I composed this discourse as an encomium for Helen and an amusement for myself.'

The lack of a total seriousness of purpose which this remark implies brought Gorgias into conflict with another of Athens' philosophical giants – if not in reality, then at least in literature. For paradoxically it is not for his own writing that Gorgias is best remembered but for his appearance in an early, angry Platonic dialogue which bears his name. Set in the immediate aftermath of one of his public lectures, it shows Gorgias waylaid and browbeaten into discussing the virtues of rhetoric. His interlocutor regards rhetoric as immoral, since by delighting the ear it can seduce its audience into choosing the worse of two courses of action – the 'techniques of a pimp', which ultimately led to the justification that 'might is right' developed by Athens' envoys to Melos in 416.

Gorgias' interlocutor was, of course, Socrates, whose life and death were to influence the course of western thought more powerfully than any of his predecessors.

SOCRATES (?469–399)
Philosopher

> *[Chaerephon] once made so bold as to ask the oracle at Delphi the question: 'Is there anyone wiser than [Socrates]?' And the priestess replied that no one was wiser.*
>
> Plato, *Apology*, 21

According to **Plato**, when Socrates was informed that the Delphic oracle had proclaimed him to be the wisest man in the world he was incredulous, observing, 'All that I know is that I know nothing.' However, making it his life's work to prove the oracle false he questioned all he met in the hope of finding someone wiser, only to discover that what in others passed for knowledge was in fact a flawed understanding based on false assumptions. Socrates' own sceptical example must inform any consideration of his life and beliefs, for he left no record, and he is only fleetingly mentioned in contemporary histories. Instead, all evidence comes from clearly slanted sources: on the one hand **Aristophanes**, intent on humour, who caricatures Socrates as a sophist; on the other his pupils Plato and **Xenophon**, both avid admirers, who tend to eulogize him.

Even from Plato and Xenophon, however, we learn nothing of Socrates' early life. His family, if not rich, seems to have been relatively affluent, and much later traditions that he and his father Sophroniscus were sculptors and his mother Phaenarete a midwife are now considered suspect. In fact, like his father, who was a close friend of the aristocratic politician Aristeides' son, Lysimachus, Socrates moved in exalted social circles, counting many of **Pericles'** coterie among his friends and acquaintances. He married well, if boldly, for his wife Xanthippe – whose aristocratic name ('Chestnut Horse'), the feminine form of that of Pericles' father, may suggest she was an Alcmaeonid – was possessed of a fiery temperament. As Socrates is said to have joked, 'Any horse I choose to own must show some spirit.' By her he had three sons, who (despite their parentage) were disappointingly dull and stupid.

Women played an unusually prominent role in Socrates' life. Plato has him name among his teachers a priestess, Diotima, who inspired his quest for the true nature of the divine, as well as Pericles' consort **Aspasia**, from whom he learned rhetoric. Other intellectuals who performed an important part in shaping Socrates' mind included Anaxagoras, with his scientific method of enquiry, and the sophist Prodicus of Ceos, who may also have tutored **Thucydides**, and whose insistence on the precise use of language influenced Socrates' own method.

Like many intellectuals Socrates regarded Athenian democracy with some suspicion. In Plato's dialogues he is heard constantly complaining that, while no one would trust unskilled artisans, in the Assembly and lawcourts they are only too willing to put matters of great importance to the vote of non-specialists. However, when called upon he proved a zealous supporter of his polis. He served as a hoplite on the campaigns at Potidaea (432), when he saved the life of **Alcibiades**, at Delium (424), and in the Amphipolis offensive under **Cleon** (422).

It was Socrates' involvement with the political and judicial life of Athens which most clearly demonstrated his character. In 406, towards the end of the Peloponnesian War, the Athenian fleet won a naval victory at Arginusae near Lesbos; but in their haste to pursue the fleeing enemy and because of an unexpected storm the strategoi failed to go to the help of shipwrecked survivors or to collect the bodies of the dead. As a result they were put on trial. By sheer chance, on the first day, Socrates found himself chairman of the Boule (a position which rotated daily), and in this capacity he successfully resisted his colleagues' demands that all eight of the strategoi involved be tried as one, arguing that this was unconstitutional. Next day, however, with Socrates no longer in charge and a more hawkish chairman orchestrating proceedings, the strategoi were condemned to death. Among them was Pericles' only surviving son, whom he had fathered by Aspasia, and whose presence among the accused may have added a sense of urgency to Socrates' desire for justice.

Socrates soon found himself embroiled in politics again. In 404, at the end of the Peloponnesian War, Sparta imposed on Athens an oligarchy known as the Thirty Tyrannoi, whose rule rapidly degenerated into despotism. As part of their attempt to implicate as many as they could in their reign of terror they ordered Socrates, together with four others, to arrest an innocent man, Leon of Salamis, so that he might be executed. Socrates refused, and escaped punishment only because the regime fell soon afterwards.

A first-century AD Roman wall painting from Ephesus of the snub-nosed Socrates, his features remarkably similar to those of surviving busts which copy portraits from his lifetime.

ΣΩΚΡΑΤΗΣ

Five years later he was not so fortunate. In 399 he was arraigned on the double charge of corrupting the young men of Athens and of not believing in the city's gods but, instead, introducing new divinities. In his unflinchingly honest self-defence he compared himself to the wrongly accused legendary hero Palamedes, and concluded with the suggestion that, as punishment, Athens should pay him a stipend for life with free meals. Despite – or perhaps because of – this Socrates was condemned to death. Resisting suggestions that he bribe his captors to let him escape, he was executed by being made to drink hemlock. In view of his supposed lack of belief in established religion, Socrates' last words are ironic: referring to a sacrifice made for deliverance from sickness, which was how he considered death, he quipped: 'We owe a cockerel to [the health god] Asclepius. Do remember to pay the debt.'

The charges which Socrates faced are suggestive both of his teachings and of his place within society. Certainly his followers included some of the most powerful young men of Athens. For, although he strenuously denied accepting fees, he did attract many of the city's elite – including not only Athens' nemesis Alcibiades but Plato's uncle Critias, the ruthless leader of the Thirty Tyrannoi. In the aftermath of that regime the politics of vengeance may very well have played an important part in Socrates' impeachment. At the same time he cannot but have made many enemies. In the wake of the oracle's declaration that he was the wisest of all men, the snub-nosed, straggly haired philosopher, whose appearance reminded aesthetically obsessed Athenians of the ugly nature god Silenus, took to accosting publicly anyone who was considered clever and interrogating them in order to discover the foundation of their beliefs. His technique, known as *elenchus*, involved the examination of a proposition through a series of interrelated questions which invariably proved it to be false, and led not only to his being nicknamed 'The Cleg', after the irritating insect which plagues cattle, but (undoubtedly) to his humiliated victims nursing grudges.

Because Socrates was focused more on refuting the arguments of others than on positing his own, and also because much of what is attributed to him may in fact be the later-developed beliefs of his pupils Plato and Xenophon, it is difficult to tell with any confidence what Socrates himself thought. However, certain ideas, some of which are clearly counter-intuitive, seem to have permeated his thinking, for example that no one chooses bad over good; that no one willingly or intentionally does wrong; that virtue equates to knowledge; that in virtue lies happiness; and that, contrary to the views of earlier thinkers, virtue is universal and objective. He appears to have believed, too, that he was protected by a personal spirit or *daemonion*, whose voice he often heard warning him against

In Jacques-Louis David's painting (1787), Socrates, surrounded by grieving disciples, stretches out his right hand to take the fatal hemlock cup, while with his left he points heavenwards.

pursuing damaging courses of action. This daemonion may have been one of the 'new divinities' referred to in Socrates' arraignment. Certainly he appears to have supposed the existence of one divine spiritual entity rather than the multitude of anthropomorphic gods worshipped by traditional Athenian religion, and, as a follower of **Pythagoras** and an initiate in the Eleusinian Mysteries, he probably believed, too, in the soul's life after death.

Indeed, it was after his own death that Socrates was to make his greatest impact. The manner of his trial and execution had a profound effect on his followers, some of whom saw it as the ultimate indictment of the Athenian democracy which had so dominated the preceding century. Now, though, with the defeat of Athens and the end of the Peloponnesian War, life in Greek poleis everywhere was changing. New allegiances were being formed, new powerbases created; and at the heart of this shifting world one of a new breed of young men in Alcibiades' mould – eager less for a life of politics than for adventure – left Athens to fight as a mercenary for a Persian prince. The young man was Xenophon, one of Socrates' disciples. The account he wrote would encapsulate the changing history of his times.

Chapter 6

Fallout

XENOPHON (c. 430–c. 354)
General, Historian, Literary Innovator

Respect for the gods, experience in the arts of war and submission before authority are certain to result in confidence.

Xenophon, Hellenica, 3.4

The fall of Athens and the implosion of her empire had immediate repercussions for the entire Greek world. As was inevitable, Sparta and her victorious allies started jockeying for supremacy; yet ironically it soon became apparent that in the east true power lay not with Greeks at all, but at the court of their old rival the Great King of Persia. In 411 Sparta and Persia had signed a treaty: in return for the financial backing of the Great King Darius II, Sparta would recognize Persia's claims to the Greek cities of Asia Minor. As a token of how seriously he took the arrangement, Darius sent his son Cyrus the Younger (a mere sixteen years old) to deal directly with the Spartans and their general **Lysander**, injecting vast amounts of cash into their war effort. Unfortunately for Sparta, however, their victory over Athens in 404 coincided not only with Darius' death but with Cyrus' fall from grace. His elder brother mounted the throne, assumed the royal name Artaxerxes (II) and stripped Cyrus of much of his authority. But, familiar with power, Cyrus was loath to relinquish it; his heart set on kingship, he plotted his revenge. With the backing of Sparta, and with his true objective hidden from all but his most trusted generals, Cyrus assembled an army. Drawn not only from his Persian subjects but from Greek mercenaries too, it assembled at Sardis, and it was here in 401 that almost by accident it was joined by a young man who would vividly chronicle its fate. He was an Athenian called Xenophon.

A man of unusual modesty and extreme good looks, Xenophon was born
into a well-to-do family in the plague years of the early Peloponnesian War. On
reaching adulthood, as part of Athens' social elite he joined the cavalry, with
which he may have ridden on a disastrous yet relatively insignificant campaign to
Ephesus and Ionia in 409. Five years later he served the Thirty Tyrannoi, imposed
on Athens after its surrender. How willing a participant Xenophon was in their
atrocities is questionable – he later tried vehemently to distance himself from
them – but his sympathies were not entirely on the side of democracy. Rumour
suggested that he was the lover of the regime's leader, Critias – he certainly
belonged to his social set for, like so many other confident, upper-class young
Athenians, Xenophon was a disciple of Critias' mentor **Socrates**. Xenophon
was not an altogether compliant pupil. When in 401 a Theban friend, Proxenus
(a student of **Gorgias** and one of the commanders of the Greek mercenaries),
suggested Xenophon join him on Cyrus' forthcoming campaign, Socrates advised
Xenophon to consult the Delphic oracle. Xenophon did, but asked not whether
he should go – rather to which gods he should sacrifice to ensure his expedition's

Xenophon was an accomplished rider; in *On Horsemanship* and *The Good Cavalry Commander* he describes cavalry processions similar to this one, shown on the mid-fifth-century Parthenon Frieze.

success. Socrates was piqued by such wilful disobedience, but Xenophon remained one of the philosopher's greatest champions.

Soon Xenophon was back in Ephesus, whose glittering temple of Artemis with its statue of the goddess festooned with bulls' testicles made a lasting impression. As he was leaving the city he saw the first of many omens which would guide him in the years to come – an eagle perched at a distance to his right, foretelling good luck mixed with suffering, which was likely to bring little profit. Undeterred, Xenophon continued to Sardis. In late spring 401 he set out with Cyrus on a campaign whose true objective soon became clear: the overthrow of the Great King of Persia. The Greek mercenaries became restive; higher pay bought their renewed support; and the summer saw them crossing the Euphrates before trudging south through unforgiving deserts in search of the enemy. At last, near the village of Cunaxa, the two sides met. Impetuous and heedless of his generals' advice, Cyrus plunged into the thick of battle, where (it was later said) he was about to cut down his brother Artaxerxes when he fell mortally wounded. In an instant all was reversed. With Cyrus' death the Greek mercenaries who had relied on him for pay and protection found themselves stranded in a hostile land, bewilderingly marooned near Babylon.

They tried to enlist with Artaxerxes, but he rejected them. All they could do was go home. But how? Hopes of safe passage were dashed when the satrap Tissaphernes treacherously lured their generals (including Xenophon's friend Proxenus) to their squalid deaths. Leaderless, the mercenaries were paralysed. But that night in a dream Xenophon saw a thunderbolt consuming his whole house. It galvanized him into action. Summoning an assembly, where he urged the men to choose new leaders, he found himself appointed general. Quite unexpectedly, having joined the expedition as a youthful adventurer, he had become the man tasked with the responsibility to lead it home.

Dogged as it was by Tissaphernes and his troops, it was a gruelling retreat, a march of many months through inhospitable terrain. As winter closed in and with all other routes denied them, the army of just over 10,000 hoplites and 2,600 light-armed skirmishers was forced to strike out north towards the snow-smothered mountains of Armenia. Here lived tribesmen so adept in guerrilla fighting that not even the Persians had tried to subdue them. Death seemed the only certainty, yet somehow against all odds, through determination and force of personality, Xenophon succeeded in leading the disparate mercenary army through a trackless icy wilderness on a journey without maps. As they marched, Xenophon constantly inspired his men with stories from history and mythology, comparing their journey to the *Odyssey*, recalling stirring episodes from the Persian Wars almost a century before and (later) recognizing Black Sea landmarks from Jason's voyage with his Argonauts. At last, they reached the mountain of Thekes. Here, as he later described in his *Anabasis* (The Journey Up-Country), Xenophon was riding with the rear of the army when he heard shouting up ahead. He thought it was enemy attackers, but 'when the noise increased and the shouting came closer, and those who were still marching started running towards those in front, who all kept on shouting, and the more there were the more the shouting grew', Xenophon galloped ahead to find out what was happening. At last he made out his soldiers' words and saw the cause of their excitement: 'The sea! The sea!' High in the hills above the Black Sea, near the Greek polis of Trapezus, amid a welter of unfettered celebration, he had brought his army back to safety.

Feelings of fraternal solidarity did not last for long. As the army marched west towards Spartan-held Byzantium, discipline broke down as the mercenaries began to show their true nature. Many little more than thugs, driven not by ideals but by a lust for booty, they behaved with no regard for law or decency, looting and pillaging not only hostile tribes but potentially friendly Greek settlements as well. For a while Xenophon considered giving his men gainful employment by founding a colony himself, but his plans were discovered and dismissed out of hand. By the time his 'Ten Thousand' reached Byzantium they were a liability.

Wisely resisting their suggestions that he expel the Spartan garrison and make himself tyrannos of wealthy Byzantium, Xenophon found the mercenaries employment under his command with a Thracian king. However, when news came that Tissaphernes' insensitive administration of Ionia had provoked war with Sparta, the remnants of the 'Ten Thousand' headed south to wreak vengeance on the man who had once sought to destroy them. On the way they attacked and held to ransom the family of a local Persian nobleman – an adventure which made Xenophon a very wealthy man. Then, with the Spartan king Agesilaus II now commanding them, they defeated Tissaphernes' troops near Sardis. Soon Tissaphernes too had paid the price of failure at the hands of Artaxerxes' executioners.

King Agesilaus II of Sparta

Agesilaus was born lame, but despite his disability, with the support of the general Lysander he became one of the two kings of Sparta in 400 when his rival Leotychidas, suspected of being the illegitimate son of **Alcibiades**, was disqualified. In 396, as Sparta sought to assert its pre-eminence in the wake of the Peloponnesian War, he attacked Persia, symbolically assembling his army at Aulis, from where the legendary Agamemnon set sail for Troy. Once in Asia, Agesilaus defeated the Persians at Sardis with the help of Xenophon's mercenaries, but he was recalled to Greece to fight in the Corinthian War, where he won the battle of Coronea (394). His long-standing enmity towards Thebes, however, led ultimately to Sparta's defeat at Leuctra (371), and the subsequent invasion of the Spartan homeland of Laconia (370/69). When Agesilaus died on campaign in north Africa in his eighties, commanding a force of mercenaries seeking to liberate Egypt from Persian rule, Xenophon (who had benefited from his friendship and patronage) wrote his eulogistic biography.

In such troubled times little remained constant for long. Irked that Sparta had broken their treaty, Persia switched sides and soon gold was pouring into Athens, Argos, Corinth and Thebes. Together they formed a coalition against Sparta. The Corinthian War (395–386) had begun. Agesilaus and his troops returned quickly to the mainland and soon at Coronea, on the reedy shores of Lake Copais, Xenophon of Athens found himself fighting for Sparta against an Athenian army. As Xenophon records, it was a bloodbath, unlike any other battle of its time: 'Locking shields, the two sides shoved forward; and so they fought and killed; and so they too were killed.' By nightfall, though badly injured, Agesilaus was victorious. Yet for Xenophon the battle had inevitable consequences. He was exiled from Athens. Having tried to lead his mercenaries home, he found he had no home of his own to go to.

In recompense for his services Sparta awarded Xenophon an estate at Scillous near Olympia, where he lived for more than twenty years with his Athenian wife Philesia and their twin sons Gryllus and Diodorus, nicknamed the Dioscuri (Heavenly Twins). In his orchard Xenophon built a shrine to Artemis, goddess of the hunt, a miniature replica of the temple at Ephesus, complete with a cypress-wood copy of the gold cult statue; and inaugurated an annual festival where local townsfolk joined his family to dedicate a tenth of all their produce to the goddess, together with such game as Xenophon and his sons had bagged on hunting trips.

The idyll did not last. In 371 Thebes defeated Sparta at Leuctra and ravaged its territory. Xenophon's estate was confiscated and he was forced to flee with his family to Corinth. Fifteen years earlier an exhausted Greece had made a lasting peace with Persia, under whose terms exiles might return to their cities. Now, allied with Sparta against their joint enemy Thebes, Athens had found pressing reasons of its own to welcome brave young fighters home. So Xenophon's son Gryllus had enlisted like his father before him in the Athenian cavalry. He was serving with his unit when, in 362, Athens faced a Theban army under **Epaminondas** at Mantinea. In a skirmish before the battle young Gryllus was killed. He was commemorated in epitaphs and eulogies and his death was shown in a painting of the battle in Athens' Stoa Poikile. Xenophon was conducting a sacrifice when he heard that Gryllus had died bravely. He did not weep, but remarked laconically, 'I knew that he was mortal.' Xenophon survived his son by perhaps seven years. Tradition suggests he died in Corinth in around 354, though

Xenophon's passion for hunting was shared by many Greek aristocrats, including the Macedonian royal family, as this mosaic from Pella, from the end of the fourth century, attests.

he may have been buried in his beloved Scillous, where later visitors were shown his tomb.

Xenophon's life was a mirror of his age. Having grown up in war-torn Athens he embodied the new realities of rootlessness which followed the collapse of empire. Yet in outlook, both politically and religiously, he was profoundly conservative – an aristocratic oligarch for whom the most important duty of a general was to ensure that proper sacrifices were offered to the gods, a pragmatist who believed that good men could commune with the divine.

For all his swashbuckling adventures Xenophon made his most lasting mark as an author. In his earliest work, *On Hunting* (dating perhaps to 390), he drew close parallels between the hunt and warfare, stressing the importance of self-discipline and strong leadership, which he saw as prerequisites for a virtuous life. He returned to this theme in *Memorabilia*, dialogues inspired by his mentor Socrates which, together with *Apologia* (a version of Socrates' defence speech at his trial), present the philosopher as a pragmatist. Critics might question whether the real Socrates used as many examples from hunting and estate management as Xenophon would suggest, and list discrepancies with **Plato's** characterization of the philosopher, but others argue that such differences merely reveal that Socrates tailored his teaching to his audience. Certainly Xenophon's Socrates had a profound influence on later Stoic philosophers.

Although Xenophon wrote in earnest only after leaving Scillous, his output was both prodigious and innovative. It included an ambitious history, *Hellenica* (Greek Affairs), a deliberate continuation of **Thucydides'** *History*, which begins almost mid-sentence where the earlier work broke off. Less scientific or sophisticated than Thucydides' account, *Hellenica* is nonetheless a vivid chronicle of the chaotic years of shifting allegiances through which Xenophon had lived, imbued with his distinctive world view and informed by his experience as a general. Curiously, despite his personal involvement in many episodes recorded in *Hellenica*, Xenophon never refers to himself by name, but as 'the leader of the Greek mercenaries', and, alluding to his own *Anabasis*, claims that its author was Themistogenes of Syracuse. Even when describing the battle of Mantinea he does not name Gryllus, writing only that 'in the fighting many good Athenians were killed'.

Xenophon's other works often reveal him to be a writer of great originality, keen to push the boundaries, developing old genres and inventing new ones. *Anabasis* (in which Xenophon places himself unashamedly centre stage) is a compelling description of the march of the 'Ten Thousand', the first surviving autobiographical history in western literature. *The Education of Cyrus*, about the childhood of the founder of Persia's empire, is a curiously hybrid work – part military handbook, part moral treatise, part historical novel, in which Xenophon revisits episodes familiar to readers of **Herodotus**, offering his own version of Cyrus' encounter with King Croesus. His *Life of Agesilaus* is arguably the first stand-alone biography, though its tone is too eulogistic to be considered objective. Indeed, throughout Xenophon's writing there is a tendency to lionize powerful men. Not only Agesilaus but Socrates, Cyrus the Younger and the Thessalian king Jason of Pherae, whose plans to conquer the rest of Greece were foiled only by his assassination, all enjoy his plaudits.

In one Socratic dialogue, *Oeconomicus* (Estate Management), Xenophon perhaps unwittingly reveals much about his own domestic life, writing that although 'when a wife is a good partner in a house, her contribution is as important as that of her husband', 'there are few people to whom a man speaks less than to his wife'. Indeed, it was horses, not wives, which gave Xenophon most pleasure. Two works are devoted to the beasts, *On Horsemanship* and *The Cavalry Commander*, where he gives enthusiastic advice on training for parades and war; while in *The Education of Cyrus* one of the characters proclaims, 'The creature I have always envied is the centaur.' Half man, half horse, like Xenophon this mythical hybrid belonged to no world other than its own. Yet in the decades which followed Xenophon's death even the real, Classical world would change beyond recognition.

LYSANDER (?–395)
Spartan General

The Spartan Eteocles was thought to have spoken on behalf of everyone when he said that Greece could never have endured two Lysanders.

Plutarch, *Life of Lysander*, 19

Lysander was born in the mid-fifth century to an ancient but impoverished Spartan family. Lacking sufficient wealth to qualify as one of the homoioi, he belonged to a class known as the *mothakes*: free men without citizen rights, dispossessed outsiders who relied on others in order to make their way in Sparta's hierarchical society. As the Peloponnesian War took its toll on the homoioi population, unimagined opportunities arose for the ambitious mothax – none more so than for Lysander, who became one of Sparta's most brilliant generals and politicians. King Agesilaus owed him his crown, yet his ruthless ambition provoked such animosity that **Xenophon** never mentions him in his biography of the Spartan king. Perhaps no wonder, then, that Lysander was the embodiment of opposites: implacably brave yet fawningly obsequious in the face of authority; a patriotic Spartan who plotted to overthrow his country's constitution; a stranger to morality who thought nothing of 'cheating boys with dice and men with oaths'.

Lysander first stepped out from the shadows of history in 407 when he was appointed admiral of the Spartan fleet and sailed east to Ephesus, which had seceded from the Delian League five years earlier. Economically isolated as a result, the Ephesians enthusiastically embraced Lysander when he promised commercial regeneration. Soon the city's wharves were once more bristling with merchant ships, while in the naval dockyards a new war fleet was being built. While in Ionia, Lysander ingratiated himself with the Great King's son and envoy, Cyrus the Younger, eagerly accepting his financial backing as Persia honoured the terms of its treaty to support Sparta. With Persian gold he raised his oarsmen's pay, boosting their morale and causing many Athenians to defect. In 406 he won a stunning victory over Athens' fleet, which led to the removal from office of its

The *Mothax* Gylippus

By the end of the fifth century irreplaceable losses in its citizen manpower caused Sparta to rely increasingly on its otherwise underprivileged class of *mothakes*. The first outstanding *mothax* was Gylippus. His father was a royal advisor who had been disgraced for accepting bribes. Nonetheless Gylippus was sent as Spartan general to Sicily in 414 to assist Syracuse during Athens' siege of the city. Here he proved to be an inspirational commander, crushing the enemy and (according to some historic records) dealing mercilessly with his prisoners. Like his father, however, Gylippus became embroiled in financial scandal. After Athens' defeat in 404, when Lysander entrusted him with shipping captured booty back to Sparta, Gylippus is said to have cut open the sacks in which the treasure was transported, removed copious quantities of silver and sewed them up again, not knowing that Lysander had made careful inventories. Gylippus' house was searched, the money was discovered hidden beneath the roof, and although Gylippus fled he was condemned to death in his absence. Was he guilty? Or was he a victim of his fellow *mothax* Lysander's rivalry? His fate is suspiciously similar to that of the legendary Palamedes, which so fascinated **Gorgias** and **Socrates** and may have inspired Lysander to plot Gylippus' downfall.

commander **Alcibiades**. Then, to his chagrin, Lysander was summoned home to Sparta, his term of office over. He left behind a toxic inheritance – out of spite he had returned his unspent monies to Cyrus and advised him to shun his successor. When within months the new admiral was killed at Arginusae both the Spartan navy and Cyrus demanded that Lysander resume his command.

Triumphant, Lysander harried the Athenian fleet until in 405 the two sides faced each other across the narrow Dardanelles at Aegospotamoi. Control of these waters was crucial to Athens' grain supply from the Black Sea. Now, with Lysander nearby, the Athenian admiral Conon should have been vigilant. Instead, he was taken unawares. After five days, in which he stubbornly refused to give battle, Lysander hoisted a bronze shield high on his ship's mast to order the attack. Off guard, the Athenians were quickly overcome and most of their ships disabled or destroyed. Although Conon and many of his men escaped, 3,000 Athenians did not. Lysander executed every one. Then he cruised the islands and Aegean coast, ordering all Athenians to return to Athens. Soon the besieged polis – its population swollen, its food supplies cut off, its surrounding territories occupied and ravaged – was starving. Lysander took his time, methodically touring cities once loyal to Athens, massacring their democratic leaders, sending entire populations into exile. Samos was depopulated, Sestus settled with Lysander's veterans, and by the time he reached Athens it was ready to surrender. When he reported to Sparta, 'Athens taken', the laconic ephors rebuked Lysander for being too verbose: 'Taken' would have sufficed.

In September 404, on the seventy-sixth anniversary of Salamis, Lysander oversaw Athens' ritual humiliation. As the remnants of its fleet were burned, and its Long Walls dismantled to the accompaniment of *auloi* (flutes), he ushered in the grim regime of the Thirty Tyrannoi. Already Lysander had installed a web of similar regimes across the Aegean, each owing its loyalty to him, a powerbase greater than any Spartan had ever controlled. At the same time he promoted his self–image. On campaign he took a poet to eulogize his victories. At Delphi he dedicated a 3 foot long (1 m) gold and ivory model trireme that had been a gift from Cyrus, and erected a statue of himself, bearded and with his hair long in Spartan fashion, flanked by his two admirals. And in Samos, now repopulated with his own supporters, the ancient festival of Hera was renamed the Lysandreia in his honour and he was worshipped as a god – the first Greek ever to be so venerated. Yet even this was not enough. Lysander's sights were set on ruling Sparta.

As things stood this was impossible. Although Lysander traced his ancestry to Heracles he was not from either of the ruling families. As a *mothax* he was not

Rubens, in his drawing of Lysander (*c.* 1600), reflects the Spartan's observation (recorded by Plutarch) that 'a good head of hair makes a handsome man more handsome and an ugly one more terrifying'.

even a full Spartan citizen. So when King Agis II died in 401 Lysander sought another solution. The succession was plagued by controversy. With Leotychidas, the heir, accused of being Alcibiades' bastard son, Lysander threw his support behind Agis' brother, Agesilaus. They had once been lovers and Agesilaus, lame from birth, was not an obvious war leader, so Lysander probably believed he could control him. He was mistaken. No sooner had Agesilaus been enthroned and sailed east to Sparta's new territories in Ionia than he began deliberately to snub Lysander. Furious but undeterred the general returned to Sparta and plotted a coup d'état.

With the help of a speech-writer, Cleon of Halicarnassus, Lysander formulated his argument: Sparta should be ruled not by hereditary kings but by the strongest candidate regardless of birth. And that, of course, was Lysander. He had already taken care to court the ephors, filling Sparta's coffers with the wealth of plundered cities while ostentatiously keeping nothing for himself. Now he lobbied the oracles of Apollo at Delphi and Zeus at the sanctuary of Dodona in Epirus and even visited the shrine of Zeus Ammon in Egypt, his luggage packed with gold, to gain the backing of the gods. But in a destabilized world the priests were wary of disturbing Sparta's status quo. They rebuffed him and reported his ambitions to the ephors. Somehow Lysander convinced them of his innocence, but his reputation had been tarnished. So, to redeem himself, he stoked the fires of war.

Argos, Thebes and Corinth, recently Sparta's closest allies in the Peloponnesian War, but now wary of her apparent lust for empire, had formed a coalition with their erstwhile enemy Athens. If this reversal were not enough, the alliance was financed by Sparta's former paymaster, Persia, against whom Agesilaus even now was massing troops in Ionia. Already a proxy conflict had flared up between Theban-backed Locris and Spartan-sponsored Phocis. Now in 395 Lysander urged the ephors to declare all-out war. They did, and soon two armies of Spartans were on the march, one commanded by their king Pausanias, the other by Lysander. It was a pincer movement, its objective: Thebes.

While besieging the Boeotian city of Haliartus, which barred the way to Thebes, Lysander learned that his communications with Pausanias had been intercepted. His strategy had been predicated on the king's support, but as the time for attack came closer Pausanias still had not appeared. Loath to delay, Lysander gave the order and the Spartans surged towards the city walls. Suddenly the gates of Haliartus swung open and its army, swollen by Thebans, poured out. Early in the fighting Lysander was cut down, his body abandoned by the walls as the Spartans fled. When Pausanias at last arrived and found a thousand Spartans dead he agreed a truce, the only way Lysander's corpse could be retrieved for burial.

Later, among Lysander's papers, Agesilaus found the speech which Cleon of Halicarnassus had penned justifying overthrowing the Spartan monarchy. He was going to publish it as evidence of Lysander's treachery when the senior ephor stopped him. Better to keep it quiet, he argued, lest another should be inspired to emulate Lysander and try to destroy Sparta from within. What neither man knew was that within a generation Sparta would be humbled, her once impregnable borders overrun by another man whom Xenophon could hardly bear to name: the Theban Epaminondas.

EPAMINONDAS (c. 418–362)
Theban General

In my judgment, Epaminondas was the most outstanding man in all of Greece.

Cicero, On the Orator, 3.139

Like the Spartan **Lysander**, Epaminondas was born into an ancient yet impoverished family. In Thebes, however, penury was not such a stigma as in Sparta. Indeed, money would never hold an attraction for Epaminondas, who considered it a virtue to live in simple austerity. As a youth he trained hard, not just in martial exercises but in dance and music. But he was particularly drawn to philosophy, idolizing his tutor the Pythagorean Lysis of Taras, spending every waking hour in the old man's company and rapidly acquiring a reputation for honesty, humanity and integrity. Yet events and a sense of public duty would not allow Epaminondas to devote his life to contemplation, and his brilliance as a military tactician would help change the face of Greece forever.

In the years after Thebes' victory over Sparta at Haliartus in 395, Greece was plunged into increasing instability as cynical alliances were formed and broken between major poleis, each still convinced in the face of bitter experience that it could gain supremacy over its rivals. To counter Sparta unexpected alliances were formed as Thebes joined forces not just with Corinth and Argos but with Athens, while in 393 Athens (backed by her erstwhile bête noire Persia) rebuilt the Long Walls, dismantled just eleven years before, and seemed set to re-establish her empire. As the allies' messy war with Sparta leached over central Greece, it was watched hungrily from the east by Artaxerxes II and from the west by Dionysius

I, the powerful tyrannos of Syracuse. By 386 it was clear that neither side could win, and peace was brokered by the Persian Great King. In their rush to sign it the mainland Greeks willingly agreed that the cities of Ionia be ruled by Persia. That Sparta, which had already counselled sacrificing Ionia in 478, had been prepared to cede the region's rights in 411 was perhaps explicable. But for Athens to agree and Greece to condone was unforgivable. So introspective and myopic had they now become that in a flourish they signed away all that their ancestors had fought so hard to gain. They should have felt humiliated, but as their horizons shrank they fooled themselves with ever more unlikely yet destructive dreams of power.

Peace did not last. In 382 a Spartan army returning from campaign in northern Greece unexpectedly attacked and captured the Cadmea, Thebes' acropolis. While many patriots fled to Athens Epaminondas stayed in Thebes, goading its young men to action. He encouraged them to wrestle in the gymnasium with their Spartan overlords and, when they won, demanded why

Thebes

The city of Thebes in Boeotia was famous in mythology as the home of Oedipus and Antigone. It was also the birthplace of the god Dionysus to which, in **Euripides'** *Bacchae*, he returns after long wanderings in Asia to wreak revenge on its citizens for not recognizing his divinity. In Classical times, however, the predominantly agricultural Thebans were pilloried by neighbouring Athenians for being backward and slow-witted. Our comparative lack of Theban literary sources (with the notable exception of **Pindar**) makes this hard to refute, but Athens' scorn was partly the result of politics. In the early fifth century Thebes had supported the Persian invasions, a decision which did little to endear it to the victorious Greeks. Nonetheless, in the First Peloponnesian War (460–446), Thebes allied with Sparta against Athens, a role it reprised in the war of 431–404. In the fourth century, under the generalship of Epaminondas between 379 and 362, Thebes' star blazed brightly as it expanded its dominance across Boeotia and beyond, but in 338 its army was defeated by Philip II of Macedon at Chaeronea. Three years later, after Thebes took part in an ill-judged revolt against Macedonian rule, **Alexander III** besieged the city, captured it and razed it to the ground. The only house he spared was Pindar's. After Alexander's death his general Cassander rebuilt Thebes, but the city never regained its former significance.

they could not therefore expel them from their city. At last the partisans led by the brilliant soldier Pelopidas returned in secret, and while one group butchered Theban quislings in their houses another (dressed as women) massacred leading collaborators at a drinking party. Next morning Epaminondas appeared beside the fighters in the agora to proclaim the liberation of his city.

Respected by Thebes' new political elite, Epaminondas was elected as one of his city's leading officials (*Boeotarchs*), and together with Pelopidas established a new crack hoplite regiment, the Sacred Band, made up entirely of 150 pairs of homosexual lovers. His belief was that, like Achilles and Patroclus at Troy (who themselves were now imagined to have been lovers), the men's mutual devotion and desire to win each others' praise would cause them to fight all the harder. At the same time, in recognition of the support which Athens had given the rebel exiles, Thebes joined the new Athenian League and together they waged war with Sparta throughout the Aegean. By 371 both sides sought an end to fighting, but when peace treaties were proposed their terms seemed calculated to destroy Thebes' hard-won hegemony of Boeotia. Epaminondas refused to sign.

Within three weeks the Spartans and their allies, 10,000 hoplites and 1,500 cavalry strong, was deep in Theban territory at Leuctra. Facing them with 6,000 hoplites and 1,000 cavalry was Epaminondas. Dangerously outnumbered, he knew that in conventional battle he would be defeated. So he changed the rules of warfare. Until now hoplite phalanxes had placed their best troops on the right wing, where they hoped to smash through their opponent's weaker left before wheeling round to attack the enemy from the rear. Now, unable to countenance great losses, Epaminondas positioned his elite troops – their ranks fifty deep with the Sacred Band at their head – on the left wing, facing Sparta's homoioi. The sheer impetus of numbers did its work. As the rest of their army attacked at an oblique angle, the Thebans, shoving and stabbing, forced their enemy to turn and flee. In the carnage 1,000 Spartan hoplites died, including 400 homoioi – a loss from which, their numbers already in decline, they would never truly recover.

Yet it was not just Sparta which had designs on central Greece. To the north the Thessalian tyrannos Jason of Pherae was planning an invasion which only his assassination prevented from being unleashed. The danger past, Epaminondas led his Thebans, still smarting from the Spartan occupation of their city, south into the Peloponnese to complete the work they had begun at Leuctra. Already the region had been buckled by tectonic shifts. Exploiting Sparta's weakness, her lesser rivals had formed a Pan-Arcadian League. Its capital at the new city of Megalopolis (founded in 371), together with Mantinea, formed a bulwark against Spartan aggression. Now, as winter approached, Epaminondas inspired the

Arcadians to do what for generations had been unthinkable: invade Laconia and strike at Sparta's heartland.

There were now fewer than 1,000 homoioi left alive. None ventured to oppose Epaminondas. Only the River Eurotas, surging in spate from the snowy heights of Mount Taygetus, prevented an attack on Sparta. As the villages of Laconia burned the Spartan women, who had never seen a hostile army, wept. Epaminondas, thwarted, continued south to Gytheon. By now his period of command was officially over, but, rather than lose momentum (and aware that the penalty for retaining his command was death), he swung his army west into Messenia, the ancient Helot country, enslaved by Sparta more than 400 years before. Now Epaminondas liberated it, and more: on the slopes of Mount Ithome, where a century before the rebel Helots made their stand, he founded Messene, its strong walls encompassing sufficient land to withstand a lengthy siege.

Back in Thebes, Epaminondas, as he predicted, was put on trial for his life. Such were his achievements, however, that he was pardoned, although he was not reappointed as a general and he next campaigned as a mere hoplite. Pelopidas, a trusted arbitrator, had made peace between Pherae and Macedon, bringing one of the latter's princes back to Thebes as hostage. Now, in 368, in the aftermath of the Macedonian king's murder, Pelopidas negotiated another settlement, but on his way home he was kidnapped and held captive by Alexander of Pherae (Jason's successor). Thebes sent an army to rescue him, but it got into difficulties when incompetent generals tried to beat a retreat, and it was only when they called on Epaminondas to take command that the troops reached safety. Early the next year he returned to Pherae as Boeotarch and, employing a strategy of wearing down the enemy rather than doing battle, he succeeded in liberating Pelopidas.

Meanwhile, Epaminondas' success in the Peloponnese had not borne fruit. The Pan-Arcadian League had been loath to trust Thebes, and in the ensuing scramble for power Athens had formed an alliance with Sparta. Things came to a head in 364, when Sparta and Elis attacked the Pan-Arcadian League at Olympia, where it had taken control of the Games. Although such military aggression was sacrilegious it was nothing compared to the desecration which followed when the League ransacked Olympia's treasuries, rich with offerings, to pay its troops. Support for the League among other Greeks cooled rapidly. Mantinea declared for Sparta. Soon the League itself seemed set to follow suit.

In 362, fearing a united Peloponnese, Epaminondas marched south. A lightning attack on a defenceless Sparta was thwarted when his plans were leaked. By the time he rejoined the bulk of his army stationed at Mantinea his horsemen there had been attacked by Athenian cavalry (the encounter in which **Xenophon's**

In Isaac Walraven's *The Deathbed of Epaminondas, Commander of the Theban Army in the Battle against Sparta* (1726), even the statues supporting the bed's canopy appear to be mourning.

son Gryllus lost his life). His men tired from their forced march and with the enemy's numbers now swollen by their allies, Epaminondas was nonetheless aware that were he not to fight his own confederates would soon slip away. Once again he put his trust in surprise tactics. Feigning retreat he suddenly wheeled round and ordered the attack. Just as at Leuctra he had reinforced his left flank, and once more his strategy paid off. But, leading his men against the fleeing Spartans, Epaminondas was struck in the chest by a spear. As he lay dying he urged his lieutenants to make peace. Although defeated, once they had regrouped the Spartans refused. What might have marked an end to Greek internecine conflict merely exacerbated it, and Thebes' brief flowering marked but another stage in Greece's spiral down to self-destruction.

However, Epaminondas did leave one lasting legacy. The Macedonian prince whom Pelopidas had brought to Thebes as a hostage had been enthralled by its revolutionary military tactics and training. Only a few years later he would use his experience to brilliant effect when, as King Philip II, he rode with his son Alexander to Chaeronea and, defeating Greece's still unwitting poleis, turned not just warfare but the Greek world on its head.

LYSIAS (445–380)
Orator and Speech-Writer

We must remember that no one is born a democrat or an oligarch; rather he favours the constitution which will benefit him most.

Lysias, *Defence Against a Charge of Subverting the Democracy*, 8

The convulsions of the late fifth and early fourth centuries affected not just poleis but private individuals. A notable example of the latter is Lysias. In the 450s his father Cephalus, a wealthy Syracusan, had settled in Athens at the invitation of its first citizen, **Pericles**. Here the family lived as part of a diverse community of metics, foreigners who, though barred from voting, contributed significantly to the economy and were closely integrated into city life. Among their friends the family counted **Sophocles**, **Socrates** and Niceratus, son of the general Nicias. Then, following the death of their father, the fifteen-year-old Lysias and one of his three brothers, Polemarchus, returned west to settle their inheritance and set up home in the Athenian colony of Thurii.

Here, in south Italy, life remained blissfully untouched by the Peloponnesian War, but Athens' defeat in Sicily in 413 caused feelings to run so high that the next year Lysias and Polemarchus, as prominent pro-Athenians, were forced to leave Thurii and return to Athens. They settled in Piraeus where, canny industrialists with a shrewd eye for profit, they set up a thriving armaments factory. At its height 120 skilled slaves manufactured shields and made the brothers rich.

But in 404, when Athens fell to Sparta, Lysias' life turned upside down. Greedy for gain the Thirty Tyrannoi drew up their first death-list. It contained the names of ten wealthy metics hostile to the new regime. Lysias and Polemarchus were among them. Late one evening the Thirty's agents knocked on Lysias' door. As his dinner guests were bundled out and armed men sent to search his factory, Lysias bribed their leader Peison with a silver *talent*, as much as a proficient artisan could earn in nine years. Greedy for more, Peison stole the contents of Lysias' strongbox: 3 talents, 400 *staters* (equivalent to 2 talents), 100 *darics* (just under half a talent) and four silver cups. When Lysias complained Peison told him to be grateful to be alive and had him frogmarched to the house

A Roman copy of a fourth-century
Greek bust of Lysias shows the
orator as he may have appeared
towards the end of his life.

of Damnippus, until recently a friend. Knowing that the front was guarded, and fearing death, Lysias crept through the building to the back and made his escape. A short sea voyage took him to Megara, where he heard the news of his brother Polemarchus' death. Arrested without charge he had been forced to drink hemlock. To compound matters further his family had not even been allowed to lay out his corpse at home; they had to hire a shed in which to mourn him. The brothers' wealth was confiscated: three houses, gold and silver, furniture, the 700 shields still in their factory and all their slaves. Golden earrings, part of her dowry, were torn from Polemarchus' widow's ears.

In exile Lysias helped engineer the Thirty's overthrow. He had already given 200 shields and money to the opposition, and now he financed 300 combatants. When democracy was restored in 403 he returned triumphantly to Athens. Thrasybulus, the liberators' leader, gratefully offered him citizenship; the Boule refused to sanction it; but, undeterred and galvanized by recent experience, Lysias entered public life. In his youth he had studied rhetoric and now he harnessed his knowledge to prosecute one of the surviving Thirty, Eratosthenes. In an excoriating speech Lysias mined his personal suffering to tell vividly of the atrocities with which Eratosthenes had been associated, demanding that the jury prove its abhorrence of the regime by condemning him to death. Sadly, their verdict has not survived, but for Lysias' burgeoning career it mattered little. He had made his mark.

Against a backdrop of growing international squabbling, life in Athens was increasingly litigious. As Athenians dragged each other through the lawcourts, their reliance on professional speech-writers grew, logographoi who could frame their arguments convincingly to influence a jury. It was a lucrative profession, and soon its leading representative was Lysias. For more than twenty years plaintiffs and accused rehearsed his speeches on charges from high treason to disability and pension fraud, from wounding with intent to uprooting a sacred olive tree. If Lysias had lost much of his wealth under the Thirty, he very soon regained it.

Away from the lawcourts Lysias delivered two other high-profile public speeches. In 392, during the Corinthian War, he was chosen to make the annual Funeral Oration for Athens' war dead. Like Pericles, he heroized the fallen, commenting that 'everywhere, in every land, our enemies mourn their dead, while glorifying the famous deeds of these Athenians...whose memory cannot grow old, while all men yearn for honour such as theirs'. At its core the speech contained a stark warning. Tracing Athens' glories from mythology (victory over the Amazons) through its heroic history (triumph over Persia) to its very recent past (the overthrow of the Thirty Tyrannoi and the start of the Corinthian War),

Lysias observed: 'How doleful, Greece, to lose such men; how fortunate the Great King not to have to fight them!'

This warning of a weak Greece vulnerable to attack from powerful neighbours formed the subject of another of Lysias' orations, delivered at the Olympic Games of 388. Here he reminded his audience:

> The Great King is our paymaster; Greece is enslaved to those who spend his money. And he has many ships. So, too, has [Dionysius I] the tyrannos of Sicily. We should, then, bury our quarrels and unite to safeguard our salvation!

Lysias' words had an immediate effect: the crowd rushed to pull down the sumptuous tents, their multicoloured fabrics shot with gold, which Dionysius' delegation had erected. Nevertheless, in Greece the internecine fighting went on unabated.

During his life and after his death Lysias' prose style was admired for its direct simplicity, his speeches studied as exemplars of the best of Attic literature. Yet they had mostly been used by Athenians to further personal interests. In the next generation the Athenian politician Demosthenes unleashed a hail of increasingly impassioned orations against the growing power of Macedon in a desperate (if misguided) bid to save not just his city but all Greece.

DEMOSTHENES (384–322)
Orator and Politician

> Had your strength matched your wisdom, Demosthenes, Greece would never have been ruled by Macedonian Ares.

Demosthenes' epitaph (said to have been self-composed),
quoted in Plutarch, *Life of Demosthenes*, 30

Demosthenes' father was a wealthy weapons manufacturer like **Lysias,** but he died when his son was only seven, leaving an inheritance worth almost 14 talents. The boy saw none of it; his guardians appropriated everything; so in 366, when he came of age, Demosthenes arraigned them. Without sufficient funds to engage a professional litigator (upon whom by now many Athenians in such circumstances relied) he chose to represent himself, and so began to train in oratory. Slight of form and with a speech impediment which made his delivery disjointed, nature was against him; but determination drove him on. Tutored gratis by the orator Isaeus and the actor Satyrus, to improve his diction and delivery he declaimed speeches by the seashore with pebbles in his mouth, while at home he rehearsed gestures in a mirror. The trial dragged on. When it was over Demosthenes had made not one but five speeches, each more confident than the last. The court found in his favour, but victory was hollow – his guardians had squandered everything and could not pay him back. There was, however, one consolation. On a pavement in Piraeus an old man told him: 'You reminded me of **Pericles**.' It was a compliment which would shape Demosthenes' life.

Inspired by his success Demosthenes embarked on the lucrative career of logographos, writing speeches for wealthy clients. It mattered little whose case he argued as long as it paid well. Indeed, he was said once to have written a compelling speech for both prosecution and defence in the same trial. Within three years he was rich enough to contribute to the funding of a state trireme. A further three years later, in 360, he could fund one on his own. Yet while Demosthenes was growing affluent in Athens, in Macedonia events were unfolding which would soon consume him.

In 359 Philip II assumed the throne of Macedon, following his brother's death in battle. Drawing on the military training he had assimilated from **Epaminondas** while a hostage in Thebes, Philip reorganized the Macedonian army, creating an elite cavalry corps, the 'Companions', and refining the infantry phalanx, which he armed with long spears (*sarissai*) up to 18 feet (5.5 m) in length. With these he won a swathe of victories, first against the local mountain tribes which had long threatened Macedon's borders, then against northern Greek cities such as Amphipolis. Soon he controlled Thrace's gold mines and in 356 he could celebrate not just victory in the Olympic horse race but the birth of his son **Alexander III**. Just four years later Philip controlled most of Greece north of Thermopylae, while to the south the mainland was once more deep in conflict. With Thebes' brief flowering crushed at Mantinea, neighbouring Phocis was making its own bid for power in central Greece, while the poleis of the Peloponnese kept up their futile infighting whenever possible. As Philip marched against the coastal cities of the Sea of Marmara there was but one voice raised in warning of his growing dominion. It belonged to Demosthenes.

In the first of a series of seven impassioned speeches (the *Philippics* and *Olynthiacs*) Demosthenes unleashed a tide of vitriol against Philip, depicting him as a power-hungry despot, a barbarian bent on the enslavement of all Greece and Athens in particular. At first the audiences were unmoved, but when Philip attacked Olynthus, Athens' ally in the Chersonese, they heeded Demosthenes' invective and went to war. From the start it was doomed to failure. Olynthus fell in 348. In Athens tensions ran so high between the doves (led by Aeschines) and hawks that, as Demosthenes entered the theatre to preside over the Dionysia, one of the appeasers, Meidias, struck him on the face. Demosthenes was delighted. Meidias was wealthy: a successful prosecution would bring both kudos and hefty damages. The case, however, was never brought. Instead, Demosthenes accepted a substantial settlement and published his undelivered speech.

Yet with Philip he would never settle. Chosen as a delegate in 347 to broker peace with Macedon, Demosthenes did all he could to undermine proceedings, and back in Athens he denounced Aeschines and his colleagues in the Assembly as traitors. Before long, Philip marched south through the pass of Thermopylae and, intervening in a war which had been maundering for ten years, defeated Phocis and summarily announced that he would preside over Delphi's prestigious Pythian Games. Demosthenes busily sowed panic throughout Athens, but when it was suggested that the city declare war he rapidly backed down. Once Philip returned north, however, Demosthenes returned to his old theme, indicting those who counselled peace, touring the Peloponnese to build alliances, reforming Athens' navy, and in 341 even leading a successful mission to retake Byzantium, still so crucial to his city's grain supply.

Later, evidence suggested that Demosthenes was in the pay of Persia, richly rewarded for sowing discontent against Macedon. Certainly this explains Demosthenes' behaviour, for at no point did the Macedonians show any desire to harm Athens. Yet, with Demosthenes fomenting rebellion in his newly won territories, Philip was forced to act. In 338 he marched south to Chaeronea. Here he found a ragged alliance of Greek poleis ranged against him: Thebans, Corinthians, Achaeans, Phocians and (with Demosthenes in their ranks as a hoplite) Athenians. The resulting battle was one-sided. While Philip's cavalry massacred the Theban Sacred Band, his phalanx caused the rest of the allied troops to flee. The conflict could so easily have been avoided, yet thanks to Demosthenes a thousand of his fellow citizens lost their lives. But not Demosthenes. Rather, he threw away his shield and joined those running for their lives in terror, his courage on the battlefield no match for his bravado on the speaker's podium.

After Chaeronea, Philip dealt leniently with Athens, returning prisoners without ransom and concluding a generous peace. At the same time, he organized the now subject Greek poleis into a league and furnished them with what he hoped would be a welcome common goal: to invade Persia and win back Ionia, ceded in 386 at the end of the Corinthian War. Despite Demosthenes' cowardice

Demosthenes strengthens his vocal
delivery by declaiming speeches on
a windswept beach near Athens
in this print after a painting by
Jean-Jules-Antoine Lecomte
du Noüy (*c.* 1900).

(and his responsibility), Athens still chose him to give the Funeral Oration for the battle's dead; and when news came of Philip's murder two years later Demosthenes, buoyed by his popularity, led his city in an obscene celebration. Although in mourning for his daughter, who had died a week before, he garlanded his head and dressed in the white robes of celebration to offer thanks for the king's death. The next year Demosthenes was quick to help incite rebellion in Greece, which balked at its lack of independence. He produced a bloodstained 'messenger' to proclaim the news that Alexander too had died. But the Thebans, who had been first to take up arms in revolt, quickly found the rumours to be false. Within weeks Alexander first captured then destroyed their city, with the loss of 6,000 lives. Initially he demanded that Demosthenes be put to death, but following an appeal on his behalf he spared him.

From now on, even with Alexander campaigning far to the east in Persia, Demosthenes was careful not to let his smouldering hostility shine out too brightly. Eventually, in 324, with insurrection simmering throughout the mainland, he found himself once more embroiled in controversy. Again the cause was money. Alexander's treasurer Harpalus arrived in Athens. Having been caught embezzling, he was on the run. At first a suspicious Demosthenes urged the People to deny him sanctuary, but when Harpalus bribed him with a silver cup worth 20 talents he quickly changed his advice, ensuring that he was among those entrusted with depositing Harpalus' remaining 700 talents in the Parthenon treasury. Shortly afterwards, when Harpalus had been killed in Crete and the money was counted, it was found that half had disappeared. Demosthenes was charged, convicted, fined and thrown into jail. By bribing his warders he escaped to exile, but within months his fortune changed. In 323, with Alexander dead in Babylon, and thanks to his impassioned praise of Athens as he wandered Greece in exile, Demosthenes was recalled to his native city and his fine cancelled. Once more he counselled war against the Macedonians. Once more Greece met the challenge. And once more, at the battle of Crannon in 322, the badly led Greeks were defeated. When the Macedonian Antipater, who now was ruling Greece, arrived in Athens he demanded Demosthenes' death. The orator had fled. They found him on the island of Poros, cowering in the temple of Poseidon. Asking for permission to write a last letter to his family, Demosthenes sucked poison from his pen. He had scarcely been carried outside before he died.

Today, as in antiquity, Demosthenes is admired for his rhetorical style and forceful arguments, while thanks to Demosthenes' attacks his adversary Aeschines remains a figure of contempt, a third-rate actor turned politician who ended his life teaching rhetoric on Rhodes. Yet Aeschines' policy of appeasement could have let Athens retain much of her prestige, whereas Demosthenes, with his quixotic nostalgia for faded glories and his inflated belief that (as a second Pericles) he could restore them, caused his city's defeat, the death of many of her sons and the complete eradication of her ally Thebes. Seduced by his own rhetoric, Demosthenes was too venal to consider its validity and too cowardly to face its consequences. However, he embodied the Athens of his age. As the philosopher Theophrastus elliptically observed, Demosthenes was an orator worthy of his city. Indeed, during the mid-fourth century philosophers often enjoyed more influence than statesmen in the courts of tyrannoi and kings – including the most famous and influential of them all: Plato and **Aristotle**.

PLATO (c. 427–348/7)
Philosopher

Cicero … said of Plato's dialogues that if Jupiter spoke it would be in language such as theirs.

Plutarch, Life of Cicero, 24

Plato was born into a proudly aristocratic Athenian family. On his father's side he traced his ancestry to the legendary King Codrus, on his mother's to the lawgiver Solon, and his childhood was spent among men who passionately believed that ruling was their birthright. In 404 the Thirty Tyrannoi boasted two of Plato's relatives among their number: his uncle Charmides and his mother's cousin, the fanatically brutal Critias. At first Plato supported them, but enduring their excesses he soon revised his views. Their attempt to implicate **Socrates** revolted him, for by now Plato had fallen under the philosopher's influence and was embarking on the cerebrations which would change not just his own life but the course of western thought.

Plato derived his nickname from his wide brows and broad shoulders (*platon* means 'broad'): as a youth he was proficient both in athletics and in the arts as a champion wrestler and an author of poetry and plays. In around 407, at the age of twenty, he was apparently intending to submit a drama for the Dionysia when he heard Socrates debating outside the theatre. The conversation so inflamed Plato's admiration that he burned his manuscript and became Socrates' most ardent

OVERLEAF Plato (third from left) converses with philosophers and orators – perhaps including Lysias (second from left) – in the Academy, in a first-century mosaic from Pompeii.

disciple. Socrates' execution in 399, so soon after the Thirty's atrocities, dismayed Plato, galvanizing his search for ultimate truths to provide a sense of justice and stability in a dangerously volatile world.

Immersed in the teachings of Socrates, **Pythagoras** and other earlier philosophers, Plato began to hone his beliefs. He attracted pupils to seminars held both at the gymnasium and in his nearby house by the Grove of Academus (the Academy), and disseminated his developing ideas in artfully written monographs. Perhaps intended as a starting point for debate, these took the form of imagined dialogues between Socrates and his contemporaries, including prominent sophists and Plato's immediate family. Although it is difficult to tell which views are Socrates' and which Plato's, the form allowed great flexibility in the exploration of topics from different viewpoints, gradually converging towards a notion of the 'truth'.

This process reflects one of Plato's most significant teachings from his *Republic*, a wide-ranging exploration of political theory. Here, Plato suggests that perceived reality is like a flickering shadow seen on a cave wall: to grasp reality we must discover both the three-dimensional object casting the shadow and the fire which causes it. Just as this fire itself is insignificant when compared to the sun, so everything possesses a pure, unchanging, ideal form, of which the imperfect physical world is just a reflection. In *Republic*, too, Plato explores his Pythagorean belief in metempsychosis, using the Myth of Er (which he invented himself, as he did the myth of Atlantis in another of his dialogues, *Critias*) to describe the soul's journey, buffeted through many physical incarnations: only through philosophy can the soul attain lasting serenity.

At *Republic*'s core was a matter of contemporary urgency: the search for an 'ideal' constitution providing political stability and security. Plato's solution is a strict hierarchy where philosopher-kings (an amalgam of his ancestors Solon and Codrus) are supported by a Guardian Council, while a distinct class of Workers generates economic activity. Slavery is absent, men and women enjoy equal rights, and frivolities such as music and drama are banned – a startlingly revolutionary vision, which Plato tried unsuccessfully to put into practice during several visits to Sicily.

In 388, aged around forty, Plato sailed to Syracuse and the court of its *tyrannos* Dionysius I. Although theirs was not a harmonious relationship (the *tyrannos* may subsequently have plotted to kill or enslave Plato) the philosopher formed a close friendship with Dionysius' brother-in-law, Dion. Twenty-one years later, with Dionysius now dead, Dion urged Plato to return to Syracuse and educate its new ruler, Dionysius II, as a true philosopher-king. Initially the young tyrannos showed promise, but when Plato tried to teach him geometry he and his courtiers lost interest. Coincidentally, Dion was suspected of treachery and exiled. Plato, disappointed, sailed home.

Still idealism outweighed experience. In 361, believing Dion had been pardoned, Plato boarded a trireme sent specifically to collect him and returned to Sicily. In a letter he described how he revealed privately to Dionysius concepts which he would never commit to writing. Although Dionysius claimed to understand them his behaviour showed that he did not. Realizing he had been summoned to Syracuse simply to lend intellectual credibility to Dionysius' regime, Plato sought permission to leave. When Dionysius refused, he found himself in effect held captive in the palace grounds. The situation within Syracuse continued to deteriorate as Dionysius became increasingly paranoid. His disgruntled mercenaries, distrusting the philosopher, plotted to kill Plato. Frantically the philosopher appealed to friends in Taras, who sent a ship to rescue him.

It was not only Dionysius who shunned Plato's teachings. In 357 Dion seized Syracuse. Instead of implementing just and equitable policies he unleashed a reign of terror. Curiously, what irked Plato most was not Dion's behaviour but Dionysius' publication of a book recording the two men's private conversations, a reminder of how words can be misinterpreted. Plato profoundly mistrusted the ambiguities of language. He had long agonized over *Republic*'s opening sentence ('Yesterday I went down to Piraeus with Glaucon, Ariston's son, to pray to the goddess and at the same time wishing to see how they would celebrate the festival which they had just inaugurated'), trying every possible word order, and he deliberately did not commit all of his beliefs to writing. Instead, he increasingly sought truth in mathematics, believing that it contained the secrets of the universe. So esoteric did his views become that a lecture he gave in old age was considered to be completely incomprehensible. It examined Plato's belief that ultimate righteousness or virtue is embodied in the concept 'One', the 'Unity', the ultimate 'Ideal', of which all other things are improperly defined divisions. Perhaps it was one of his 'unwritten doctrines' or arcane teachings, communicated verbally only to his most trusted pupils.

After Plato died in 348/7 his nephew Speusippus became head of the Academy. Plato's philosophy continued to be taught, its influence spread by his students across the Greek world. The most notable of these pupils would, like Plato, educate a king, and strive to make sense of the chaos of Greek life not only by delving deep into metaphysics but by seeking order in the physical world around him. His name was Aristotle.

ARISTOTLE (385/4–322)
Philosopher

Cicero called Aristotle 'a river of flowing gold'.

Plutarch, *Life of Cicero*, 24

From childhood Aristotle was familiar with both politics and science – realms which would soon be transformed beyond all recognition, the one by his most famous student, the other by himself. Born in Stagira in the northwest Chersonese, Aristotle probably spent his youth in the Macedonian capital of Pella, where his father Nicomachus was court physician to King Amyntas III, and the future Philip II was his slightly junior contemporary. In 369, in the wake of Amyntas' death, Philip was taken south to Thebes as hostage. Two years later, at

A marble copy of a bronze bust by the famed fourth-century artist Lysippus possibly flatters Aristotle, whom contemporaries described as small-eyed and prematurely balding.

the age of seventeen, Aristotle too left court, for Athens, the Academy and **Plato**. Physically he was the antithesis of his muscular and distinguished teacher. Small-eyed, spindle-legged and prematurely balding, he curled what hair he had, dressed foppishly and flaunted ornate jewelry.

Aristotle stayed in Athens for twenty years, first as star pupil then as lecturer. His vision of the world, however, diverged from that of his master. While Plato delved ever deeper into the theoretical, Aristotle came to believe that true understanding could be gained from the application of reason to a close observation of the material world. Comprehension, not just of nature but of man's behaviour too, could be gained through a structured classification and analysis of data. On Plato's death in 348/7 Aristotle decamped from Athens (resounding to **Demosthenes'** thundering orations against Macedon) to Assos in the Troad and the patronage of Hermias, a eunuch, ex-slave and former student of the Academy, who tried to reign as a philosopher-king. Both here and across the narrow straits on Lesbos with his friend and colleague Theophrastus, Aristotle pursued studies in marine and terrestrial biology, an idyll made complete when, in a rare love match, he married Hermias' niece Pythias. When Hermias was betrayed to the Persians and crucified a few years later, Aristotle set up a statue to his friend at

Theophrastus and the Study of Character

Born Tyrtamus, Theophrastus received his nickname ('Godlike Speaker') from Aristotle, perhaps when they studied at Plato's Academy. Later, in his native Lesbos, Theophrastus conducted ground-breaking research into botany, again with Aristotle, at whose Lyceum in Athens he subsequently taught, succeeding its founder as its head. An outstanding scientist and philosopher, Theophrastus wrote on topics ranging from botany and physics to stones and sensations, ethics and metaphysics. But it is for his *Characters* that he is best remembered.

Plato's *Republic* contains characterizations of the democratic and oligarchic types, and Aristotle's *Nicomachean Ethics* includes thoughts on a range of characters, but Theophrastus' *Characters* develops the idea further. Perhaps the notes for a lost work on ethics, it presents thirty thumbnail sketches of general personality types. Most are unpleasant – such as the boor, the superstitious man, the gossip and the flatterer – but all are described with flair and humour and shed valuable light on contemporary life. Theophrastus' studies reflect a growing fascination in personality, exemplified in the comedies of his pupil **Menander**.

Delphi and composed a poem in his honour, which compared his undying fame to that of Achilles.

In the winter of 343/2 Aristotle was summoned to Pella to assume the coveted post of tutor to Philip II's thirteen-year-old son, **Alexander III**, a chance to succeed where Plato had failed and shape the ideal ruler. Away from the court, in tranquil Mieza, he fired the prince and his companions with a passion for discovery and scientific knowledge and a hatred of Hermias' killers, the Persians. Barbarians, he taught, were by nature slaves (mere 'animate gadgets'), no better than dumb beasts – a dubious proposition at a time when Demosthenes was describing the Macedonians themselves as barbarians. Then in 336, with mainland Greece conquered and Philip dead, Alexander assumed the throne. The time for tutorials was over. As Alexander marched on Persia, Aristotle packed his bags and sailed with wife and infant daughter for Athens.

East of the city near a gymnasium by the grove of Apollo Lycaeus (the Wolf God) he founded a new seat of learning, the Lyceum. At its heart was a garden, a haven for contemplation and a source of plants for study, whose covered walkway (*peripatos*), paced during lectures, gave its name to Aristotle's students: the Peripatetics. Unlike Plato's Academy the Lyceum, with its distinct curriculum, attracted experts like Theophrastus to teach and research. Part-funded by Macedon and with new scientific specimens for study arriving regularly from Alexander's campaigns, it became arguably the western world's first university.

Politics, however, still intruded. In 327 Aristotle's nephew Callisthenes, accompanying Alexander on campaign as his official historian, was implicated in a plot and executed. Alexander, paranoid and petulant because Aristotle would not recognize his divinity, accused him of complicity. In 323 rumour even suggested that Aristotle helped engineer Alexander's death. Aristotle's enemies quickly moved against him. Claiming that in his poem to Hermias Aristotle had praised that king as more than human, they accused him of impiety, a dangerous charge closely mirroring the accusations levelled against **Socrates**. Proclaiming his desire to prevent Athens sinning a second time against philosophy, Aristotle fled to his mother's native island of Euboea, where he died the next year.

Aristotle's will reveals much about his character. The remains of his beloved wife Pythias (who had died young) were to be buried with him 'as she herself requested'. The mother of his son Nicomachus, a slave woman called Herpyllis with whom he had lived once he was a widower, should be freed and given the choice of either his garden guest-house on Euboea or his father's home in Stagira. And Theophrastus, his successor at the Lyceum, should become his daughter's kyrios. As befitted a polymath, Aristotle had thought of everything.

In Raphael's *The School of Athens* (1509–10), Plato points heavenwards, while his pupil Aristotle presses his palm towards the ground, gestures which reflect their respective interests in metaphysics and the natural world.

Aristotle's Written Legacy

After Aristotle's death his writings passed first to his successor Theophrastus, then to the family of Theophrastus' nephew, who stored them in a damp cellar in the Troad, where they mouldered, inaccessible and forgotten. Eventually they were rediscovered and bought by a wealthy Athenian. After the sack of Athens in 86 by the Roman general Sulla, they were shipped to Rome, where they provoked immense excitement. Cicero, himself a philosopher and famed for his literary style, described them as 'rivers of gold'. All were early treatises, written before Aristotle's return to Athens in 336, and intended for a general readership including, perhaps, Alexander. As their content was not thought as significant as his later works, they were not widely copied so have not survived in their original form. Instead, all we possess are notes (either his own or his students') of Aristotle's later lectures at the Lyceum, scholarly and dry, possessing little of his famous stylistic charm. Nonetheless, these proved highly influential both to medieval Christian scholars and (translated into Arabic) in Islamic madrasas, while his methodology imbues scientific research to this day.

Aristotle's genius defies hyperbole. He has been called the greatest teacher who ever lived and the last man to encompass all contemporary knowledge. Even incomplete, his written legacy is unsurpassed. Entire, it included works on politics and ethics, mathematics and astronomy, theology and metaphysics, meteorology, biology, zoology and botany, all subjected to intense analytical scrutiny. He even tried (with less success) to apply his techniques to literature. The heir to philosophers such as **Empedocles** (to whose four elements he added a fifth, *aether* or heavenly fire) and Plato (like whom he strove to identify the ideal political constitution – assembling 158 examples in the process), Aristotle surpassed all who had gone before.

In teachings ranging from the size and distance of heavenly bodies to mankind's status as an animal (the only one which lives in poleis and is therefore 'political'), Aristotle revealed a world view which transcended anything previously imagined. Although he was still wedded to Classical notions such as the geocentric universe, the cultural superiority of Greeks and the acceptance of slavery, his contribution to subsequent philosophical and scientific understanding was unprecedented. So too was the climate of state-sponsored intellectual enquiry, which ensured that his ideas could be developed and which was supported avidly by many of his pupils, not least his most famous: Alexander.

Chapter 7

The Age
of the Dynasts

ALEXANDER III (356–323)
King and Conqueror

Where is Great Alexander? Great Alexander lives and reigns!

Modern Greek folk saying

During most of the first half of the fourth century Macedon was in crisis. The death of King Archelaus I in 399 was followed by decades of internecine struggles. Eventually in 359 a brilliant twenty-three-year-old strategist became first regent and then king. As Philip II he reorganized the army, reconciled Macedon's warring tribes, cemented foreign alliances and annexed widespread territories by force. In 356, while campaigning against Potidea, he learned of two splendid victories – his horse's at Olympia; his general Parmenio's in battle in Illyria – and of the birth of his son, Alexander.

Alexander traced his lineage to gods and heroes – to Heracles and Zeus through Philip, and through his mother, the Epirote princess Olympias, to Achilles. In Macedon (which still resembled the societies of Homeric epic) such kinships were taken seriously. Adopting Achilles' motto 'always to be best', Alexander sought to rival the legendary hero.

When Alexander was eight a horse-trader came to court touting a spirited black stallion. No one could master it, until Alexander begged to try, promising to pay the price of the horse as forfeit if he failed. Recognizing that the stallion was frightened of its own shadow, Alexander turned its head towards the sun and coaxed it into letting him mount. As the boy galloped across the plain, Philip's courtier, Demaratus of Corinth, bought the horse as a gift for Alexander. Delighted, he named it Bucephalus (Ox Head), after the distinctive shape of its white blaze.

Alexander's early education was shaped by his mother Olympias, who inculcated in him mystical Dionysiac beliefs, while her kinsman Leonidas supervised tough lessons in physical endurance. As an accomplished composer and singer to the lyre Alexander had already studied Homer (as well, perhaps, as **Euripides**, **Herodotus** and **Xenophon**) by the time, aged thirteen, he came under the tutelage of **Aristotle**, the greatest intellectual of his age. In the 'Precinct of the Nymphs' at Mieza, Alexander studied (sometimes reluctantly) with a tight-knit circle of close friends, many of whom later became his generals and rivals for his empire on his death.

At the age of sixteen Alexander – small, unusually clean shaven and restless, his head tilted up and to the left, his mane of golden hair cascading to his shoulders, his eyes, one blue, one brown, suggesting a sensitivity belied by his ruthlessness – exploded onto the Greek stage. Appointed regent while Philip campaigned against Byzantium, he crushed a rebellion among their northern tribes, renaming their city Alexandropolis. Two years later, in 338, he led the

Olympias

The daughter of the Epirote king Neoptolemus, Olympias was eighteen when she married Philip II of Macedon in 357, having perhaps met him at the Mysteries of Samothrace. The next year she gave birth to Alexander. She was a devotee of the orgiastic cult of Dionysus, and reputedly furthered Alexander's interests by damaging with drugs the brain of Arrhidaeus, the polygamous Philip's eldest son by another wife. In 336, having been briefly exiled when Philip married once again, she was probably complicit in his assassination, killing Philip's widow and her son days later by roasting them alive.

During Alexander's campaigns Olympias' relationship with Antipater, his lieutenant in Greece, was stormy. After both men died she allied herself to Antipater's successor Polyperchon. She was desperate to ensure the succession of Alexander's infant son and in 317, after bitter fighting in which she accompanied the army into battle, Olympias had Arrhidaeus and his wife murdered, and unleashed savage reprisals against many Macedonian nobles, including Antipater's family. Besieged by Antipater's son Cassander in Pydna in 316, she surrendered on condition that she be spared. But Cassander reneged on the agreement and had her condemned in a show trial. She was stoned to death by her victims' relatives.

cavalry charge against the Theban Sacred Band at the battle of Chaeronea, splintering resistance and heralding the new dawn of Macedonian supremacy over Greece. The victory was commemorated at Olympia in a shrine containing gold and ivory statues of Philip, Olympias and Alexander, which suggested their divinity. Within months, however, Philip divorced Olympias and took a new bride, Cleopatra. When her uncle drunkenly predicted the birth of a 'legitimate' heir, Alexander stormed out in fury.

Tensions exploded in June 336. In the theatre at Aegae crowds gathered to celebrate the marriage of Philip's daughter to Olympias' brother, the king of Epirus. As Philip arrived, followed by the bridegroom and a still seething Alexander, one of his bodyguards suddenly stabbed him. In the confusion the assassin was killed. The truth died with him. While official explanation was personal revenge for the bodyguard's gang-rape by Philip's entourage, Olympias crowned the dead assassin's head and offered annual libations in his memory.

Alexander rapidly asserted his authority. Backed by his father's general Parmenio, he was undisputed king of Macedon within three months; within a year he had crushed insurrections in Thrace, Illyria and Greece, and razed to the ground the ancient city of Thebes, whose alliance with Persia against his Macedonian 'tyranny' had provoked his fury; and by spring 334 he was poised to embark on what he considered to be his destined mission: the invasion of Persia. In 337 at Corinth, Philip and his subject Greek League had already declared war on Persia, vowing to liberate Ionia and exact vengeance for Xerxes' burning of Greek temples in the Persian Wars. For Alexander there was another appealing dimension: Persia was heir to Troy, and Alexander's ancestors Heracles and Achilles had similarly punished Troy's wrongdoing. Symbolically, it was at Troy that Alexander first set foot in Asia. Where Xerxes had slaughtered a hundred oxen before he marched on Greece in 480, Alexander now sacrificed for victory at Athene's altar, in return receiving from the priests a shield believed to date back to the Trojan War, a talisman for his campaign of retribution.

Within days, some 60 miles (100 km) east of Troy on the banks of the River Granicus, the Macedonians routed a Persian army, its numbers swollen by Greek mercenaries led by their brilliant commander Memnon of Rhodes. His name was resonant. At Troy, Achilles had killed another Memnon, and Granicus, Alexander's creative antiquarians obsequiously assured him, was fought a millennium to the month after Troy's sack. The conqueror swung south. At Sardis and Ephesus he was welcomed; in Caria Queen Ada, desirous of his patronage, adopted him as her son; but Miletus vacillated. As Persian ships patrolled the coast its governor barred the gates. Not trusting his outnumbered fleet, Alexander conducted his siege operations exclusively by land, and soon he was victorious. It was a turning point. Alexander disbanded his fleet, resolving not to meet the Persians at sea but to destroy their harbours until, without safe haven, their ships capitulated. At Halicarnassus, as autumn drew in, Memnon held out for two months before Alexander's siege engines forced him to flee the burning city. Winter saw no let-up as Alexander pressed on south until all the coast as far as Side was his. Then inland at Gordium he mustered his army.

Here Alexander was shown a wagon, its yoke secured by an elaborate knot of cornel bark. Whoever could undo it, legend told, would rule all Asia. Unable to untie it, yet desperate to succeed, Alexander drew his sword and sliced through the knot. A thunderstorm that night showed Zeus' approval, soon confirmed by news of Memnon's death and Persia's consequent confusion. But, marching south in the autumn of 333, Alexander was dangerously outmanoeuvred when a vast Persian army under the Great King, Darius III, unexpectedly appeared behind his lines by the banks of the River Issus. Rapidly Alexander wheeled and, rallying his men with a rousing speech reminding them of the heroic battles of Xenophon's *Anabasis*, he led a terrifying cavalry charge across the river against the Great King himself. For a moment the two were within striking distance, but then Darius turned and fled. He left 100,000 soldiers, the vast bulk of his army, dead, while in his tent his wife and womenfolk, abandoned, trembled at their fate. They need not have worried. Thanks to Olympias' influence, Alexander treated women with respect. Queen Stateira and her daughters were no exception.

As more cities opened their gates and treasuries, Alexander took from Damascus a jewelled casket for his treasured copy of the *Iliad* (containing notes by Aristotle). But Persia's western cities, Phoenician Tyre and Gaza, still held out. Siegecraft proved Alexander's tenacity and brutality – a causeway thrown half a mile (800 m) into the sea at Tyre, and the crucifixion of its captured soldiers; a huge mound piled against the walls of Gaza, whose governor Alexander dragged dead behind his chariot as Achilles had dragged Hector. With Persia's last Asiatic ports taken, the road to Egypt lay open. At Memphis in a winter ceremony in 332/1 Alexander was crowned pharaoh and worshipped as a god, the son of Amun-Ra (known to the Greeks as Ammon). For unlike Egypt's Persian rulers, insensitive to its customs and religion, Alexander flamboyantly embraced the country's ways and earned its loyal respect.

OVERLEAF: On a Pompeian mosaic, probably inspired by a late fourth-century Greek painting, Alexander and Bucephalus plunge into the thick of the fighting at Issus in search of the terrified Great King Darius III.

Early in 331, near the Nile's western mouth, at the only deep-water harbour on the northeast coast of Africa, Alexander founded a new city, Alexandria-by-Egypt, where Greek and Egyptian temples stood side by side. Then, diverting south from a journey to Cyrene, he trekked 300 miles (480 km) across the desert to Siwah and the shrine of Zeus Ammon, where he apparently experienced a mystical epiphany. Thereafter he openly proclaimed himself the son of Zeus, wearing the symbolic ram's horns of Zeus Ammon and fixing others cast in gold onto Bucephalus' headpiece

But Alexander still required one final victory over Persia. Hearing that Darius had marshalled a new army, he marched east to the Euphrates to do battle that October on the plain at Gaugamela. The vastness of Darius' force – said to number up to 250,000 infantry and more than 30,000 cavalry, though some in antiquity claimed it totalled a million – supported as it was by scythed chariots and elephants gave even Alexander pause. But with careful tactics and reckless bravery, and the air so thick with dust that troops fought almost blind, the Macedonians again broke the Persian lines and Darius fled. Triumphant, Alexander led his men to Babylon, which surrendered with lavish theatricality. By December he was ensconced on the Great King's golden throne in Susa (though his feet did not reach the footstool, and a table had to be substituted). The sight of Alexander enthroned in glorious splendour caused Demaratus of Corinth to burst into tears of joy.

In January 330, with the statues of the tyrannicides Harmodius and Aristogeiton, stolen by Xerxes 150 years before, already on their way from Susa back to Athens, Alexander rode in triumph through Persepolis, Persia's ceremonial capital. It was the goal which his men had marched for and now he gave them their heads. An orgy of looting culminated in the wanton torching of Persepolis' ornate palace. With tall columns and glazed walls, broad staircases flanked by carved reliefs of guards and subject emissaries, and a hundred-pillared audience room capped with an exquisitely worked cedar ceiling, the complex had been breath-taking. Now it lay deep in ash, destroyed, some said, in calculated vengeance for Xerxes' burning of Greek temples, or perhaps in an act of drunken vandalism.

The campaign continued: with Darius alive, Alexander could not claim to have defeated him. So the Macedonian pursued his fleeing rival east until, after a frenzied dash through the desert near Damghan (in modern Iran), he found the still-warm corpse of Darius sprawled in the back of an ox-cart, murdered by treacherous satraps. In that instant, with the Persian empire in effect dead too, Alexander's intentions changed. No longer merely a conqueror, he proclaimed himself Darius' successor and avenger, and during a welcome rest by the southern shores of the Caspian Sea he revealed what his new role would entail.

Throughout his long campaign Alexander had demonstrated his intention not only to defeat but to govern. Wherever he went he appointed Persian satraps (reinstating many who had served Darius) to rule alongside Macedonian military governors. But to earn the Persians' respect he must adopt their traditional trappings of power. So he began to dress partially in Persian attire and wear the cloth diadem reserved for kings, to keep aloof from his courtiers and to refer to himself in letters as 'we'. Even more controversially, he tried to introduce the practice of *proskynesis*, a ritual gesture of obeisance which the Persians traditionally made before their king but which the Greeks reserved for gods. Pleasing the Persians, it infuriated many Macedonians. An assassination plot was soon uncovered. Its alleged instigator, Philotas, was one of Alexander's closest officers and the son of his general Parmenio. All implicated were summarily executed, including Parmenio himself, whom Philip had once praised saying, 'In Athens they elect ten generals a year; I have found only one.'

Now pursuing Darius' assassins, Alexander continued to press east. From Kandahar he descended into Bactria through the hostile Hindu Kush, its gruelling winter crossing cheered only by the sight of a grim mountain on whose peak, they said, Prometheus was chained to suffer his eviscerating punishment for giving fire to mankind. Across the River Oxus, Alexander learned that Bessus, the last assassin and the self-proclaimed heir to Darius' empire, had been captured. Still he pressed on, until, beyond the River Jaxartes and victorious over the Scythians, he was told the momentous news: even Dionysus in his Asian wanderings had not come as far as this!

As fighting continued unabated, Alexander became increasingly unpredictable. After his garrison was massacred in Samarkand in 328 he murdered in a drunken brawl his general Cleitus, who had made his opposition to Alexander's adoption of eastern ways all too clear. But Alexander's genius had not deserted him. The more inaccessible a fortress, the more he yearned to take it. By 327 all Soghdiana, one of Persia's most easternmost provinces, was his, a conquest celebrated by Alexander's marriage to the beautiful Roxane, daughter of a tribal chief. The first of Alexander's wives, she alone bore him a child, the ill-fated Alexander IV.

Yet still Alexander would not turn back, driven by a desire to reach the furthest Ocean – for the Greeks the limit of the earth. For two years Alexander rode on with his increasingly disgruntled army. From the Punjab east through the

Swat Valley he devastated any city which would not embrace him – like Aornos (Pir Sar), perched on a seemingly impregnable rock, which it was said not even Heracles had captured, but which Alexander did, thanks to the brilliance of his engineers. Having outdone his divine ancestor, Alexander took to wearing Heracles' lion-head helmet. Further plots against him were unmasked: the royal pages were accused and executed, and Aristotle's nephew Callisthenes, the campaign's official historian, was charged with complicity and killed. But until 326, when he came to the River Hydaspes, Alexander lost none of those he loved. Here, though, after a night of pouring rain and deafening electric thunderstorms, his old horse Bucephalus died from wounds sustained in victory against the Indian king Porus. Mourning, Alexander founded a city, Bucephala, in his honour. Within months it was washed away in floods.

When Porus surrendered he had appealed to Alexander to treat him 'like a king'. Although Alexander responded by making Porus his ally, his notion of kingly behaviour was increasingly eccentric. In monsoon rains he marched to the Hyphasis, the ancient river border of Persia's empire. Worn down by the weather, a march of more than 11,000 miles (17,500 km) and eight years of fighting, his men refused to continue. Sulking in his tent like a recalcitrant Achilles, Alexander learned the omens were unfavourable. Submitting to both army and gods he erected twelve tall altars by the swollen river's bank and gave the order to turn back. At the Hydaspes he ordered the construction of 1,800 ships. With his baggage train shadowing him on the shore, he sailed south towards the Indus and the sea. The boredom of the eight-month voyage was alleviated only by the occasional massacre of Brahmin insurgents along the way. At Multan, Alexander leapt alone from the ramparts into the fighting and was wounded in the chest. For a week his life hung in the balance. Although he survived, his mobility was restricted. At last, at the Indus' mouth, he saw a miracle. The distance between dry land and sea's edge changed throughout the day. Nothing like this ever happened in the Mediterranean or Caspian. For the first time the Macedonian had observed a tide. Surely this was the Ocean!

Alexander's troops, though, had little reason to rejoice. Partly in revenge for their mutiny at the Hyphasis, Alexander chose as his homeward route some of the most inhospitable terrain in Asia: the Gedrosian desert, a place of blistering, shifting sands, where flash floods raced from distant mountains and swept baggage trains and followers to their destruction. For eight weeks in 325 they laboured on this infernal march, until they were reunited with their fleet. They celebrated in traditional Macedonian style (with drink), and in a wild Dionysiac procession wound their way back to the luxuries of Peria.

Alexander thrusts his spear at a falling Persian on the so-called Alexander Sarcophagus. The battle of Issus was fought near Sidon, where this late fourth-century carving was discovered.

But Alexander found Persia in poor shape: the rule of law had fractured; Macedonian governors had behaved high-handedly; Persian satraps had been feathering their nests. Alexander rapidly purged the disgraced officials, both Persian and Macedonian. Then in 324 at Susa, in an unprecedented sacrament designed to cement relations between east and west, almost a hundred of Alexander's closest officers married Persian brides. Alexander himself married two, including one of Darius' daughters. He gave another to Hephaestion, his life-long friend and lover, who had accompanied him on campaign and whom he had recently appointed as his second-in-command. The honeymoon was short-lived. That autumn, Hephaestion fell ill and died at Ecbatana. Hysterical with grief Alexander cut his own and his horses' hair and rode beside the catafalque to Babylon where he sacrificed 10,000 animals and celebrated funeral games, successors to Achilles' rites for dead Patroclus.

Meanwhile, as Alexander's generals were summoned to a conference at Babylon, rumours abounded of new ambitious plans: a voyage around Africa, a campaign to conquer Carthage, an expedition to the Caspian Sea. Building works were mentioned too: a pyramid for Philip in Macedon, a new temple to Athene at Troy, further temples at Delos and Delphi, the sculpting of Mount Athos to show a seated Alexander holding a whole, inhabitable city in his outstretched hand. Then, after a voyage on the Tigris, Alexander announced the real plan: an invasion of Arabia. Preparations were almost complete when Alexander fell ill – a sudden pain at a drinking party, then a slow decline. Already there had been omens of his death: a soldier inadvertently placing the diadem on his head as he rescued it from the Tigris, and a prisoner found seated inexplicably on the throne were both thought to presage the transference of royal power, while earlier that year as the Indian *gymnosophist* ('naked philosopher', or *sadhu*) Calanus committed suicide by self-immolation rather than grow old in ill health, he announced that he would meet Alexander again in Babylon. Now, with his officers demanding to see him, a sad procession passed by the weakening king's bed. At last on 10 June 323, in Babylon, Alexander died.

Perhaps, already weakened not only by the wound at Multan three years earlier but by his heavy drinking, he had succumbed to malaria caught on a recent voyage on the Euphrates. Perhaps, some whispered, his death was Dionysus' punishment for Alexander's destruction of the god's beloved Thebes. Or perhaps (like Hephaestion, so it was rumoured) he was poisoned. Suspects included Alexander's generals, summoned to Babylon for a conference where they feared they might be deposed or killed, among them Antipater (who did not obey the summons) and his son Cassander (who did). Some even said that Aristotle provided the poison in revenge for the killing of his nephew Callisthenes.

In death as in life Alexander was worshipped as a god, an honour previously enjoyed by the Spartan general **Lysander**, while both Dionysius I and II of Syracuse and Alexander's father Philip II had paraded their divinity in works of art. Already in 334 at Ephesus Alexander's offer to rebuild the temple of Artemis had been rejected because it was not right for one god so to honour another. After the oracle at Siwah, when city after city declared he was a god, he seems increasingly to have believed in his own divinity. In 324 he had it proclaimed at the Olympic Games that all Greek poleis were to worship him. Even Sparta obeyed, observing, 'If Alexander wants to be a god, let him be a god.'

The arsonist Herostratus, who set fire to Artemis' great temple at Ephesus in 356 – traditionally on the day of Alexander's birth – claimed he did it so that his name would live forever. Alexander shared his ambition. Except at Siwah, his court historians were constantly present, tailoring their accounts to suit his desires, emphasizing his brilliance while disparaging officers like Parmenio who fell from favour. When Callisthenes was killed, Alexander's private secretary and cavalry commander Eumenes inherited his position. But Eumenes' record of events was suspect. He detested Hephaestion, and was implicated in Alexander's death. There never was a true, objective, contemporary history, and subsequent accounts by Alexander's generals only muddied the waters further.

Nothing, however, can diminish Alexander's brilliance. As a general and tactician he has had few equals. As a propagandist he was supreme. Even as an administrator he showed talent, inventing systems which should, if followed sympathetically, have worked. Shrewdly, he adapted existing structures, careful never to offend unless offence would bring results. Pragmatically, he founded cities at key locations throughout his empire. Although seldom on new sites, they bore his name in order to reinforce his kudos. Far-sightedly, he attempted to unite conquerors and conquered through marriages and by melding old traditions into new ones. For many this was a step too far. Proud of their history and long used to independence, Greeks and Macedonians alike found Persian practices such as proskynesis hateful. Whether the prospect of their universal adoption led to Alexander's poisoning cannot be known, but no matter how men viewed him when alive, his legacy was profound. Not only had he brought Greek culture into lands which until now few Greeks had heard of, but within a few short years he had broadened Greek horizons and set a new benchmark against which every ambitious conqueror to come would measure his success. Within months of his death his memory took on almost magical powers. As the empire fractured into bitter fighting one general, Ptolemy, even tried to bolster his legitimacy by stealing Alexander's corpse.

PTOLEMY I (367–283)
General and Dynast

For Ptolemy to have lied would have been shameful, since like Alexander he was a king.

Arrian, Campaigns of Alexander, 1.1

On his deathbed in 323 **Alexander** gave his signet ring to Perdiccas, his second-in-command, but bequeathed his empire 'to the strongest'. Within days, as he had predicted, the 'great funeral games' began. Heralding the Hellenistic Age, these wars of his successor generals were long and bloody. When they were over, the Greek world was reshaped beyond all recognition, its culture flourishing in lands which a century before no Greek had even visited, its cultural heart transferred

Ptolemy I's coinage shows him as a Hellenistic monarch, his elephant headdress an allusion to Alexander's Indian campaign in which he had served.

from mainland Athens to Egyptian Alexandria. This relocation was in part the work of Ptolemy I.

Ptolemy was probably related through his father Lagus to Alexander. Although older than him by eleven years he was part of the young prince's retinue. When Alexander became king, Ptolemy rose with him. Later, he wrote of how, riding with Alexander to the oracle of Zeus Ammon at Siwah, two talking serpents showed them the way; but it was only after Philotas' plot against Alexander's life in 330 that Ptolemy achieved a top command. He was entrusted with arresting Bessus, one of the assassins of Darius; led an advance guard to occupy strategic heights at Aornos, the mountain citadel in Swat; fought beside Alexander at the battle of the Hydaspes; and bravely led his troops against the stronghold of Sangala shortly before the mutiny at the River Hyphasis.

In a conference at Babylon immediately after Alexander's death Ptolemy, who was ill-disposed to Perdiccas, proposed that power be shared by a military junta. Given the egocentric volatility of most of those involved such a solution was unworkable. Instead, Perdiccas was appointed regent for both Alexander's unborn child and his brain-damaged brother Arrhidaeus, while other generals were chosen to govern the empire's sprawling territories. To Ptolemy went Egypt, where Cleomenes, whose greed was as legendary as his loyalty to Perdiccas, was lording it as governor. He made an unreliable lieutenant. Within a year Ptolemy had executed him.

As fault lines widened and the successors sought to strengthen their claims, Ptolemy encouraged rumours that he was Philip II's illegitimate son, Alexander's half-brother. But he was determined to enhance his status even further. In 321 he learned of Perdiccas' intention to repatriate Alexander's embalmed remains to Macedon. Claiming that Alexander had wished to be buried at the oracle of Zeus Ammon, he dispatched a crack cavalry division to intercept the royal catafalque in Syria. They found the body lying on a bed of spices, the golden coffin draped in purple, laid in a golden shrine with ornate columns and adorned with winged Victories and sculptures showing Alexander's triumphs, the glittering bier pulled by sixty-four mules, each with a golden bell around its neck. Before Perdiccas could stop them Ptolemy's men had seized the body and were galloping back to Egypt and to Memphis. The next year Perdiccas, still seething, ordered his troops across the Nile, but the crossing was disastrous and in the ensuing chaos he was assassinated. Offered the role of regent in his stead, Ptolemy refused. It was a wise decision.

In the brutal years which followed, Alexander's erstwhile empire boiled. As giant bubbles of conflict seethed and burst throughout all Asia and Greece, first one pretender then another, driven by power-hungry paranoia, led his troops to battle. From Megalopolis to Babylon and beyond, phalanxes clashed, cavalry charged and elephants lumbered through the carnage, increasingly sophisticated siege engines battered city walls, and in ruling families children, siblings, partners and parents found ever more exquisite ways to kill each other. The prize which most of the successors sought was total power. Ptolemy, however, though not averse to foreign intervention, was for the most part content with ruling Egypt and the wealthy buffer zones around it. Generally he remained aloof, watching for weaknesses and judiciously exploiting opportunities to consolidate his position and annex new lands, until Cyrene and Cyprus, Phoenicia and Palestine, all rich in resources, were under his rule.

In 306, however, he was defeated in the waters off Cyprus by Demetrius the Besieger, the flamboyant son of Alexander's general Antigonus the One-Eyed. But when Demetrius went on to lay siege to Rhodes, Ptolemy was able to win through and liberate the islanders. In gratitude they named him 'Saviour' (*Soter*) and worshipped him, erecting at their harbour mouth a colossal bronze statue of the sun god Helios, 105 feet (32 m) tall, which would become one of the wonders of the ancient world. In 301 Antigonus, by now the most powerful of the successor kings, was killed when his rivals united against him at the battle of Ipsus. The east was again carved up, and for sixteen years Ptolemy renewed and strengthened his authority, carefully choosing allies and causes to support. Such were the twists of politics that in 298 he formed an alliance with Demetrius (whose brother-in-law **Pyrrhus** he entertained as hostage); but by 288 he was attacking him again, sending his fleet north against the Peloponnese to dissuade Demetrius from invading Asia. Then, in 285, two years before his death, Ptolemy made a surprising move. He abdicated, passing power to his younger son, whose name, Ptolemy II Philadelphus (Brother-Loving), belied his hatred for his elder and less stable sibling, Ptolemy the Thunderbolt.

Ptolemy I was not just a fighter. Ruling 4 million subjects, he needed to govern well. Mostly he retained the systems which he inherited, adding a top layer of Greek and Macedonian bureaucrats, but interfering little with traditional ways of life. Thus in Egypt there were two official languages, Egyptian and the *Koine* ('common [language]'), a form of Greek first used in Philip II's court but now increasingly adopted throughout the east Greek world; two calendars; two legal codes; and two religions. Yet there was some integration. To help unite his peoples Ptolemy promoted worship of the god Serapis, whose iconography fused elements from Greece and Egypt, establishing a vast temple complex in his honour at Alexandria, the city which since 313 had been his capital.

In lands made fertile by draining and irrigation, between the teeming Lake Mareotis and the Mediterranean Sea, Alexandria now boasted two great harbours, wide boulevards and elegant buildings. Two hundred thousand Egyptians, Greeks and Jews – each living in segregated areas – were turning it into the most prosperous city in the Greek world. Soon a towering lighthouse, nearly 400 feet (120 m) tall, would beckon sailors from across the Mediterranean, but already in the palace quarter there were wonders enough. At its heart was the *Soma*, where the remains of Alexander lay in a golden casket, having been conveyed in great solemnity from Memphis. Nearby was Ptolemy's greatest and most visionary foundation, the most pre-eminent seat of learning in the ancient world. Ptolemy had known **Aristotle** in Macedon. In Alexandria he employed Aristotle's student Strato (who would succeed Theophrastus as the Lyceum's head) as his sons' tutor. Now he invited another Aristotelian to supervise the institution of a Temple of the Muses (*Museum*), a state-funded research centre which would attract the finest practitioners and scholars in the fields of literature and science and so make Alexandria the intellectual capital of the world. The man he appointed was Demetrius of Phalerum.

Worship of the god Serapis – burgeoning with the promise of fecundity and harmony between Greeks and Egyptians on this wax-painted Egyptian panel from *c.* AD 100 – was promoted in Ptolemy's Alexandria.

DEMETRIUS OF PHALERUM (*c. 347–c. 283*)
Governor of Athens and Scholar

The celebrated Demetrius of Phalerum, accused of being the first to set rhetoric on a downward path, was in fact highly talented and eloquent and should be remembered.

Quintilian, *Institutes of Oratory*, 10.1

Demetrius was born in the Athenian seaside suburb of Phalerum to Phanostratus, a man of modest means, and studied under Theophrastus. At the Lyceum he may have known Cassander, a pupil of **Aristotle** and son of **Alexander III's** 'General in Charge of Europe', Antipater. Then, in the last days of Alexander, Demetrius left the cloistered Lyceum and entered politics. By 324 he was already a fine orator when he addressed the Assembly as it debated its response to the arrival in Athens of Alexander's fugitive treasurer, the corrupt Harpalus. His advice is not recorded, but given the Lyceum's pro-Macedonian bias it is likely that he argued against harbouring the renegade. It mattered little. Athens was soon at war.

Alexander's death in 323 inspired the diehards. Hoping that they could shake off the yoke of Macedon, 10,000 Athenians marched with their allies north to Lamia and besieged Antipater; but the next year the Macedonians regrouped and at Crannon they dealt the allied Greeks a crushing blow. The flame of Athenian freedom, once a beacon to all Greece, was extinguished. Henceforth the city would be known less for its politics than for past glories, winning a growing reputation as a seat of learning. In 319 Antipater died, designating as his heir not his son Cassander but his general Polyperchon, thus inevitably sparking further conflict. By the end of 318, aided by the powerful Antigonus the One-Eyed, who ruled much of western Asia, Cassander had seized control of Greece. He immediately propelled Demetrius centre stage.

Demetrius' career had been chequered. One of Athens' negotiators after Crannon, he had narrowly survived a death sentence passed by Polyperchon. Now in 317 Cassander appointed him governor of Athens. For ten years he ruled as a 'philosopher-king', labouring to re-establish Athens' prosperity and political pride. The presence of a Macedonian garrison lent stability to Athens and allowed the city to boom. Yet **Demosthenes'** nephew Demochares, demonstrating his fellow intellectuals' scorn for economics, sneered at Demetrius' 'boast that the Agora was plentifully supplied with cheap goods and a profusion of all of life's necessities'. Others (though perhaps confusing him with his namesake, the Besieger) reproved the profligacy of Demetrius' private life, its sumptuous banquets and numerous affairs both with boys and with women who swooned over his eyes and eyelids. They accused him of vanity, of dying his hair blond, of using rouge and of erecting 360 statues of himself throughout the city. Publically, however, Demetrius both curbed and pandered to Athens' love of the extravagant. On the one hand he introduced laws regulating not only the cost of funerals and memorials but also the magnificence of women's clothing. On the other he presided over lavish civic processions – one was even preceded by a giant mechanical snail secreting slime.

While Demetrius governed Athens, Cassander consolidated his position in wider Greece, killing not only Olympias, Alexander III's mother, but Roxane, his wife, and their son, his heir and namesake. But Cassander's power soon waned. In 307 Demetrius the Besieger (perhaps wearing his trademark cloak showing the solar system embroidered in gold thread) took Athens, erected a statue of himself beside those of the tyrannicides, and set up home with his mistress in the Parthenon. Ousted, Demetrius of Phalerum was allowed safe passage to Cassander's recently rebuilt Thebes, where he stoically learned of his own statues' toppling.

In 297 he received a summons from **Ptolemy I** to compose new forms of worship for the god Serapis, and perhaps draw up new laws for Alexandria. It is likely that he was also asked to help found Alexandria's pioneering Museum. Half research centre, half universal library, the Museum (including its covered walkway) was partly inspired by Aristotle's Lyceum. Funded by Ptolemaic gold it became the Hellenistic world's leading centre of learning. Close to the royal palace, the

Not every statue of Demetrius was toppled. A Roman copy of a Hellenistic bust shows him in the guise of earnest philosopher.

The Great Library of Alexandria, showing scholars reading while staff access manuscript scrolls from shelves, was published in a nineteenth-century illustrated history by Otto von Corvin.

Museum contained a botanic garden, a zoo, a lecture theatre, a dissection room, an astronomical observatory and accommodation for the thousand scholars and staff who worked there. At its heart was the famous Library, which later claimed to hold a copy of every book ever written, 500,000 papyrus rolls, a unique repository of learning and cultural achievement. In fact, avaricious for the best possible editions, Ptolemy III later 'borrowed' definitive manuscripts of Athens' fifth-century tragedians for copying, then preferred to pay a 15 talent indemnity rather than return them. Besides Greek literature the Library contained works from other cultures. Demetrius may have supervised the

Agathe Tyche

The wars of Alexander and his successors caused many to question old certainties. Suddenly Good Fortune (*Agathe Tyche*) or Lady Luck, an irrational feminine force, seemed to underpin the universe. Demetrius of Phalerum cited recent history as evidence of how Fortune demonstrated her power through the unexpected:

> *If fifty years ago a god had revealed the future to the Great King or the king of Macedon do you think they would have believed that now Persia's very name would be no more, when once it ruled the world, while the Macedonians, whom nobody had heard of, would now rule everything?*

As Tyche's cult spread, her statues appeared in temples, and soon each polis had its own protecting Fortune whose iconography showed her often crowned with city walls and bearing attributes associated with the region. In colonnades, gymnasia and private houses mosaics and inscriptions bore the talismanic words: 'Agathe Tyche'.

Jewish Old Testament's translation into Greek, named the 'Septuagint' from the seventy scholars who worked on it.

Demetrius found time for his own scholarship too. Inspired by Aristotle he collected and classified works by other authors, producing the first 'edition' of Aesop's fables. He wrote widely, covering topics from love and old age to rhetoric, his governorship of Athens and the *Iliad* and *Odyssey*. Discussing Fortune (*Tyche*), whom he described as 'blind', he encapsulated the sometimes nihilistic views of his age: 'We can reach no covenant with Fortune; she accomplishes the opposite of our expectations.'

In the end Demetrius' own good fortune changed. He outspokenly urged Ptolemy I to reconsider abdicating in favour of his younger son Philadelphus, arguing that to share power was dangerous and that it was better that the eldest son inherit. When Philadelphus did attain the throne in 285 he suspected Demetrius' loyalty and placed him under house arrest. Two years later Demetrius was dead, ostensibly bitten while asleep by a snake, though perhaps the victim of assassination. For it was a dangerous time to be involved in politics. Many found it preferable to escape into a world of make-believe, as contemporary arts and literature – not least the comedies of Demetrius' friend Menander – attest.

MENANDER (342–291)
Comic Playwright

Why would any educated man go to the theatre unless to see Menander?

Plutarch, *Summary of a Comparison Between*
Aristophanes and Menander, 3

Like many influential men in the late fourth century Menander belonged to the
Lyceum, where his friend Theophrastus was director. He came from a literary
family, and although little is known of his father Diopeithes, his uncle Alexis was
a prolific comic dramatist. So it was not surprising that at the Lenaea in 321 the
twenty-one-year-old Menander entered his first comedy, *Orge* (Anger). Six years
later at the same festival he won first prize with *Dyskolos* (Grumpy Old Man), a
romantic situation comedy in which a rich urban Athenian glimpses, falls in love
with and succeeds in marrying a country girl despite the antisocial behaviour of
her father, the eponymous 'grumpy old man'.

Although the next year Menander triumphed at the more prestigious City
Dionysia, he won the victor's crown only eight times in a career which spanned
over a hundred comedies. His genius was not unrecognized, however. Keen to
make his court a haven for intelligentsia (especially those associated with the
Lyceum), **Ptolemy I** offered Menander tempting incentives to move from his
house in Piraeus to Alexandria. Menander refused, partly perhaps, as the writer
Alciphron later imagined, because of weak health ('which my enemies term
effeminacy and posturing'), partly because he could not bear to leave his mistress
Glycera's arms, 'so much safer and sweeter than the patronage of kings and
satraps'. Yet he could not cheat Tyche. In 291 Menander drowned while swimming
in the sea off Piraeus. Five centuries later his tomb was still to be seen on the road
to Athens near the cenotaph of **Euripides**, a tragedian whom Menander admired
and whose influence on comedy had been surprisingly profound.

Menander's comedies are very unlike those of **Aristophanes**. Fifth-century
participatory democracy allowed comedians (with some impunity) to present
hard-hitting political satire, mercilessly lampooning public figures, some of whom
appeared under their real names in the *dramatis personae*. After Athens' defeat
in 404, however, comedy began to favour a gentler and more genteel approach,
while the chorus, so central to early drama, was confined to singing unrelated
songs during intermissions between 'acts'. Plot-lines changed too. Dominated not
by feisty political activists but by romantic love, they revolved around domestic
life, often in rustic settings, where (as in Euripides' late plays) themes that once

Glycera

In the 320s the hetaera Glycera ('Sweetie') was at the centre of scandal when **Alexander III's** increasingly extravagant and autocratic treasurer Harpalus, learning of her beauty, summoned her to Tarsus as his consort. Here he insisted on her being addressed as 'queen', greeted with proskynesis and presented with crowns. Sadly, Glycera's bronze statue erected near Tarsus paled into insignificance beside monuments to Harpalus' dead inamorata, Pythonice, which cost 200 talents and included a temple to her as Aphrodite. Summoned like Glycera from Athens, Pythonice's enemies named her 'thrice slave, thrice harlot'.

On Harpalus' downfall, Glycera returned to Athens, where she acquired a reputation not only for her mastery of the erotic arts but for her cultured intellect. Her well-known association with Menander was not always harmonious. When Philemon, an older and more popular comic playwright and a rival for Glycera's affections, wrote praising a hetaera for being good, Menander replied in one of his own dramas: 'There is no such thing as a good woman.'

dominated tragedies – mistaken identity, children ignorant of their real parents, mankind's manipulation by the gods – had happy endings.

Deliberately remote from real events, Menander's comedies contained no references to the seven-year famine which gripped the Mediterranean in the 320s, the wars of Alexander's successors, Greece's 20,000 displaced refugees or the reforms of Menander's friend **Demetrius of Phalerum**. Rather, the violent upheavals of the age invited escapism. Tyche pervades Menander's plots. She delivers the prologue to *Aspis* (Shield), while a character in *Dyskolos* (Grumpy Old Man), which was performed in 315 and is Menander's only comedy to survive complete, exclaims:

> It seems to me that everybody's luck must change, no matter if he's prospering or poor. If lucky, he'll remain lucky as long as he doesn't harm others unjustly. But when luck leads him to wrongdoing, he can expect to see his fortune changing for the worse.

The comedy of Menander and his contemporaries was almost entirely populated by recurring stock character types – cooks, wily slaves, hetaerae,

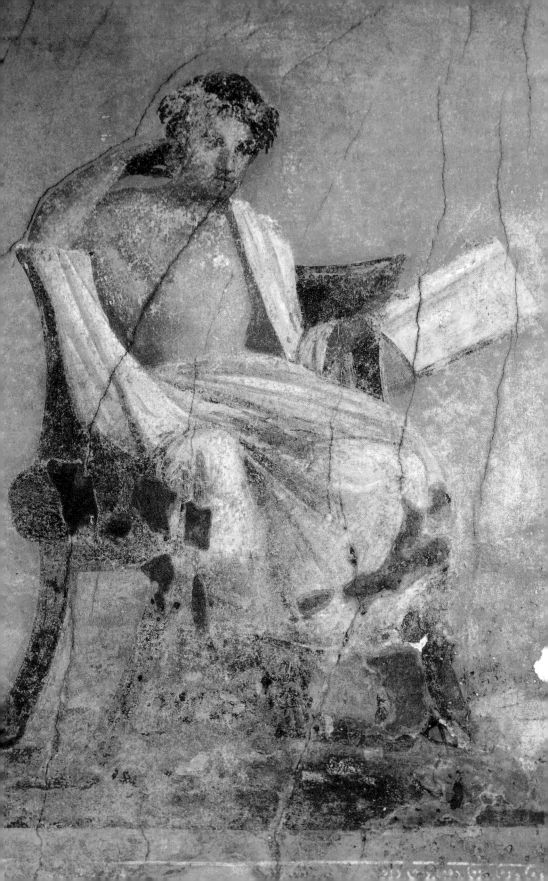

bumptious soldiers, sponging parasites – and given Menander's grounding in ethics it is perhaps no coincidence that some of his plays' titles, *The Boor, The Flatterer, The Sanctimonious Man*, reflect those of Theophrastus' *Characters*. With their clear, unfussy style, often tailored to suit specific character types, circumstances and emotions, many of Menander's lines were collected and quoted by later generations. Caesar appropriated 'let the die be cast!'; St. Paul borrowed 'bad company corrupts good character'; while 'those whom the gods love die young' remains in common currency.

Menander's influence on literature was profound. Roman comedians mined his plays for inspiration, and the rhetorician Quintilian praised his representation of real life, power of invention and elegant style. An anecdote suggests Menander's methodology. Asked how a script was progressing, he replied: 'It's done. I've sketched out the storyline. All that remains is to write the words.' Working from a creative outline inwards towards ever greater detail and refinement, Menander was striving for an artistry which, belying its technical brilliance, would suggest an easy realism. In doing so he resembled the greatest painter of his day, Apelles.

APELLES (PRE 360–?C. 295)
Artist

Apelles of Cos surpassed all other painters who came before or after him.
Pliny the Elder, Natural History, 35.36

Although Apelles was universally recognized as the greatest painter of antiquity tantalizingly little is known about his life and none of his artworks survive. However, his influence on painting and the evolving iconography of power meant that he played a pivotal role in defining his age.

Cos, Colophon and Ephesus all claimed to be Apelles' birthplace. As a young man the artist studied under the Macedonian Pamphilus, a member of the influential school of Sicyon. Pamphilus may have introduced Apelles to Philip II's court, where his work achieved such success that by the time of Philip's assassination in 336 Apelles had executed several portraits of the king. Wishing to ensure a tight control over his image as a youthful heroic conqueror, Philip's

A mid-first-century AD wall painting from Pompeii shows a young man, traditionally identified as Menander, garlanded and reading a manuscript.

successor **Alexander III** publicly forbade anyone but Apelles to paint him, while Lysippus, another product of the Sicyonian school, was granted exclusive rights to sculpt him.

Apelles' paintings of Alexander were renowned. Some were (or were later interpreted to be) allegorical: in one Alexander rode in a chariot with Victory at his side; in another he was accompanied by Triumph, while War and Fury, chained, crouched on a pile of weapons. In the most famous of these works, later housed in the temple of Artemis at Ephesus, Alexander appeared as Zeus hurling a thunderbolt so realistic that later viewers thought it reached out towards them. Although it had cost him 20 talents, Alexander was initially unimpressed. But when Bucephalus recognized himself and whinnied excitedly, Apelles observed sardonically, 'Your horse, king, is a better critic than you are.' Another time, at the painter's studio, Alexander was expressing his ill-conceived views on art when Apelles quietly requested him to stop, lest the assistants (grinding pigments nearby) laugh at him. But when Apelles was commissioned to paint a nude of Alexander's early mistress Campaspe and fell in love with her the king gave her to him as a gift.

Alexander's courtiers, eager for a portrait by the royal favourite, commissioned Apelles, too. Among them were Cleitus, whom Alexander later killed in a drunken brawl, and Antigonus the One-Eyed, whom Apelles painted in three-quarter view to hide his deformity. Not everyone appreciated him, however. After Alexander's death a storm forced Apelles to put in at Alexandria, where a malicious rival assured him that **Ptolemy** had invited him to dinner. Ptolemy, who loathed Apelles, was outraged and ordered him to identify the mischief maker, at which the artist sketched so lifelike a portrait that all recognized the culprit. During the same visit Apelles was reportedly accused of plotting against Ptolemy, a charge of which he was acquitted, but which inspired his allegorical *Calumny*, in which a king with ass's ears was shown listening to personifications of Slander, Ignorance and Suspicion.

Among Apelles' most famous works were many with religious subjects: *Sacrifice in Cos, Artemis Surrounded by Sacrificing Virgins, Procession of the Priest of Artemis at Ephesus* and *The Birth of Aphrodite*, which showed the goddess in a seashell, having risen from the waves. Although his model was probably Campaspe, his inspiration may have been Phryne, an Athenian hetaera who specialized in untying her hair and bathing naked in the sea during the Eleusinian Mysteries and the festival of Poseidon. (Thanks to her profession Phryne was so rich that she offered to finance the rebuilding of the walls of Thebes which Alexander had destroyed.) At his death Apelles left incomplete another *Birth of*

Botticelli's *The Calumny of Apelles* (c. 1494) was inspired by the Roman author Lucian's description of
Apelles' painting, *Calumny*, itself prompted by a false charge laid against Apelles before Ptolemy I.

Aphrodite, commissioned by the islanders of Cos. No one of sufficient talent could
be found to finish it.

Apelles achieved an impression of realism through judgment (especially,
he claimed, knowing when to stop), technique and imagination. Using only
four colours (red ochre, yellow ochre, gypsum white and charcoal black), he
finished his paintings with a dark amber varnish, which lent them a unique
luminosity, but whose recipe died with him. In a treatise *On Art* Apelles described
how he practised continually ('not a day without a line'), striving to achieve
perfection because he was painting 'for eternity'. Sometimes his techniques were
unconventional – the splatter of a sponge flung at a painting of an exhausted
horse brilliantly conveyed the foam at the beast's mouth. The second-century AD
sceptical philosopher Sextus Empiricus (a follower of Pyrrho, who accompanied
Alexander to India and conversed with the gymnosophists) believed Apelles' act

to be born from furious frustration. He used the episode to illustrate how, once one has give up, one's goal can sometimes be achieved by chance, when least expected. He called this consummation *ataraxia*. But ataraxia was not only the preserve of sceptics. In its sense 'freedom from anxiety' it was the goal of one of Apelles' most visionary contemporaries, Epicurus.

EPICURUS (341–270)
Philosopher

His energetic life-spirit prevailed, and he advanced beyond creation's burning walls to range in mind and spirit across its boundless entirety.

Lucretius, *On the Nature of Things*, 1.72–74

Epicurus was born on the island of Samos to an Athenian settler family, one of four brothers, whose father was a schoolmaster and mother performed occasional priestly rituals. Baffled as a boy by Hesiod's account of Chaos (if nothing existed before Chaos, from what was Chaos formed?), Epicurus studied with the Platonist Pamphilus until in 323, aged eighteen, he sailed to Athens for his two-year military service. Whether he (or his contemporary **Menander**) fought in the crushing defeat of Crannon in 322 is unknown, but he probably frequented both the Academy and Lyceum during his time in Athens.

When he returned east Epicurus discovered that his family had been expelled from Samos and had relocated to Colophon on the Ionian coast. Here Epicurus studied under Nausiphenes of Teos, a follower of Democritus, who proclaimed death to be a state of 'unperturbedness', and that the physical world was formed of atoms which, falling uniformly through the void, temporarily coalesce to create objects or creatures. Although partly the answer which Epicurus had been looking for, he refined it to account for free will by suggesting that atoms (including those forming our minds) can swerve. The mind can partially regulate this swerve, to allow individual thoughts to be formed and choices made.

In 311, when he was thirty, Epicurus established a school at Mytilene on Lesbos. Somehow he soon offended the citizens and authorities, and was compelled to relocate first to Lampsacus on the Dardanelles and finally in 306

Epicurus, whose goal in life was 'ataraxia' or freedom from anxiety: a Roman bust copied from an original dating to Epicurus' lifetime.

Stoicism

Stoicism originated around 300 and was named after the Athenian Stoa Poikile, where its founder Zeno of Citium taught. It posited a universe guided by divine Reason or *logos* (a term used in John's Gospel, sometimes translated as 'the Word'). A virtuous, happy life is led in accordance with this logos, while emotions such as desire, fear, pain and even pleasure, which interfere with its pursuit, should be avoided. By cultivating wisdom, courage, justice and self-control Stoics sought a mental and spiritual equilibrium, *apatheia* (freedom from passions) – assisted by the type of meditations made famous by the Roman emperor Marcus Aurelius (r. AD 161–80).

Stoics believed in a divine fire, or (according to Zeno's successor Chrysippus) a mixture of fire and air called *pneuma* ('breath' or 'spirit', a word used in the New Testament to mean the 'Holy Spirit'). Pneuma is present as the soul in all living beings (human or animal, slave or free), but on their physical death it becomes re-assimilated into the universal pneuma. Periodically the universe is cleansed by fire as part of an infinite cycle of decay and regeneration. Elements of Stoicism prefigure Christianity, though for Stoics the pneuma was impersonal and the fiery cleansing of the universe unconnected to moral judgment.

to Athens. Between the city and Piraeus he bought a house with a garden where he lectured and by whose door was inscribed, 'Friend, rest awhile: our greatest goal is happiness.' Here he wrote most of his works, whose titles included *Atoms and the Void*, *On Love*, *On Fate* and *On Kingly Power*, as well as numerous letters, three of which survive. Claiming that he was an autodidact, in none of his writings did he reference previous authors.

Epicurus and his followers, including a banker, a mathematician, a satirist and his own brothers, lived together in his house, a self-sufficient community where slaves and free debated as equals. Female students also lived with them, the object of much prurient suspicion, especially as some may have been practising hetaerae. One, Leontion, was later grudgingly praised for her elegant prose style but condemned for her effrontery in criticizing Theophrastus. In fact criticism was a hallmark of Epicurus himself. He vilified Theophrastus, Nausiphenes (an 'illiterate', a 'jellyfish' and a 'porne'), **Aristotle** (a 'desperate drug-dealer'

– a reference perhaps to his alleged role in **Alexander III's** death) and the philosophers of the Academy ('flatterers of [the Sicilian tyrannos] Dionysius').

Surprisingly, given his splenetic outbursts, Epicurus' ultimate goal was freedom from anxiety, which he named 'ataraxia'. This could be achieved by following his *Tetrapharmacus* or four canons, namely: (i) since gods exist in sublime tranquillity they are unconcerned about mankind's actions, so we need not fear them; (ii) since we are formed of atoms which disintegrate on our death, nothing of us remains to be punished in the afterlife, so we need not fear death; (iii) since anyone can acquire the basics of life, by not striving for excess happiness comes easily; (iv) suffering can easily be endured since nothing lasts forever and pain can be mitigated through contemplating happiness. This last was a precept of consolation to Epicurus himself, who was afflicted by kidney stones for many years. When he was dying he wrote of how he relieved his suffering by cheerfully meditating on his own philosophy.

Although not the first to suggest the significance of atoms, Epicurus' application of the hypothesis to human behaviour was novel. It was a reaction not only to his disease but to contemporary politics, where the attraction of the untroubled life must have been great. His pronouncements (that wise men should withdraw from public life, since desire for political power is unnatural and painful, and that the gods exist beyond the turbulence of worldly tribulations) are a direct challenge to the self-declared divinity of Alexander and his successors. Epicurus was not alone in reassessing the world around him: while new philosophical doctrines such as Stoicism advocated self control and Cynicism rejected wealth and power, private citizens increasingly withdrew from politics, preferring to channel their energies into enhancing their cities or homes.

After his death, Epicurus was honoured by his followers, who erected statues in his honour, wore signet rings bearing his likeness and, following the terms of his will, celebrated both his birthday and the twentieth of each month with reunions. Thus a philosophy suggesting that the divine plays no part in human life acquired the nature of a sect: by demonstrating that mortals can live free from distress Epicureanism made gods not of conquerors but of citizens and slaves. As **Plato** and Aristotle fell out of fashion, the philosophical schools of the late fourth century dominated intellectual life not just in Greece but in the increasingly powerful civilization with which the Greeks would soon come into disturbing contact: Rome.

Chapter 8

In the Shadow
of Rome

The terrifying Pyrrhus' features are idealized, in part to recall his cousin Alexander III, in this Roman copy of a contemporary statue.

PYRRHUS OF EPIRUS (319–272)
King and General

All Pyrrhus' victories were (as the saying goes) Cadmean. Although he defeated the enemy he could not subdue them, since their territory was so large, and he suffered the calamities which normally come with defeat.

Diodorus, *Library of History*, 22.6

With his terrifying appearance and curious upper jaw, possessing not separate teeth but a continuous strip of serrated bone, **Alexander III's** second cousin, Pyrrhus, was also his distorted mirror image. Like Alexander he traced his lineage to Achilles, whose son Neoptolemus was also known as Pyrrhus. He shared Alexander's restless energy, too, and his brilliance on the battlefield – the great Carthaginian commander Hannibal thought him the finest general of all. But he lacked the patience to build on success, and his battles were won so dearly that, while Greeks named such victories 'Cadmean' (after Thebes' legendary founder, who lost all his troops in winning his city), today we call them 'pyrrhic'.

In the wars of Alexander's successors, one of the most alluring prizes was Macedon. Soon after it fell to Cassander in 316, the general crossed west to his recently executed enemy Olympias' homeland of Epirus to hunt down her cousin King Alcetas and his three-year-old son Pyrrhus. In a frantic dash to safety three of Alcetas' men galloped with the child through driving rain to the court of King Glaucias of Illyria. Despite Cassander's offer of bounty, Pyrrhus stayed there for the next nine years. In 307 Glaucias annexed Epirus and placed the twelve-year-old Pyrrhus on its throne. Soon the young king was forming his own alliances. In 303 he arranged for his sister Deidameia to marry Demetrius the Besieger during a festival at Argos. But only the next year the Epirotes, backed by Demetrius' enemy Cassander, deposed him. Pyrrhus made haste to Athens, where Demetrius was preparing to sail to Asia to support his father Antigonus the One-Eyed against a rare coalition of Alexander's successors, which had been marshalled by Cassander. In 301 Demetrius and Pyrrhus fought at the battle of Ipsus, leading the cavalry charge which routed the enemy's left flank. But rather than immediately turn and harry the rear of the enemy's phalanx, they pursued too far; when they did finally wheel round their path was blocked by elephants. Terrified, their horses bolted, and on the battlefield the eighty-year-old Antigonus fell in a hail of javelins, cut off but confident that his son would rescue him.

In 298, under a treaty between Demetrius and **Ptolemy I**, Pyrrhus sailed to Alexandria as a token of Demetrius' goodwill. He impressed his hosts. Queen Berenice gave him her daughter Antigone in marriage; and Ptolemy provided Pyrrhus with sufficient expertise and soldiery to allow him to return as joint king of Epirus in 297. Soon Pyrrhus had engineered his co-ruler's demise, and in gratitude to his sponsors he named his firstborn son Ptolemy and a newly founded city Berenice. But Cassander's death the same year kindled a new war. His two sons quarrelled. One, Antipater, promptly murdered their mother; the other, Alexander V, appealed for help to Pyrrhus and Demetrius. Pyrrhus swiftly reinstated Alexander as joint ruler of Macedon. Demetrius was even more decisive. In 294 he killed Alexander V, exiled Antipater and seized the throne of Macedon for himself.

The coup brought Demetrius into conflict with not only Pyrrhus but Lysimachus, the powerful overlord of Thrace and the Ionian coast. In one of a series of opportunistic raids, as Demetrius invaded Epirus and Pyrrhus marched to meet him, the armies missed each other. Instead, Pyrrhus found Demetrius' lieutenant whom, like a Homeric hero, he challenged to single combat and defeated. In admiration Pyrrhus' army bestowed on him the title 'Eagle'. Hostilities infected palace politics as well. When Antigone died in 295, Pyrrhus married not one but three princesses. But one of them – Lanassa, the daughter of the Syracusan tyrannos Agathocles – was piqued not to be held in greater honour. She stormed out of Epirus to Macedon, where she gave Demetrius not just herself in marriage but, as her dowry and an earnest of goodwill, the island of Corcyra.

By 288, however, Demetrius felt confident enough to contemplate invading Asia. It was the moment everyone was waiting for. Backed by Ptolemy I, Lysimachus and Seleucus (who ruled Alexander III's vast eastern empire), and encouraged by a dream in which Alexander promised to support him, Pyrrhus struck before Demetrius could march. Demetrius' Macedonians defected en masse. Although Demetrius escaped, raised an army with his son Antigonus

Gonatas and attacked Asia, he was defeated and captured by Seleucus. Imprisoned for two years, Demetrius drank himself spectacularly to death.

Sadly Pyrrhus was no strategist. Having finally seized control of Macedon, he agreed to share it with Lysimachus. The arrangement could not last. When hostilities broke out Pyrrhus was driven back to Epirus, but Lysimachus failed to deliver the coup de grâce. Instead, he crossed to Asia to face Seleucus, and in 281 at Corypedium near Sardis he was killed in battle. But before Seleucus could claim Macedon's empty throne he was murdered by one of his own entourage: Ptolemy the Thunderbolt, who had abandoned Alexandria in anger when Ptolemy I refused to make him his successor. Now the Thunderbolt was crowned king of Macedon. It was an outcome no one had foreseen. Its aftermath was equally unlikely: rather than fight Pyrrhus for Macedon, Ptolemy offered the Epirote some of his own troops. For, still desperate for adventure, Pyrrhus had set his sights on a new adventure which held out the potential for great glory as the leader of a panhellenic campaign to assist Taras in its war against the growing power of Rome.

In the past ten years south Italy had come increasingly within Rome's sphere.

Early Rome

According to legend, while Rome's territory was settled by the Trojan hero Aeneas, the city itself was founded by Romulus on 21 April 753. In the seventh century Rome, like the surrounding region of Latium and Campania to the south, was subject to the Etruscans. But in 510 its citizens expelled its king Tarquinius the Proud, and four years later formed the Latin League with the rest of Latium's now free cities. In 396 Rome, the League's dominant member, won a major victory over the Etruscans and further expanded its territories, but six years later the city and surrounding areas were briefly occupied by Gallic invaders. Once the Gauls had returned north Rome recovered faster than its neighbours, imposed its will on both the Latins and Etruscans and consolidated its power. In 348 it concluded a treaty with Carthage which allowed it to spend the next sixty-five years conquering the Italian peninsula without fear of Carthaginian attack. In 283 Rome aided Thurii and other Greek colonies against the south Italian Lucanian people, an alliance which prompted nearby Taras to fear for its security and enlist the help of Pyrrhus of Epirus.

In 291 Rome had assimilated Campania (including the Greek city of Cumae), and in 283 the poleis of Thurii, Locris, Rhegium and Croton had concluded an alliance with Rome against the Lucanians, who were threatening their borders. The treaty also brought Rome into conflict with Taras, which had been at odds with its Greek neighbours for two decades. Now, in 280, suspecting that barbarian Rome might use the war as an excuse to annex their own city, the Tarantines, isolated and fearing for their proud independence, placed their trust in Pyrrhus.

For Pyrrhus, Taras' salvation was part of a larger plan. He confided to his chief negotiator Cineas his plans to conquer Sicily and Carthage, too – a western campaign to mirror Alexander's in the east. When he was victorious, Pyrrhus said, he would 'drink and be happy', to which Cineas (an Epicurean) observed, 'We could do that now, without the bloodshed.' His words had little impact. Pyrrhus' troops were already embarking: 20,000 infantry, 3,000 cavalry, 2,000 archers and twenty elephants, creatures never before seen in Italy. The crossing was disastrous. Storms swept the ships off course; only good fortune prevented their destruction. Finally they reached Taras, a city steeped in luxury, where Pyrrhus imposed such strict discipline on the population that there were many who regretted their decision to enlist his help.

With Pyrrhus' army on Italian soil, Rome was soon on the march. As 45,000 Roman troops commanded by the consul Laevinus, one of the two senior Roman magistrates, converged on Heraclea, 40 miles (64 km) west across the gulf, Pyrrhus, with his now combined force of 35,000 men, rode out to meet them. Observing the Roman army in their regimented ranks beyond the River Siris, he presciently remarked, 'Barbarians they may be, but there is nothing barbaric about their discipline.' While Pyrrhus awaited his allies, the Roman infantry seized the moment and splashed across the river. His purple cloak shimmering with gold embroidery, Pyrrhus ordered the attack, plunging his horse deep into the melee, the perfect target for any Roman bent on glory. Aware of the king's danger, a bodyguard insisted they swap armour. Immediately the recipient was killed. Meanwhile, with the Roman shield wall steadfastly resisting the Greek phalanx, Laevinus sent his cavalry curving around Pyrrhus' right flank to attack the Greeks from the rear. He had not anticipated the elephants. When the Romans' horses saw and smelt the beasts they panicked, careering towards their own lines, causing mayhem. Pyrrhus pursued them, and as the horsemen thundered towards them the Roman infantry broke. The evenly balanced battle turned into a rout.

As south Italy rallied to Pyrrhus' side Cineas travelled to Rome with gifts of money for the city's senators, dresses for their wives and offerings of peace. The peace terms were not entirely unattractive, and only the intervention of their blind colleague Appius Claudius hardened the senators' resolve: until Pyrrhus returned to Greece, Rome would remain at war. Pyrrhus was not slow to respond. Leaving Campania, which had resisted both his attacks and his blandishments, he led his army to Praeneste, from where Rome itself was visible just 20 miles (32 km) away. Scenting the overthrow of their old rival its citizens welcomed him enthusiastically and soon Greek troops were just 4 miles (6.5 km) from Rome. It was as close as Pyrrhus came. Rome's walls were strong and winter was fast approaching. Already another Roman army was massing to the north, while in the south the rump of Laevinus' defeated force hungered for revenge. Giving the order to withdraw, Pyrrhus left Praeneste to its fate. In Campania he met Laevinus' army, but after terrifying each other with their war cries neither side could face battle, and Pyrrhus slipped back to Taras unopposed.

Talks continued throughout the winter. Pyrrhus tried to bribe a Roman delegate with gold, to terrify him by having an elephant (concealed behind a curtain) unexpectedly trumpet in his ear, and finally to seduce him with Epicurean philosophy. All failed. In 279 the two sides clashed at Asculum in Apulia. So large were their armies that each side's battle line stretched over 4 miles (6.5 km). Since Heraclea the Romans had devised defences against elephants, covered wagons manned by archers and equipped with swivelling sharp-barbed poles, some bound with flaming pitch-soaked rags. The blueprints no doubt generated much excitement, but they had no effect. After a hard-fought struggle in which the Roman infantry punched a hole half a mile (800 m) wide through the Greek phalanx, Pyrrhus' elephants again came to the rescue. But his casualties were hideously high. Congratulated on his victory, Pyrrhus bitterly remarked, 'Another like this will ruin us.'

Then news came which caused Pyrrhus, never tenacious at the best of times, to switch his focus. In Macedon, Ptolemy the Thunderbolt had been killed in battle against Gaulish raiders. The throne which Pyrrhus craved was empty. But a second dispatch was even more intriguing: an invitation from Sicilian Greeks to help resist a Carthaginian siege of Syracuse. Pyrrhus could not resist. Defeating Sicily and Carthage was part of his grand plan, and who better to rule Syracuse than his son Alexander, grandson of Agathocles, the city's late tyrannos? Imposing a garrison on Taras, in 278 he set sail for Sicily.

The siege was quickly raised and across Sicily poleis, hoping that he would be their island's liberator, flocked to Pyrrhus' side. As the Carthaginians withdrew before Pyrrhus' elephants and well-drilled phalanx, only Lilybaeum in the far west held out. But eulogies of Pyrrhus as the 'king of Sicily and Epirus' were premature. His fortunes changed. Built on a low spit of land, Lilybaeum was washed on two

A mid-second-century terracotta figurine shows a war elephant, equipped with a howdah (itself perhaps a Macedonian invention), trampling a Gallic warrior.

sides by the sea. Had Pyrrhus' fleet been dominant he might have taken it; but it was not. Carthage ruled the waves. Pyrrhus' patience frayed. Never one to buckle down to lengthy graft when new wars beckoned, he raised the siege, demanding from the Sicilians ships and money for his next campaign: an attack on Carthage itself. It was not an impossible strategy, but Pyrrhus' overweening treatment quickly alienated his allies. While he ruthlessly punished his own supporters for failing to provide the materiel he had requested, Carthage and the Mamertines of southern Italy engaged in a campaign to woo the now disgruntled poleis. Lacking the resources to sail against Carthage or the acumen to rule Sicily, in 276 Pyrrhus quit the island. Thanks to his cloddish character he failed to grasp his prize.

Back on Italian soil and marching to Taras, his army was harassed by Mamertines until Pyrrhus furiously challenged their hulking champion to single combat. Before the Mamertine had time to think, Pyrrhus split the man's head in two. Thereafter the journey progressed unhindered. Yet Pyrrhus' funds were dangerously low. To pay his troops he plundered the wealthy temple of Persephone at Locris, an ill-considered move. Bad omens suggested the goddess was displeased, the Greeks viewed his behaviour with foreboding, and as Pyrrhus marched north against Rome's replenished legions he failed to give thought to his destination's ill-starred name: Maleventum (Bad Outcome).

On his arrival there, he tried to launch a surprise attack by night behind Roman lines, but the necessary manoeuvring took longer than expected and Pyrrhus' torches failed. When he finally attacked next morning the Romans were expecting him. Worse, they had discovered means of terrifying elephants: fiery missiles, pigs smeared with tar and set alight, their dying squeals sowing panic. The elephants ran amok, trampling friend and foe alike, and by sunset neither side had won. It had been Pyrrhus' last chance to triumph over Rome. Accepting the inevitable, and with a fraction of his original army still alive, he returned to Epirus. Within five years the Romans possessed all southern Italy, and in recognition of their victory over Pyrrhus renamed the site of their last battle with him Beneventum (Good Outcome).

Unfazed, Pyrrhus turned his sights on Macedon, where Antigonus Gonatas was now king. Desperate for victory, his ranks swollen by cheap but deadly Gaulish mercenaries (whom he happily allowed to plunder the royal tombs at Aegae), Pyrrhus overran Thessaly and much of Macedonia, pursuing Antigonus to the sea. But once more Pyrrhus showed little interest in ruling his new territories. When his ally the thuggish pretender Cleonymus appealed for help to gain the Spartan throne (and to recover his estranged wife), Pyrrhus readily agreed, and soon, with speed and subterfuge, the Epirotes were encamped outside the city walls which Sparta, for centuries so well protected by its hoplites' spears, had only recently been forced to build. With much of Sparta's army on campaign in Crete, the terrified Gerousia (Senate) was edging closer to capitulation when a woman burst into their chamber. Brandishing a sword she swore that she would rather kill herself than surrender.

The Spartans rallied. By night, as Cleonymus' wife stood waiting in her room, a noose around her neck, preferring death to conjugal embrace, the women of Sparta buried wagons in deep pits as elephant traps. The next day's fighting ended inconclusively, but at dawn Pyrrhus broke through and entered the city. Then, according to the Spartans, Agathe Tyche intervened. As Pyrrhus' horse was shot from under him, news came that the Spartan army had returned. During the desperate retreat north Pyrrhus' son Ptolemy was killed in an ambush. Berserk with rage, Pyrrhus cut down the Spartan general, and in the lull which followed held a lavish funeral for his son. And then, responding to a call to intervene in its domestic politics, he continued his march to Argos.

Here he found the heights above the city already occupied by Antigonus, who since Cassander's death had assumed the throne of Macedon and the ambition to rule Greece. Leaving Helenus, his youngest son, to guard their nearby camp, in the dead of night Pyrrhus led a detachment of his troops to Argos, where his allies unlocked the gates. As soldiers stumbled through the darkened streets, an elephant became stuck fast in the gateway. Its distressed trumpeting awoke the city. As the enemy rushed to arms, all was confusion: soldiers lost in twisting alleyways; others falling into open water channels which crisscrossed the city; still others not knowing who was enemy or friend. At sunrise in the agora Pyrrhus saw a sight which made him freeze: a statue of a wolf savaging a bull, a long-prophesied omen presaging his death. Horrified, he sent a messenger to order Helenus, his youngest son, to retreat from his position outside the city walls while he evacuated Argos. The order became garbled. Instead, Helenus advanced into the city along the same road by which his father's men were trying to escape. As they met in chaos, no one could hear the frantic orders. The weight of men pressing forward caused those in the centre to be crushed so tightly that they wounded comrades with their unsheathed blades; and in the ghastly ruckus, as elephants stampeded and stones and missiles rained down from rooftops, Pyrrhus fell, struck by a roof tile. An enemy soldier recognized him, dragged him into a doorway and messily hacked off his head. When Antigonus was presented with it he was appalled. He accorded the mutilated corpse a royal cremation. While Helenus took his father's ashes in an urn back home to Epirus for burial, Antigonus rode into Macedon, its undisputed king, to found a dynasty.

Mourning its master's fate, Pyrrhus' pet eagle starved itself to death. Yet the bird's sorrow was not universally shared. In an age of self-seeking sociopaths Pyrrhus' egocentric and ultimately worthless savagery was unsurpassed. Content with nothing less than constant war he was incapable of exercising any of the arts of peace essential for good government. In fact, when once asked which of two aulos-players deserved a prize, he growled, 'Polyperchon.' (Polyperchon was a general. Kings, he implied, did not waste their time with aulos-players.) Not that Pyrrhus was averse to literature. He penned a tract, *On Generalship*, which was used throughout the following centuries as a handbook by would-be conquerors, as well as a set of memoirs, which proudly chronicled the swathe of misery for which he was responsible.

APOLLONIUS OF RHODES (PRE 270–?235)
Poet and Scholar

In teeming Alexandria flocks of tame scholars grow fat, forever squabbling in the Muses' birdcage.

Timon of Phlius, quoted in Athenaeus, *Banquet of the Sophists*, 1.22

While Hellenistic warlords such as **Pyrrhus**, delighting in their trail of havoc, dragged out their dismally destructive lives, others still appreciated the civilizing joys of culture – especially in Alexandria, where scholars like Apollonius of Rhodes found solace for the present in the past.

Few facts are known for certain about Apollonius, but his work and that of his colleagues significantly influenced literature not only in Greece but in Rome. Two brief biographies survive, one of them fragmentary, which agree in basic detail. He was born in or around Alexandria in the early third century to a family which may have been linked to the Ptolemies. Eager to embark on a career of letters, in his early adult life Apollonius formed an association (albeit increasingly strained) with Callimachus, one of the most outstanding literary scholars at the Library, perhaps taking lessons from the older man and assisting him in his onerous duties.

For Callimachus was tasked with cataloguing the Library's collection. The result is the first such inventory in the western world. Callimachus' 120-volume *Pinakes* (Tablets) arranged the collection by genre. In time the constantly updated catalogue would list 500,000 manuscripts by their first line and author's name, as well as providing a brief synopsis. Like many of his colleagues Callimachus was a prolific original writer too, producing works ranging from short occasional verses to his four-book *Aetia* (Causes) – collected elegies tracing the origins of cities and arcane rituals – and *Hekale*, a thousand-line poem about an adventure of Theseus, characterized by a deliberately elliptical style. For Callimachus, poetry must be 'slender', bejewelled with clever and well-chosen imagery; the 'trickling water of a pure fountain', he wrote, was preferable to Homer's 'turbulent Euphratean flood'. Where possible, brevity should reign supreme and a 'big book' was a 'big disaster'. Such dogma may have set Callimachus at odds with Apollonius, and there is a suggestion of a scholarly spat. For Apollonius' best-known work, *Argonautica*, which recounts the story of Jason's quest for the golden fleece in the Black Sea kingdom of Colchis, was an epic in the Homeric mould.

The first, youthful version of *Argonautica* was so derided that in embarrassment Apollonius fled Alexandria for Rhodes, where he earned a living teaching rhetoric. Meanwhile, he revised his poem, republishing it to such acclaim that he was awarded citizenship, and naming himself thereafter Apollonius of Rhodes. The revised *Argonautica*, which survives complete in four books totalling almost 6,000 lines, is the quintessential work of its time. Indebted to the *Odyssey*, it intertwines the scholarly and romantic, a self-conscious *homage* to Homeric tropes incorporating an Alexandrian love of causation, deep psychological insight and a rich seam of urbane humour. At its core is Medea's sudden love for Jason, which causes her heart to 'palpitate, restive as a streak of sunlight which gyrates against a wall as twisting water poured into a pail or cauldron sends it flying'.

Jason is an unprepossessing, self-questioning hero. In contrast to the brave Achilles or the wily (*polymechanos*) Odysseus, he is often at a loss (*amechanos*), relying heavily on his fellow crewmen (many of whom, like **Alexander III's** quarrelsome successors, were considered at least semi-divine). Only in romance does Jason excel. In a passage consciously mirroring the *Iliad*'s description of the shield forged for Achilles by the blacksmith god Hephaestus, Apollonius writes of Jason's cloak, elaborately woven by Athene, which he dons to woo Hypsipyle, the queen of Lemnos. For all its romanticism, *Argonautica* does not eschew the dark concerns of contemporary life. A brutal killing brings nightmares and prospects of dire punishment, though hope lies in the belief that while 'Zeus detests murder, he still can love the murderer'. Elsewhere, similes remind us of the volatile real world. When Jason, made temporarily heroic thanks to Medea's magical intervention, cuts down a fearsome army that has sprung from ground sown with a dragon's teeth, Apollonius likens him to:

> *a farmer, menaced by border conflicts, grabbing a freshly sharpened sickle and rushing to take in unripe crops, not waiting for the proper time or for the sun to fatten them, lest the enemy should get there before him.*

Apollonius draws on other literature and traditions too: **Euripides'** *Medea* is never far away; a description of the strange customs of the Mossynoecoi recalls the *Anabasis* of **Xenophon**, who had partially followed Jason's course and encountered this same people; one passage references a Celtic version of a myth; another draws on the wisdom of 'priests in Egyptian Thebes [Luxor]'. There are allusions to the visual arts and architecture. A passage describing Eros playing knucklebones with Ganymede may recall a famous sculpture by Polycleitus; the hostile bronze giant Talos resembles the colossus in Apollonius' adopted Rhodes; and a description of Apollo's bow flashing through the mist to guide lost sailors evokes the lighthouse of his native Alexandria.

Thanks to the success of the revised *Argonautica*, Apollonius returned home in triumph to be appointed head of the Library and Museum, to tutor Ptolemy III, and to write more poetry. He was already well aware of the demands of courtly life. In *Argonautica* he explained the ceaseless toil of busy servants with the almost throwaway line, 'They were working for a king.' Apollonius served as Librarian until 235, perhaps the year he died, when he was succeeded by Eratosthenes – nicknamed 'Beta' because, despite being a good all-rounder, he was second best in every discipline (though as the first to calculate the circumference of the globe to an error of just 1.6 per cent, he deserved at least beta plus).

As Librarian, Apollonius rubbed shoulders not only with writers like Theocritus but also with the myriad scientists who flocked to the 'Muses'

Theocritus, Idylls and Mimes

Among Alexandria's literary community, the Syracusan Theocritus is best remembered for his development – or invention – of a genre long central to the western literary tradition: bucolic poetry (from *boukolia*, 'cattle-herd'), also called 'idylls' (from *eidullion*, the diminutive of *eidos*, 'form'). In keeping with much Hellenistic literature, these relatively short works present escapist visions, rural scenes populated by lovelorn shepherds (like Daphnis) or mythical figures like the Cyclops Polyphemus, singing to soothe his passion for the nymph Galataea.

Another genre of poetry practised by Theocritus which gained fresh life during the period was the *mime* ('imitation'), with its characteristic urban settings. One, in which two women converse as they make their way to the palace of Ptolemy II and a festival of Adonis, sheds valuable light on Alexandrian life. It tells of busy streets ('The crowds! The horses! The heavy boots! The men in uniform! The never-ending boulevard!') and linguistic snobbery (Syracusans, who do not speak Koine, are scorned for their dialect). Most revealing of all, however, is the freedom of movement which the women enjoy – a remarkable contrast to Athenian life of the fifth and early fourth centuries. This picture is reinforced in the *Mimes* of Herodas, another Alexandrian, whose poems are infused with a fascination for character and reveal much about women's lives, showing them at the temple of Asclepius in Cos, at the shoe shop (buying autoerotic aids) and at home, where one mistress orders a faithless male slave to receive 2,000 lashes.

birdcage' (as the Museum became known). Among them was Aristarchus, the first astronomer to propose a heliocentric universe. Others, specialists in engineering, were called upon to enliven the flamboyant processions in which Alexandria delighted. The most famous was staged by Ptolemy II in 285. According to ancient accounts (whose accuracy is now questioned) it included exotic animals; performers dressed as Victories and satyrs; a mechanized statue, 12 feet (3.5 m) tall, which rose automatically, poured milk from a shallow golden dish and then sat down again; a wineskin sewn from leopard pelts, with a capacity of 30,000 gallons (136 cu. m), which trickled wine along the whole course of the procession; and a 300 foot (91 m) golden phallus tipped with a gold star. Such peacetime parades provided opportunities to showcase cutting-edge inventions, but most practical science was focused on warfare, and here no one was more creative than Archimedes.

ARCHIMEDES (c. 287–212)
Mathematician and Inventor

Give me somewhere to stand and I can move the world.

Archimedes, quoted in Pappus of Alexandria, *Collection*, 8

Archimedes was born in Syracuse, where his father Pheidias, an astronomer, was closely related to the city's ruler Hieron II. A general in **Pyrrhus'** army, Hieron became commander and then tyrannos of Syracuse after the Epirote abandoned Sicily in 276. As a boy Archimedes must have endured the Carthaginian siege of 278 before watching Pyrrhus' siege train lumber west to Lilybaeum. Later, in more peaceful Alexandria, he may have studied under Euclid, the great geometer, pure mathematician and author of the influential *Elements*, whose thirteen volumes cover everything from geometric algebra to spatial geometry by way of ratios, proportions and square roots.

Back in Syracuse, Archimedes pursued pure mathematics, where systems of his own invention allowed him to compute considerably larger (and smaller) numbers than his predecessors. His treatises revolutionized the subject. In *Sand-Reckoner*, drawing on Aristarchus' vision of heliocentricity, he computed the number of grains of sand in the universe as 8×10^{63}; in *Measuring the Circle* he calculated the value of π to between 223/71 and 22/7; and in *The Sphere and the Cylinder* he demonstrated that the ratio of both surface area and volume of a sphere placed within a cylinder of the same height and width is 2:3.

Practically, too, Archimedes excelled. His revolving hollow celestial globe (turned by a handle) illustrated the relative movements of the sun, moon and five visible planets with remarkable accuracy. Challenged to determine whether a crown was made of pure gold, Archimedes did so by working out how to measure its density and volume. He probably suspended the crown from one end of a set of scales and a solid gold bar of equal weight from the other, then lowered both into water. Being more dense, pure gold would displace more water than gold-plate. Traditionally Archimedes discovered how to calculate volume while immersing himself in a bath. Perceiving the resultant water displacement he is said to have run naked through the streets exclaiming, 'I have found it!' (*heureka!*).

Archimedes was a prolific inventor. He designed the block and tackle, the first odometer and the compound pulley, which allowed the lifting of heavy weights, and successfully explained the working of levers, observing, 'Give me somewhere to stand and I can move the world.' With Hellenistic Greece's fad for building ever bigger and more spectacular creations (such as Rhodes' colossus and Alexandria's lighthouse), Archimedes was required to put his inventions to practical use. Hieron II commissioned him to design and build a titanic three-storeyed ship, the *Syracusia*. With twenty banks of oars, it contained a dining room, library, gymnasium, shrine to Aphrodite, salt-water fish-tank, gardens, vine-shaded walkways and a floor mosaic illustrating the entire *Iliad*. The heavy ship inspired two inventions: a windlass to drag it to the sea and Archimedes' eponymous screw, a cylinder housing a rotating blade, to empty the bilge-water. It also doubled as a warship. With stables for twenty horses and barracks for marines, it carried state-of-the-art weaponry, including catapults designed by Archimedes capable of firing stones weighing 180 pounds (82 kg) and arrows 18 feet (5.5 m) long over 200 yards (183 m). The *Syracusia*, however, was a white elephant. No port in Sicily was large enough to take it, so it was filled with grain, renamed the *Alexandria* and presented as a gift to Ptolemy III – whose son later commissioned an even larger ship to trump it.

As artillery and siege engines became ever more sophisticated, Archimedes found himself in ever greater demand, especially when Syracuse was dragged into

'Do not disturb my circles': a mosaic (now believed to date from the seventeenth century) shows a soldier at the capture of Syracuse surprising Archimedes at his studies before killing him.

war with Rome. In 263 the Syracusan tyrannos Hieron II had concluded a treaty with Rome, which was waging war with Carthage over Sicily, as a result of which Syracuse continued to enjoy power over the southeast of the island. But Hieron died in 215 and his successor Hieronymus, prompted by Hannibal's victory at Cannae and the Macedonian King Philip V's support of Carthage, dramatically switched sides. In 214 Rome besieged Syracuse.

Again Archimedes' ingenuity was called upon. To repulse Rome's fleet he positioned catapults of varying ranges on Syracuse's walls, while smaller versions nicknamed 'scorpions' fired through specially created loopholes. Tradition suggests, too, that he set fire to enemy ships attacking the city from the sea by using concave mirrors to focus the sun's rays onto their tarry hulls. For closer combat he suspended iron claws on chains, which were swung out on poles to grab ships' prows and pull them out of the water. He employed similar techniques on land, where huge swinging beams were hung with heavy weights to smash into the Roman siege engines.

But in 212 Syracuse fell, captured as it celebrated the festival of Artemis. Archimedes died in the resultant butchery, perhaps trying to protect his scientific instruments. One tradition suggests that the Roman commander Marcellus ordered Archimedes to be captured alive so that Rome could benefit from his military acumen, but when the legionaries found him, deep in thought drawing geometrical shapes in the sand, he bade them stand back with the command, 'Do not disturb my circles.' Incensed by his lack of respect they killed him. In 75 the Roman philhellene Cicero found Archimedes' tomb, now overgrown with brambles, by Syracuse's Agrigentine Gate. He recognized it from its marker: a slender column, topped with a stone sculpture of a cylinder in which was housed a sphere.

ATTALUS I (269–197)
King and General

Trembling at the words of the Great Goddess, Attalus exclaimed, '…Rome demands our heritage.'

Ovid, *Fasti*, 4.326

From Greek Italy and Sicily, Rome's shadow lengthened eastwards, finding kings eager to form alliances amid threats of local wars. Among them was Attalus I of Pergamum, a relatively new kingdom in northwest Asia Minor.

After the battle of Ipsus in 301 Pergamum was governed by the eunuch Philetaerus, first on behalf of Lysimachus, then (from just before the battle of Corypedium in 281) for the successors of Seleucus, who ruled over much of Asia Minor. His overlords' lack of tight control allowed both Philetaerus and his nephew Eumenes I (r. 263–241) to administer Pergamum as their personal fiefdom. The province flourished, but tranquillity came at a price. Threatened by Gaulish tribesmen who, recently migrating from the north, had settled nearby, Eumenes preferred to pay tribute than to do battle, a controversial policy which his nephew the twenty-eight-year old Attalus I quickly overturned on his accession.

Decisive, heroic, his hair coiffed in the style of **Alexander III**, in 241 Attalus led his army into battle with the Gauls by the headwaters of the River Caicus. Victorious, he was acclaimed as 'Saviour' and proclaimed himself 'King'. But the Gauls took reprisals. They allied themselves with Antiochus the Hawk – younger brother and sworn enemy of the Seleucid king – who from his lair at Sardis launched an attack on Pergamum, the prelude to a long campaign. From the Bosphorus to Caria, battles were fought and victories won, until by 228 Attalus controlled all of western Asia Minor north of the Taurus Mountains. Attalus' increasing power provoked the Seleucids, and after a lengthy war he was forced to concede most of his hard-won lands in a treaty with Antiochus III in 213.

Undaunted, Attalus now turned his attention west. Since 219 he had been affiliated to the mainland Greek Aetolian League, whose war with the raffish King Philip V of Macedon (known in happier days as 'The Greeks' Beloved') had ended in defeat in 217. Two years later Philip signed a treaty with the then ascendant Carthage, but in 211 the Aetolian League, still bent on victory, responded by concluding an alliance with Rome. Attalus embraced their cause. In 210 he captured the island of Aegina, where the next year he and the Roman general met to discuss strategy. But the war did not go to plan and Attalus returned to Pergamum, which was being threatened by Philip's brother-in-law King Prusias the Lame of Bithynia. For four years the conflict consumed Attalus' attention, and when in 205 a blanket peace was made, it was met with general relief.

That same year Rome, whose priests had proclaimed that the presence of the Great Goddess of Mount Ida (near Troy) would make the city invincible, enlisted Attalus' help in acquiring from Phrygia a large black meteor worshipped as the embodiment of the great mother goddess Cybele. Later Roman poets imagined the goddess exclaiming to a hesitant Attalus, 'Rome deserves to be home to all the gods.' So in 204 the stone was installed in the temple of the Magna Mater (Great

Mother) on Rome's Palatine Hill and annual games instituted in her honour. Her priests, who castrated themselves in religious ecstasy, provided endless fascination to the more sober Romans.

In 201 war returned to the Aegean. When Philip captured Samos and besieged Chios, islands dangerously close to Pergamum, Attalus and his Rhodian allies met the Macedonians in a sea-battle off Erythrae. Cut off from his fleet and pursued by Philip's ships, Attalus fled for shore, where he had the royal coffers broken open and their treasures scattered on the beach to distract his pursuers. Philip's men nevertheless followed Attalus to Pergamum where, finding the citadel impregnable, they devastated the surrounding countryside. Attalus sought help from Rome. It did not come, but already Philip had moved on. Next year his confederates invaded Attica. Athens desperately appealed to the Aetolian League. By chance Attalus was close by on Aegina. His arrival in Athens was met with a hero's welcome. He processed up the Sacred Way, feted by crowds of cheering citizens, to offer sacrifice for victory on the Acropolis. Later the Athenians named a new tribe in his honour.

In 200, with Carthage defeated, Rome finally declared war on Philip and summoned Attalus, now nearly seventy years old, to support it. In a lengthy campaign which threatened to engulf the whole Aegean neither side struck a decisively crushing blow. Then in 198 Philip's allies the Peloponnesian Achaean League announced that they were considering switching sides. A team of negotiators met them at Sicyon. It included Attalus, who so impressed the Achaeans that they erected a colossal statue of him in the agora, inaugurated sacrifices in his honour and enlisted their troops to his cause. Nonetheless, they failed to capture hostile Corinth, and early the next year a delegation went to Thebes to try to win Boeotian backing. Attalus was first to speak. Reminding his hosts of his services to Greece, he was warming to his theme when he suddenly collapsed, one side entirely paralysed by a massive stroke. He was taken back to Pergamum, where he died that autumn. His throne passed peacefully to his son Eumenes II. Thanks to its alliances the kingdom thrived, its artistic life flourished, and when Eumenes' grandson Attalus III died without heirs in 133, he shrewdly bequeathed Pergamum to Rome.

In autumn 197, as Attalus lay dying at Pergamum, Rome's elephants defeated Philip in the mists at Cynoscephalae. Rome allowed the humbled Macedonian monarch to keep his throne, but forced him to become a Roman ally; and in 195 they ordered him to march against his former confederate, the Spartan king Nabis, in a war whose surprising victor would be neither Nabis, Philip nor a Roman, but an adopted citizen of Megalopolis.

Under Attalus I, Pergamene art attained remarkable heights: this Roman copy of a victory monument shows a Gaul committing suicide, having first killed his wife.

PHILOPOEMEN (253–183)
Statesman and General

One Roman praised Philopoemen, saying that after him Greece produced no
great man worthy of his country's name, but that he was the last of the Greeks.

Plutarch, *Life of Philopoemen*, 1

Faced with the rise of Rome, some Greeks remembered past glories with
nostalgia. Among them was Philopoemen, adopted son of the Peloponnesian city
of Megalopolis and devotee of the Theban general **Epaminondas**. Philopoemen's
father Creugas was a Mantinean exile. When Creugas died the tall, slim-
waisted yet somewhat plain-featured boy was adopted by Cleander, a leading
Megalopolitan, who entrusted the boy's education to two local philosophers.
Products of the Academy, both were zealous champions of liberty and democracy,
and inculcated in Philopoemen a love of thrift and honest toil which led him in
later life to enjoy working on his smallholding. But in these troubled times war
soon impinged on Philopoemen's life and, keen to devote his life to the heroic
ideal of fighting for his city, he was soon devouring books on tactics and the
campaigns of **Alexander III**.

In 223 Megalopolis was attacked by the Spartan king Cleomenes III.
Thanks to his land redistribution, austerity measures and military reforms,
Sparta was regaining the status it had enjoyed before **Pyrrhus'** invasion of 272.
Now, eager to expand into the Peloponnesian territories of the Achaean League,
Cleomenes occupied its capital Megalopolis' agora in a night attack. Entering
history for the first time, Philopoemen organized a mass evacuation of the
bewildered citizens, resisting Spartan attack even when his horse was shot from
under him. Once they were safely in the nearby city of Messene, he persuaded
his compatriots to resist Cleomenes' peace offers, suggesting that this would lead
to enslavement.

Uniting with a league of Greek poleis led by the Macedonian king Antigonus
III Doson, Philopoemen and the Achaeans joined battle with the Spartans
near Sellasia in the foothills of Mount Parnon. Discipline was far from tight;
communications failed; and seeing his allies dangerously pressed Philopoemen
wilfully ignored orders and led a cavalry charge. Later, as he dismounted to fight
on foot, both his thighs were skewered by a javelin. But he simply snapped it
in two, removed the pieces and rejoined the rout and massacre of the Spartans.
Praising Philopoemen's pluck, Antigonus offered him a high command in his own
army. He refused.

Instead, Philopoemen sailed to Crete where he spent the next ten years fighting as a mercenary while furthering Macedon's interests on the island. When he returned in 210 he found the Achaeans, as a result of their alliance with Antigonus' successor Philip V, at war not only with the more northern Aetolian League but with Rome. As Achaean cavalry commander, Philopoemen rode at Philip's side, and by the banks of the River Larissus near Elis he increased his kudos by transfixing the enemy commander with his spear. In the months that followed Philopoemen restructured, re-equipped and revitalized the Achaean army, for Sparta was stirring once again. After Sellasia, Cleomenes had fled to Alexandria, and an ambitious mercenary called Machanidas had overthrown the constitution and proclaimed himself Sparta's sole king. Now he was keen to expand his rule across the Peloponnese by defeating the Achaean League. In 207, when he attacked one of their cities, Mantinea, Philopoemen's army met him nearby. The battle ended only when the two commanders fought in single combat. As Machanidas' horse struggled up a ditch Philopoemen drove his spear deep into the Spartan's chest, a moment commemorated in a bronze sculpture dedicated by the victorious Achaeans at Delphi. Soon afterwards, at the Nemean Games, Philopoemen was lionized as the saviour of Greece. His name alone inspired such confidence that later, when the Achaeans switched allegiance, Philip, in terror, tried to poison him. For now, though, Philopoemen continued to harry the Spartans as they tried to take Messene; and after a protracted war in 201 he put a temporary end to their ambitions by defeating Nabis, the Spartan king who, like his predecessor Machanidas, had installed himself

Pierre-Jean-David d'Anger's statuette of Philopoemen (1837) shows the general, heroically nude, plucking a javelin from his thigh at the battle of Sellasia.

as sole and unconstitutional ruler. But in 199, despite signs that Nabis' hunger for power remained unchecked, Philopoemen responded to a request for help from the people of Gortyn in Crete and once more departed for that island. When he returned to the mainland six years later he found that Greek life and politics had radically changed. The Achaeans were now allied to Rome, and had welcomed their legions into the Peloponnese; and in Sparta Nabis was staging a last stand.

During Philopoemen's Cretan sojourn Nabis had enjoyed mixed success. Alliances with first Philip and then Rome had soured, but, taking heart from the legions' temporary withdrawal from Greece in 194, Nabis had regrouped. Now reappointed strategos of the Achaean League, Philopoemen was tasked with eradicating him. Initially his efforts failed, and when he did enjoy success the newly returned Roman general Flaminius not only jealously prevented him from pressing his advantage but made peace with Sparta. In truth Rome had other concerns. The Aetolian League had allied with the Seleucid king Antiochus III (protector of Rome's bête noire Hannibal), who was even now invading mainland Greece. But Antiochus was trounced at Thermopylae in 191 and driven back to Anatolia, where, after another three years of repeated defeats, he surrendered.

Meanwhile, in 192 Nabis reneged on his treaty with Rome and appealed for help to the Aetolians. Instead, they murdered him and occupied Sparta. In the confusion Philopoemen too marched south, and with a judicious mix of promises and threats he secured Sparta's allegiance to the Achaean League. For a time Philopoemen championed Sparta's cause against Roman interference, but faced with renascent Spartan nationalism he was forced to act severely. In 188 he demolished Sparta's walls, annulled what remained of its constitution, abolished the Agoge and sold 3,000 of its most recalcitrant citizens into slavery. In Megalopolis he used the money raised by the sale to build a portico.

Five years later Messene rebelled from the Achaean League. Philopoemen, old and ill, bestirred himself for battle once again. In fighting near Messene he was thrown from his horse and captured. Led through the city, he was flung in chains into an airless subterranean cell grimly nicknamed the *Thesaurus* (Treasury), where he was forced to drink hemlock. Grief-stricken, the Achaeans overran Messene, threw their prisoners into chains and took their revenge. Recovering Philopoemen's corpse, they cremated it and ceremonially conducted the ashes home to Megalopolis. As the honour guard of cavalry, resplendent in full armour, clattered north through Achaea's towns and villages, the streets were thronged with mourners desperate to touch his urn. At his tomb, where his ashes were buried in state ceremonial, the prisoners of war were stoned to death.

Nabis' Wife

The historian **Polybius** recounts how Sparta's despotic and avaricious king Nabis devised a curious automaton, dressed in rich robes and formed in the likeness of his wife Apega. Should any Spartan refuse his requests for money, Nabis introduced him to the automaton, quipping, 'If I can't persuade you, I think Apega will.' Believing it to be the queen the hapless victim would offer his hand in greeting, at which the automaton would throw its arms around him and hug him in a close embrace. But beneath the robes, the arms and breasts were bristling with iron spikes. As Nabis turned a handle the automaton drew in its victim ever tighter until he agreed to whatever the king requested.

Though powerless to resist Rome's advance, Philopoemen warned constantly of its ambitions, prophesying that its influence would spell the end of Greek independence. Less than forty years after his death Romans had annexed Greece and would have destroyed Philopoemen's tomb had not one man, the historian Polybius, persuaded them against it. His words were surely passionate. For as a youth Polybius had carried his great hero's urn, garlanded in wreaths and ribbons, on its final journey from Messene, little knowing that in his lifetime he would see Philopoemen's prophecy come true.

POLYBIUS (200–118)
Politician and Historian

[As Carthage burned] Scipio quoted: 'The day will come when sacred Troy will fall and Priam and his people all be killed.' When Polybius asked what he meant, Scipio quite openly confessed that when he thought of human fate he feared for Rome.

Appian, Punic Wars, 132

Politics was in Polybius' blood. His father Lycortas was an influential Megalopolitan, a close associate of **Philopoemen**, and in 183 the seventeen-year-old Polybius probably rode with the cavalry in the battle for Messene, from where he carried the general's ashes home to Megalopolis. Later, he idolized Philopoemen in a three-volume biography, a self-confessed 'encomium, a rather exaggerated account of his achievements'.

The young Polybius was impressive. Polished and well-educated, he was considered sufficiently distinguished by the age of twenty to serve on an embassy to Alexandria; while at thirty he was appointed second-in-command of the Achaean League. His period of office coincided with renewed hostilities between Macedon and Rome, which viewed the policies of Philip V's successor, Perseus, as provocative. A war, which began in 171, ended in 168 at Pydna when the Macedonian phalanx was almost annihilated by Rome's well-drilled legions. Macedon was partitioned, its most patriotic families deported and Perseus led in triumph through the streets of Rome. When Epirus fell the next year, many of its citizens were sold into slavery. Although the Achaean League stayed scrupulously uninvolved, for the Romans nothing less than active backing was enough. In 167 a thousand of the League's best men were rounded up and sent as hostages to Rome. Among them was Polybius. An advocate of neutrality, he now paid the price.

In fact, he was well treated. Clever and beguiling, Polybius won access to the homes of Rome's elite, and before long was employed to tutor the sons of Pydna's victor Aemilius Paullus, forming such an attachment to his son Scipio Aemilianus that he boasted that their bond was famous throughout 'Italy, Greece and beyond'. For a Greek with an eye to history it was a heady friendship, allowing access to state archives in the pursuit of research and enabling Polybius to witness at first hand the fall of a mighty civilization. Under the peace terms following Hannibal's defeat in 201, the Carthaginians had been compelled to pay Rome an annual indemnity for fifty years. Now that this period was over, each side watched the other with suspicion. In 149, as the senator Cato urged tirelessly that 'Carthage must be destroyed', Rome found excuses to attack its old enemy. After an uncertain start, in 147 a new general was sent to take command: Scipio Aemilianus. With him sailed Polybius.

Having already given Scipio sound political advice ('never leave the Forum without making a new friend'), Polybius proved his tactical worth, too. He was a great admirer of **Archimedes**, and like him was a keen deviser of military stratagems, inventing a system to deliver encrypted signals over long distances using code books and torches. In 146, after a gruelling siege, Carthage fell. At Scipio's side, Polybius witnessed the general Hasdrubal's surrender, his wife's desperate suicide (in shame she killed their children before hurling herself into the blazing temple of the healing god Eshmoun) and the wholesale destruction of the city. While the surviving Carthaginians were sent into slavery, statues, costly furniture and fabrics, all the treasures of the once-proud city, were loaded onto Roman ships. The pillage lasted for seventeen days before the city was set ablaze. By the time the last Romans left, not a trace of once-proud Carthage remained.

Soon Greece, too, would fall. With Carthage destroyed and with an eye to further wealth, Rome began provoking the Achaean League. As winter neared, the League took up arms. In response the consul Mummius marched on Corinth, the richest city on mainland Greece. In battle the Achaean cavalry turned tail and fled; their phalanx held out longer, but with grim inevitability the Roman legions broke their ranks. Corinth shared the fate of Carthage, and soon Polybius was watching as the first of a great haul of Greece's artworks were roughly seized and packed in crates, ready to be shipped to Rome. No other polis dared resist. Greek independence, for which its peoples had fought countless wars, was over. For Athens and many Achaean states the year quite literally marked the end: records called the next year 'Year One'.

Respected by both sides, Polybius succeeded in lightening the yoke, curbing the victors' worst excesses and helping smooth the transition to occupation. At least six grateful cities set up statues in his honour. But already he was planning his *Universal History*, an account of Rome's growth to supremacy. By 144 he had left Greece again and was immersed in research: scouring Rome's public records; interviewing veterans, generals and politicians; travelling to sites of battles and campaigns to understand at first hand how geography had helped shape outcomes. From Sardis to Alexandria and across the Alps (in an attempt to reconstruct the route of Hannibal's attack on Italy), Polybius 'asked what had happened from those who had been present and personally inspected the terrain'.

The resulting forty books (of which only five survive in their entirety) were a tour de force. Although at their core were fifty-three momentous years from 220 (just before the outbreak of Rome's second war with Carthage) to the battle of Pydna in 168, they encompassed much else as well: an eyewitness account of Carthage's defeat, an analysis of the Roman constitution, digressions on geography, staunch criticisms of the work of fellow historians, all underpinned by the author's struggle to understand why history had turned out as it had. Part of the explanation, Polybius believed, lay in Rome's 'mixed constitution' and its avoidance of an otherwise inevitable political decline from monarchy to tyranny, aristocracy, oligarchy, democracy and finally mob rule – a deterioration which is curiously similar to Hesiod's cycle of the Ages. For Polybius, truth based on methodical research was more important than seductive style or entertaining speeches and digressions. Myths and gods play no part in his *Universal History* though, true to the spirit of the age, Tyche does. So does character. Thus, as **Xenophon** did for the subject of his *Education of Cyrus* (or Lysimachus for his study of *The Education of Attalus I*), he mined the early life of Scipio to try and unearth the causes of his greatness. That he praises Scipio and disparages his own detractors is to be expected: even Polybius could not escape the conventions of his day. As he admitted (and we would surely agree if such famous ancient works as Timaeus' *Life of Pyrrhus* or Theopompus' fifty-eight-volume *History of Philip II* survived), biography was closer to encomium than to objective history.

Polybius died, aged eighty-two, when he was thrown from his horse as he returned home from a country ride. Recently he had found good reason to reflect on Tyche. In 133, in part prompted by Attalus III's bequest, Rome was convulsed by the beginnings of social unrest. Led by Scipio Aemilianus' brother-in-law Tiberius Gracchus, the People demanded greater rights and the redistribution of wealth and state-owned land. It was not a cause which the patrician Scipio could espouse. Welcoming the news of Gracchus' assassination, he was not afraid to confront the mob. When he was found mysteriously dead on the morning of an important speech, no one doubted that he had been murdered. The conqueror of Carthage had met a squalid death. Facing his assassins, Polybius would possibly not have been surprised. For Tyche must have her way. As a student of Polybius he knew the opening of his *Universal History*:

> *For public life there is no better education than history, and nothing can more readily teach us how bravely to endure the fickleness of Fortune than the record of other men's misfortunes.*

A Roman copy of a lost second-century relief shows
Polybius in heroic pose, a spear resting on his
shoulder, his shield and helmet at his feet.

Chapter 9

Lives in
a Mirror

Greece, once captured, captured her fierce conqueror and introduced her arts to rustic Latium.

Horace, *Epistles*, 2.1.156–57

I n the century following Attalus III's bequest of Pergamum to Rome in 133, the Mediterranean world continued to be wracked by war. Initially uncertain how to respond to the consequences of a rapidly expanding empire, the Senate and People of Rome found themselves first fighting their Italian allies, then embroiled in civil wars between ambitious generals vying for total power and defending their newly won territories from attack.

In 87, with Mithridates, king of Pontus, threatening the Roman provinces of Asia and Greece, Rome's general Sulla marched on rebel-held Athens. The next year, after a long siege, the starving citizens sued for terms. If they hoped that by reminding Sulla of their ancient glories they might persuade him to treat them leniently they were wrong. Sulla was unimpressed. Athens' walls were undermined and in the night the legions poured through the now opened gates. Soon hobnailed sandals splashed through the blood which, we are told, gushed down the lanes near the Acropolis. Much of the city was burned and many of its artworks looted. In battles at Chaeronea and Orchomenus in Boeotia, Sulla crushed all Greek resistance, and across Asia and the Aegean his troops reimposed Roman rule, exacting heavy penalties.

A generation later, Rome's civil wars again spilled into Greece: at Pharsalus in 48 Caesar crushed his rival Pompey; at Philippi in 42 Octavian took vengeance on Caesar's assassins; and in 31 off Actium he smashed the fleet of his arch-rivals, Antony and Cleopatra, not only the last Ptolemaic queen but the last Hellenistic ruler of an independent Greek kingdom. Three years after her 'suicide' in 30,

One of the most sublime examples of Roman art, the Ara Pacis Augustae (Altar of Augustan Peace), consecrated in 9 BC, borrows Greek iconography to proclaim Roman dominance over the Hellenistic world.

Octavian became Rome's first emperor, and taking the title Augustus heralded centuries of Roman Peace (*pax Romana*) throughout much of the Greek world. While in Alexandria after Actium, the victorious Octavian (like countless dignitaries before him) had been taken to view **Alexander III's** body in its Soma. As he bent over it, he snapped off the nose. If this was a deliberate attempt to break Alexander's talismanic power, it failed. Although the might of Rome had conquered Greece, centuries of Greek influence would permeate Roman culture.

While cities like Athens, Pergamum and Alexandria found new roles as heritage sites or university towns, and once-independent states like Macedon turned into Roman provinces, a passion for Greek art gripped Rome. Looted statues and paintings adorned not just the city's temples but the chic villas of the rich and powerful. Greek architecture flowered in Rome, and even the pragmatic Augustus was shamed into transforming city-centre buildings from native brick to Grecian marble. Greek technology fascinated, too. A sundial 'liberated' from Catana intrigued Rome's public even though, angled incorrectly for Rome's latitude, it told the wrong time; while captured siege engines were paraded in triumph, their workings to be studied, refined and utilized in new and even more deadly machines. It was arguably Julius Caesar who most Hellenized Rome. His visit to Alexandria was more stimulating than Octavian's, his relationship with Cleopatra more productive. Returning home he brought specialists from the Museum (including the astronomer Sosthenes, who helped him reform the calendar), stratagems for draining marshes and plans for a library to house both Latin and Greek literature.

By the time of Caesar, Greek literature had long been known in Rome. In the third century a Sicilian Greek – known by his Latinized name, Livius Andronicus (*c.* 280–*c.* 200), and perhaps enslaved in 272 shortly after **Pyrrhus** had abandoned Taras to the Romans – translated the *Odyssey* into Latin verse and introduced Greek drama into Rome. Although the titles of his *Gladiolus* (Little Sword) and *Ludius* (Gladiator) were Latin, in form they resembled the comedies of **Menander** and greatly influenced Latin authors such as Plautus (*c.* 254–186) and Terence (?185–159). Livius also wrote (or translated) tragedies with plots straight from Greek mythology (*Achilles, Ajax* and *The Trojan Horse*), which heralded Rome's complex literary relationship with Attic tragedy. Others whom Greeks once called barbarians enjoyed their tragedies now, too. In 53 Orodes II, king of the Parthians, the Persian peoples who had now conquered the Seleucids and whose empire stretched west to the Euphrates, admired a performance of **Euripides'** *Bacchae* which used as a prop the recently severed head of his enemy, Rome's general Crassus.

Meanwhile, the native Italian Ennius (*c.* 239–*c.* 169) wrote *Annales* (Annals), a Homeric-style epic tracing the thousand-year history of Rome from the sack of Troy. Together with Homer and Apollonius, *Annales* inspired Virgil (70–19) to write the most quintessentially Roman epic of them all, the *Aeneid*. Other Greek genres were avidly adopted, too. Virgil used Theocritus' bucolic poetry as the model for his *Eclogues*, while Hesiod's *Works and Days* influenced his *Georgics*. In lyric poetry Catullus (*c.* 84–54) translated and adapted Sappho's verse, acknowledging his debt by referring to his beloved as 'Lesbia'. Other Greek lyricists influenced Horace (65–8), Tibullus (*c.* 55–19) and Ovid (43–AD 17), protégés of Augustus' 'Minister of Arts', Maecenas (?70–8). A century later, the rhetorician Quintilian (*c.* AD 36–*c.* AD 100) could boast, 'In Elegy, we rival Greeks.'

This rivalry was felt in historiography and biography, too. Roman historiography was unknown until the late third century, when Quintus Fabius Pictor traced Rome's history from its foundation to the defeat of Hannibal. Instructively, he wrote it in Greek. But not until Livy (59–AD 17) composed his sweeping history of Rome in 142 books did Roman historiography truly find its voice. Both Livy and his successor, the brilliantly wry Tacitus (*c.* AD 56–AD 117), drew deeply on Greek models, their narratives peppered with speeches, character assessments and geographical digressions. Tacitus also wrote biography, or rather encomium *à la Grecque*, in the form of a eulogy on the life of his father-in-law the general Agricola.

'It is hard for thee to kick against the pricks': Michelangelo's fresco, *The Conversion of Saul* (*c.* 1542–45), shows the apostle struck profoundly (if temporarily) blind on the road to Damascus.

Biography had to wait well over a millennium until it approached the form we recognize today. Content to borrow from the Greeks, the universal historian Nepos (*c.* 110–*c.* 25) wrote anecdotal *Lives of Famous Men*, whose scope included both Romans and Greeks. In his preface he announced his purpose: to educate 'those [Romans] who are ignorant of Greek and so judge all men by their own standards'. More influential were the biographies of the Greek philosopher and polymath Plutarch (*c.* AD 46–*c.* AD 120). Seeking both to celebrate and reconcile the two cultures, he composed a series of *Parallel Lives*, pairs of biographies of Greeks and Romans with similar characters and achievements – Alexander III and Julius Caesar, Demosthenes and Cicero, Lysander and Sulla and so on – most of them accompanied by a brief comparative essay. Even mythical characters appeared in his list, like Rome's and Athens' early kings, Romulus and Theseus.

To *be* Greek had always been to *speak* Greek, and it was perhaps the widespread adoption of the Greek language which in the end did most to propagate Greek culture. After Alexander, Koine became the *lingua franca* of the Greek east, while the worship of Dionysus unified the eastern Mediterranean. By the first century, Roman admiration for Greek culture meant that Greek became the preferred language for their elite. Indeed, Caesar's biographer Suetonius took pains to record that as he fell to the assassins' blades the quintessential Roman's last words were not Shakespeare's Latin *'et tu, Brute'*, but the Greek *'kai su, o pai'* ('even you, my son?').

To ensure their widest promulgation the first books of Christianity, too, were composed in Koine – not only the encomiastic biographies of Christ that are the Gospels but the letters of Paul and the brief history of the spread of early Christianity, *Acts of the Apostles*. In time the new religion would not only adopt many useful Greek ideas and adapt Greek gods and heroes as its saints but suppress many inconvenient Greek truths and discoveries, reverting to a concept of history informed not by Thucydides' rational causation but by Herodotus' divine intervention.

Already the account of the conversion of Paul (or Saul as he then was) to Christianity, describing his experience of a miracle on the road to Damascus, plunges us back five centuries to the world of Epizelus with which this book began. For, in the magisterial King James translation:

Suddenly there shined round about him a light from heaven: And he fell to the earth, and heard a voice saying unto him, Saul, Saul, why persecutest thou me? And he said, Who art thou, Lord? And the Lord said, I am Jesus whom thou persecutest: it is hard for thee to kick against the pricks… And Saul arose from the earth; and when his eyes were opened, he saw no man.

No one can look with impunity on the divine. Saul had been struck profoundly (if temporarily) blind.

Consciously or not, the words ascribed to Jesus allude directly to Greek tragedy: 'Better to give prayer and sacrifice than to kick against the pricks, for you are a mortal and Dionysus is divine.' Thus just outside Damascus the risen Christ, whose blood was transubstantiated in the grape, referenced Euripides' *Bacchae*, and the Greek world stepped sublimely through the looking glass towards a transformed future.

Maps

BELOW

Map of the Greek world from Magna Graecia
to the coast of Asia Minor.

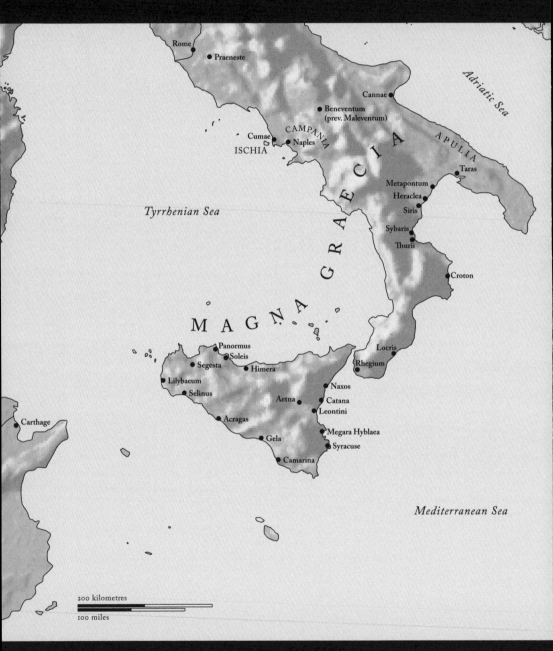

Rome

Praeneste

Cannae

Beneventum
(prev. Maleventum)

Adriatic Sea

CAMPANIA

APULIA

Cumae
Naples

ISCHIA

Taras

Metapontum

Heraclea

Siris

Tyrrhenian Sea

Sybaris

Thurii

Croton

M A G N A

G R A E C I A

Panormus

Soleis

Locris

Segesta

Himera

Rhegium

Lilybaeum

Naxos

Selinus

Aetna

Catana

Leontini

Acragas

Megara Hyblaea

Gela

Syracuse

Carthage

Camarina

Mediterranean Sea

200 kilometres

100 miles

Byzantium

Bosphorus

THRACE

Strymon

Abdera

Amphipolis

THASOS

Aegospotamoi

Cyzicus

Mieza Pella

MACEDON

Stagira

SAMOTHRACE

Granicus

Aegae

TENEDOS

Sestus

TROAD

Olynthus

Sigeum Troy

Pydna

Athos

Assos

THESSALY

LEMNOS

LYDIA

EPIRUS

MAGNESIA

Aegean Sea

Pergamum

Dodona

Arginusae

LESBOS

Eresus

Aegae

SCYROS

Mytilene

CORCYRA

Clazomenae

Corypedium Sardis

Actium

IONIA

CARIA

PHOCIS

EUBOEA

CHIOS

ITHACA

LOCRIS

Delphi

BOEOTIA

Erythrae

Teos

Colophon

Thebes

Ephesus *Maeander*

Athens

SAMOS

Olympia

Corinth

CEOS

RHENEA

Mycale

Miletus

PELOPONNESE

Argos

DELOS

Halicarnassus

MESSENIA

Sparta

PAROS

NAXOS

COS

Amyclae

MELOS

Cnidus

RHODES

CRETE

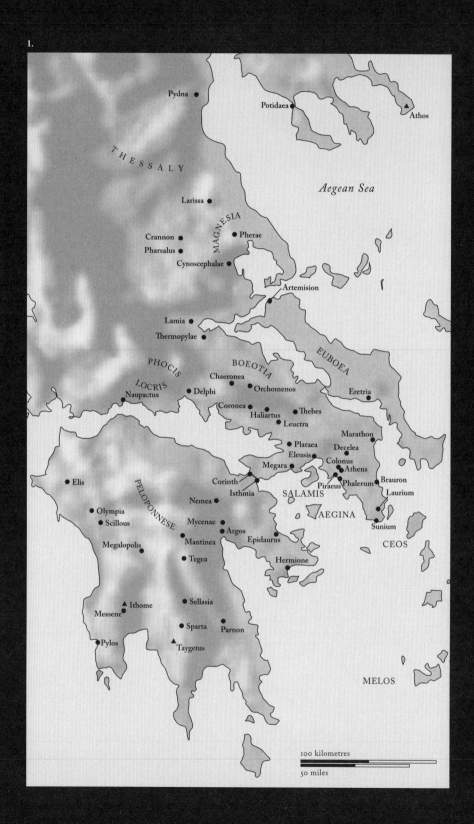

1.

Pydna

Potidaea

Athos

T H E S S A L Y

Aegean Sea

Larissa

MAGNESIA

Crannon
Pherae
Pharsalus
Cynoscephalae

Artemision

Lamia
Thermopylae

PHOCIS
BOEOTIA
EUBOEA

Chaeronea
LOCRIS
Delphi
Orchomenos
Eretria
Naupactus
Coronea
Thebes
Haliartus
Leuctra

Marathon
Plataea
Decelea
Eleusis
Colonus
Megara
Athens
Corinth
Piraeus
Phalerum
Brauron
Isthmia
SALAMIS
Laurium
Elis
Nemea
PELOPONNESE
AEGINA
Olympia
Mycenae
Sunium
Scillous
Argos
Epidaurus
CEOS
Megalopolis
Mantinea
Tegea
Hermione

Ithome
Sellasia
Messene
Sparta
Pylos
Parnon
Taygetus

MELOS

100 kilometres

50 miles

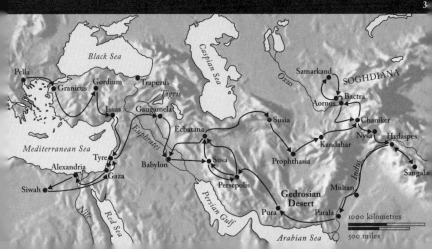

Glossary

Achaean League confederacy of Peloponnesian states, principally existing between 280 and 146.

Acropolis literally 'high city', often an easily defensible rocky outcrop, the site of temples, most famously the Acropolis of Athens.

Agoge brutal educational system for training Spartan males.

Agora marketplace and social hub of polis life.

Alcmaeonid member of one of the most wealthy and powerful Athenian families, which included Pericles and Alcibiades.

Artemision temple of Artemis (at Ephesus).

Ataraxia freedom from anxiety.

Athene Polias Athene in her role as protectress of the city of Athens.

Athene Promachus Athene 'who fights in the front line of battle'.

Aulos (*pl.* **-oi**) flute.

Barbarian literally, someone whose language sounds like a sheep's bleating, thus a non-Greek speaker.

Boeotarch one of a number of officials elected annually to rule Thebes and its territories.

Boule Athenian legislative council, consisting of 500 citizens chosen by lot.

Delian League alliance of mainly Ionian poleis, under the leadership of Athens, formed in the fifth century in the aftermath of the Persian Wars.

Demos the People, often a euphemism for a city's poor or lower classes.

Dionysia or 'City Dionysia': international dramatic festival of Dionysus held in Athens in March/April.

Dithyramb hymn to Dionysus.

Elenchic method philosophical method of eliciting the truth through question and answer.

Encomium speech or writings in praise of the dead.

Epinicean ode Poem celebrating a victor in one of the panhellenic games.

Ephor one of five Spartan 'overseers', or senior magistrates, elected annually, with powers extending even over the kings.

Eponymous archon leading political official in Athens, after whom the year was named.

Gerousia Spartan 'senate': a body of thirty elders with the power to propose and veto motions in the Assembly.

Gymnosophist literally 'naked philosopher': one of a number of Indian *sadhus* encountered by Alexander III during his conquests.

Hades god of the Underworld; by extension, the Underworld itself.

Helot member of the Spartan underclass of slaves.

Hero human being accorded semi-divine status for his actions, and as such the object of veneration.

Hetaera (*pl.* **-ae**) courtesan.

Homoioi literally 'equals', Sparta's elite citizen class.

Hoplite heavily armoured infantry soldier equipped with a large round shield (*hoplon*)

Isonomia literally 'equality under the law' – often interpreted as meaning 'democracy'.

Koine literally 'common': a form of Greek, originating in the court of Philip II of Macedon, which became prevalent across the Hellenistic world.

Kudos glory or praise won for great achievements.

Kyrios (male) head of family; guardian of its womenfolk.

Lenaea dramatic festival of Dionysus held for a domestic audience in Athens in January/February.

Logographos (*pl.* **-oi**) in the sixth century, a chronicler or antiquarian. Later, a speech-writer.

Metempsychosis transmigration of the soul from one body to another after death.

Metic foreign national living and working in Athens.

Metropolis (*pl.* **-eis**) literally 'mother city': the founding city of a colony.

Ostracism Athenian process by which a leading politician could be banished for ten years without suffering any loss of money, possessions or prestige.

Panathenaic Festival Athenian religious and athletic festival including a procession to the Acropolis in honour of Athene. The four-yearly Greater Panathenaic Festival aspired to be part of the circuit of the panhellenic games.

Panhellenic Games international athletic games open to all Greeks; those held at Olympia, Delphi, Nemea and Isthmia were the most prestigious.

Phalanx hoplites or heavy infantry drawn up in a rectangular formation, usually to fight.

Polis (*pl.* **-eis**) city-state: i.e. an area of agricultural land together with the urban centre which governed it.

Porne common prostitute.

Probouloi magistrates with special powers appointed in Athens in 411 to address the crisis situation of the Peloponnesian War.

Proskynesis ritual gesture of obeisance associated in Greece with gods, but in Persia with the Great King.

Proxenos a citizen of one polis who represents the interests of another.

Prytaneum town hall or administrative centre of a polis.

Satrap Persian regional governor.

Satyr play light-hearted comedy based loosely on mythology, in which the chorus represented satyrs, rampantly anarchic half-men half-beast followers of Dionysus, performed after a tragic trilogy.

Soma literally 'Body', the name given to Alexander's mausoleum in Alexandria.

Sophist philosopher, usually one who travelled widely and earned money as a professional teacher. Originally the term possessed none of its later pejorative overtones.

Stoa Poikile 'Painted Stoa': a colonnaded arcade in Athens, famous for its paintings of famous events from history and mythology.

Strategos (*pl.* **-oi**) general (one of ten elected annually in Classical Athens). Later, one of the leading officials of the Achaean League.

Talent unit of weight or currency, in Athens equalling 57 lbs (26 kg). One silver Attic talent was the equivalent of nine years' earnings for a skilled workman.

Tetralogy series of four plays (three tragedies and a satyr play) performed on one day.

Trireme Greek warship with three banks of oars, and a reinforced metal 'beak' with which to ram enemy vessels.

Tyrannos (*pl.* **-oi**) in the sixth and early fifth centuries, sole (unelected) ruler of a polis, used almost interchangeably with 'king'. From the late fifth century onwards, a tyrant in the modern sense.

Xoanon sacred and often very ancient wooden statue of a deity.

Timeline

Entries referring to the subjects of the fifty lives are **bold**.

776	Olympic Games inaugurated.
c. 710	Foundation of Croton.
688	Foundation of Gela.
c. 657	Foundation of Byzantium.
632	Cylon's failed coup in Athens. Alcmaeonids exiled.
c. 630	Foundation of Cyrene.
post 630	**Birth of Sappho.**
?c. 605	**Birth of Peisistratus.**
c. 600	Foundation of Massalia.
594	Alcmaeonids return to Athens.
582	Pythian Games and Isthmian Games inaugurated.
c. 573	Nemean Games inaugurated.
c. 570	**Death of Sappho. Birth of Pythagoras.**
570	**Birth of Cleisthenes.**
561–556	**Peisistratus' first period as tyrannos of Athens.**
556	Greater Panathenaic Games inaugurated.
555–?	**Peisistratus' second period as tyrannos of Athens.**
c. 555	Miltiades the Elder becomes tyrannos of Chersonese. **Birth of Milo.**
547	Cyrus the Great of Persia defeats Croesus of Lydia to assume control of Ionia.
546	Alcmaeonids again exiled from Athens. **Peisistratus becomes tyrannos of Athens for third time.**
?540	**Milo's first victory at Olympia as a boy wrestler.**
c. 540	**Polycrates becomes tyrannos of Samos. Birth of Leonidas.**
?536–520	**Milo's run of Olympic victories as an adult wrestler.**
534	City Dionysia dramatic festival inaugurated in Athens.
530	**Polycrates makes an alliance with Cambyses of Persia. Pythagoras flees Samos for Croton.**
528	**Death of Peisistratus. Succession of Hippias as tyrannos of Athens.**
525	With Spartan help, Samian opposition tries unsuccessfully to oust Polycrates.
525/4	**Birth of Aeschylus.**
524	Cumae defeats an Italo-Etruscan army. **Birth of Themistocles.**
c. 522	**Birth of Pindar.**
522	**Death of Polycrates.**
521	Darius I becomes Great King of Persia.

c. 520	Cleomenes I accedes to throne in Sparta.
516	**Miltiades (the Younger) becomes tyrannos of Chersonese.**
514	Assassination of Hipparchus.
513	Darius I's expedition against Scythia.
c. 510	**Birth of Cimon.**
510	Croton defeats and destroys Sybaris. Scythians overrun Chersonese. Carthaginian victory over Greeks at Segesta. **Expulsion of Hippias from Athens. Start of Histiaeus' captivity in Persia.**
508	Sparta invades Attica and temporarily seizes Acropolis.
507	**Democratic reforms of Cleisthenes in Athens.** Athens offers earth and water to Persians at Sardis.
?507	**Death of Cleisthenes.**
506	Sparta's abortive mission to overthrow Athens' fledgling democracy.
499	Greek poleis of Ionia revolt against Persia.
498	Ionian and Athenian troops burn Sardis. **Histiaeus escapes from Persian captivity. Pindar's first victory ode performed.**
497/6	**Birth of Sophocles.**
c. 495	**Birth of Empedocles.**
495	**Birth of Pericles.**
?494	**Execution of Histiaeus by Persians.**
494	Sack of Miletus ends Ionian Revolt. Spartan victory over Argos at battle of Sepeia.
493	**Miltiades flees to Athens. Themistocles elected eponymous archon.**
492	First (abortive) Persian invasion of Greece.
491	**Gelon becomes tyrannos of Gela.**
490	Second Persian invasion of Greece defeated at battle of Marathon. **Miltiades elected strategos. Death of Hippias. Birth of Protagoras.**
489	Assassination of Cleomenes I. **Prosecution and death of Miltiades. Accession of Leonidas to throne of Sparta.**
c. 487	Ostracism introduced in Athens.
486	Comedies first performed at City Dionysia.
?c. 485	**Death of Pythagoras.**
c. 485	**Birth of Euripides.**
485	Xerxes becomes great king of Persia. Ostracism of Xanthippus. **Birth of Gorgias.**
c. 484	**Birth of Herodotus.**
483	Syracuse under Gelon takes control of neighbouring cities. Athens begins building new fleet.

c. 480	**Birth of Pheidias.**		Return of Cimon from exile.
480	Third Persian invasion of Greece. Battle of Thermopylae. Athens captured and burned. Greek victory over Persians at Salamis. Greek victory over Carthaginians at Himera. **Death of Leonidas at Thermopylae. Sophocles leads victory celebrations at Athens.**	450	Athenian expedition against Persians in Cyprus. Legislation restricting citizen rights in Athens. **Death of Cimon on campaign in Cyprus. Aspasia brought to Athens. Birth of Alcibiades.**
479	Greeks defeat Persians at battles of Plataea and Mycale. Athenian capture of Sestus from Persians.	449	Peace of Callias ends hostilities between Delian League and Persia.
478	Pausanias accused of collaborating with Persians. Delian League founded. **Death of Gelon. Accession of Hieron as tyrannos of Syracuse.**	448	Outbreak of Sacred War for control of Delphi, involving Sparta and Athens.
		c. 447	**Herodotus settles in Athens.**
476	**Cimon 'discovers' 'bones of Theseus' on Scyros.**	447	Athens defeated by Boeotia at battle of Coronea. **Alcibiades orphaned when his father is killed at Coronea.**
474	Etruscans defeated at battle of Cumae by Syracusans and south Italian Greeks.	*c*. 446	**Birth of Aristophanes.**
472	The tyrannos Thrasydeus overthrown in Acragas. Athens prevents Naxos from leaving Delian League. **Pericles produces first performance of Aeschylus'** *Persians*.	446	Thirty Years Peace between Sparta and Athens. **Foundation of Pericles' 'panhellenic' colony of Thurii.**
		445	**Pericles divorces his wife in order to live with Aspasia. Birth of Lysias.**
471	**Themistocles ostracized and flees to Persia.**	*c*. 422	**Death of Pindar.**
c. 470	**Birth of Aspasia.**	442	Inauguration of Lenaea comic drama festival in Athens. **Ostracism of Pericles' rival, Thucydides son of Milesias. Pericles unsuccessfully prosecuted for misappropriation of Delian League funds. Sophocles appointed one of ten Hellanotimai. Euripides wins first prize at City Dionysia for first time.**
470	**Pindar's victory ode for Hieron celebrates Greek victories of Himera, Cumae, Salamis and Plataea.**
?469	**Birth of Socrates.**
468	**Cimon engineers Sophocles' first dramatic victory at the City Dionysia.**	*c*. 441	**First performance of Sophocles'** *Antigone*.
?467	Greek victory over Persians at battle of Eurymedon.	441–431	**Pericles elected strategos annually.**
		441	**Sophocles appointed strategos.**
467	**Death of Hieron.**	440	Athens crushes revolt by Samos from Delian League. **Pericles and Sophocles lead Samian campaign.**
466	Establishment of democracy in Syracuse.
465	Murder of Xerxes and accession of Artaxerxes I as Great King of Persia.	438	**Consecration of Parthenon and Pheidias' statue of Athene. First performance of Euripides'** *Alcestis*.
464	Earthquake at Sparta. **Cimon assists Spartans in crushing Helot rebellion.**
		c. 435	**Death of Empedocles.**
463	**Cimon prosecuted by Pericles for dereliction of duty, but acquitted.**	432	Athens imposes a trade embargo on Megara. Athenian victory over Corinth at battle of Potidaea. **Socrates saves Alcibiades' life at Potidaea.**
462	Reform of Council of the Areopagus in Athens.
461	**Cimon ostracized.**	431	Beginning of (second) Peloponnesian War. **First performance of Euripides'** *Medea*.
?460	**Birth of Zeuxis.**
460	Outbreak of (first) Peloponnesian War. Start of Athens' Egyptian campaign.	*c*. 430	**Death of Pheidias. Lysias emigrates to Thurii. Birth of Xenophon.**
459	**Death of Themistocles while Persian governor of Magnesia.**	430	Outbreak of plague in Athens. **Pericles fails to be re-elected strategos; delivers his Funeral Oration.**
458	**Aeschylus'** *Oresteia* **first performed.**	429	**Death of Pericles from plague. First performance of Sophocles'** *Oedipus Tyrannos*. **Thucydides contracts plague, but survives.**
457	Spartan victory over Athens at battle of Tanagra.
456/5	**Death of Aeschylus in Gela.**	428	**First performance of Euripides'** *Hippolytus*.
454	Athenian defeat in Egypt. Delian League Treasury transferred to Athens.	*c*. 427	**Birth of Plato.**
		427	Athens defeats rebellious Lesbos. Civil war on Corcyra. **Gorgias arrives in Athens to**
451	Five-year truce between Athens and Sparta.

solicit aid for Leontini against Syracuse. First performance of Aristophanes' debut play, *Banqueters*.

426 | End of plague in Athens. **First performance of Aristophanes' *Babylonians*. Cleon prosecutes Aristophanes.**

425 | Athenian victory over Sparta at Pylos. **Cleon captures Spartan homoioi on Sphacteria. First performance of Euripides' *Hekabe* and Aristophanes' *Acharnians*.**

424 | Athens defeated by Boeotians at battle of Delium. Sparta captures Amphipolis from Athens. Spartan massacre of Helots. **Socrates serves on Delium campaign. Thucydides elected strategos, fails to prevent loss of Amphipolis. First performance of Aristophanes' *Knights*.**

423 | **Thucydides exiled from Athens.**

422 | Sparta prevents Athenian recapture of Amphipolis. **Death of Cleon at Amphipolis. Socrates serves on Amphipolis campaign.**

421 | Peace treaty between Athens and Sparta (Peace of Nicias).

420 | **Death of Protagoras.**

419 | **First performance of Aristophanes' *Clouds*.**

c. 418 | **Birth of Epaminondas.**

418 | Athenian defeat by Sparta at battle of Mantinea.

416 | Athenian capture of Melos. Last ostracism from Athens. **Alcibiades' victory in Olympic chariot race; Euripides composes victory ode to celebrate.**

415 | Athens sends an expedition to Sicily. **Alcibiades defects to Sparta. First performance of Euripides' *Trojan Women*.**

414 | **First performance of Aristophanes' *Birds*.**

413 | Defeat of Athenian Sicilian expedition. Thracian massacre of schoolboys at Mycalessus. Archelaus I assumes throne of Macedon.

412 | **Alcibiades defects to Persia. Lysias returns to Athens.**

412/11 | **Sophocles appointed one of ten probouloi overseeing Athenian war effort.**

411 | Suspension of democratic constitution in Athens in favour of oligarchic rule. Sparta signs treaty with Persians. **Alcibiades reinstated as strategos by Athenian troops in Ionia. First performance of Aristophanes' *Lysistrata* and *Thesmophoriazusae*.**

410 | Athenian victory over Spartan fleet at battle of Cyzicus. Restoration of Athenian democracy.

408 | **Gorgias' speech on Greek unity at Olympic Games. First performance of Euripides' *Orestes*. Euripides leaves Athens for court of Archelaus I of Macedon.**

?407 | **Plato becomes a follower of Socrates.**

407 | **Alcibiades returns to Athens; granted extraordinary powers. Lysander appointed Spartan strategos in Ephesus.**

406 | Athenian victory over Spartan fleet at battle of Arginusae. Trial and execution of Athenian strategoi. Carthaginians return in force to Sicily. **Lysander defeats Athenian navy at Ephesus. Alcibiades flees to Chersonese. Death of Euripides in Macedon.**

405 | Athenian fleet defeated by Spartans at battle of Aegospotamoi. Dionysius I becomes tyrannos of Syracuse. **Sophocles leads chorus in mourning Euripides' death. First performance of Euripides' *Bacchae* and Aristophanes' *Frogs*. Death of Sophocles.**

404 | Defeat of Athens ends Peloponnesian War. Athens' Long Walls destroyed; democracy suppressed and rule of Thirty Tyrannoi established. Artaxerxes II becomes Great King of Persia. **Socrates refuses to collaborate with Thirty Tyrannoi. Lysias escapes Thirty Tyrannoi to Megara. Death of Alcibiades in Phrygia.**

403 | Overthrow of Thirty Tyrannoi and restitution of democracy in Athens. **Lysias returns to Athens.**

402/1 | Death of Agis II provokes succession crisis in Sparta.

401 | Cyrus the Younger's expedition against Artaxerxes. Defeat and death of Cyrus at battle of Cunaxa. **March of the Ten Thousand under command of Xenophon. Xenophon joins Cyrus the Younger's expedition. First performance of Sophocles' *Oedipus at Colonus*.**

?c. 400 | **Death of Aspasia.**

400 | Agesilaus II becomes king in Sparta.

399 | Death of Archelaus I of Macedon. **Trial and execution of Socrates.**

397 | Dionysius I besieges Carthaginian city of Motya.

396 | Spartan victory over Persians at Sardis.

c. 395 | **Death of Thucydides.**

395 | Corinthian War begins. Theban victory over Sparta at battle of Haliartus. **Death of Lysander at Haliartus.**

394 | Spartan victory over Athens at battle of Coronea. **Xenophon fights with Spartans at Coronea, is exiled from Athens.**

393 | Athens rebuilds Long Walls.

?392 | **First performance of Aristophanes' *Assembly Women*.**

392 | **Lysias' Funeral Oration for Athenian war dead.**

388 | **First performance of Aristophanes' *Plutus*. Lysias' oration of Greek unity at Olympic Games. Plato travels to court of Dionysius I of Syracuse.**

c. 386	Death of Aristophanes.
386	Peace treaty brokered by Artaxerxes II (King's Peace) ends Corinthian War in return for ceding of Ionia to Persian control.
385/4	**Birth of Aristotle.**
384	**Birth of Demosthenes.**
382	Spartans occupies Thebes. Birth of Philip II of Macedon.
380	**Death of Gorgias. Death of Lysias.**
378	Pelopidas and his allies liberate Thebes. Founding of new Athenian League.
375	Birth of Olympias.
371	Theban victory over Sparta at battle of Leuctra. Founding of Megalopolis. **Xenophon takes refuge from Thebans in Corinth.**
c. 370	Founding of Pan-Arcadian League.
370	Jason of Pherae's abortive invasion of Greece.
370/69	Theban invasion of Laconia.
369	Founding of Messene. Philip II of Macedon taken as hostage to Thebes. **Epaminondas pardoned for exceeding limits of his command.**
368	Pelopidas captured by Alexander of Pherae.
367	Death of Dionysius I of Syracuse. **Epaminondas liberates Pelopidas from captivity. Plato's first visit to court of Dionysius II of Syracuse. Aristotle goes to Athens and the Academy. Birth of Ptolemy I.**
366	**Demosthenes' first speech in Athenian lawcourts.**
364	Sparta and Elis attack Pan-Arcadian League at Olympic Games.
362	Victory of Thebes and Pan-Arcadian League over Sparta and Athens at battle of Mantinea. **Death of Epaminondas at Mantinea.**
361	**Plato's second visit to court of Dionysius II of Syracuse.**
360	Death of Agesilaus II in Egypt.
359	Philip II becomes king of Macedon.
357	Dion ousts Dionysius II and takes control in Syracuse. Philip II captures Amphipolis and Pydna. Marriage of Philip II and Olympias.
356	Destruction of Artemision in Ephesus. **Birth of Alexander III of Macedon.**
c. 354	**Death of Xenophon.**
354	Dion assassinated.
351	**Demosthenes' *First Philippic*.**
348	Philip II captures and destroys Olynthus. **Alexander masters his horse Bucephalus.**
348/7	**Death of Plato. Aristotle goes to live with Hermias in Assos.**
c. 347	**Birth of Demetrius of Phalerum.**

347	Demosthenes undermines Athenian peace negotiations with Philip II.
346	Philip II assumes control of Pythian Games. Restoration of Dionysius II as tyrannos of Syracuse.
344	Dionysius II deposed as tyrannos of Syracuse.
343	Death of Dionysius II in exile.
343/2	**Aristotle becomes Alexander III's tutor.**
342	**Birth of Menander.**
341	Athenian recapture of Byzantium led by Demosthenes. Execution of Hermias of Assos by Persians. **Birth of Epicurus.**
340	**Alexander III (as regent) defeats northern tribes and founds Alexandropolis.**
338	Victory of Macedon over Greek poleis at battle of Chaeronea. Philip II marries Cleopatra. **Demosthenes delivers Funeral Oration for Athenian dead at Chaeronea.**
337	Philip II and Greek League declare war on Persia.
336	Philip II assassinated. **Alexander III becomes king of Macedon. Aristotle returns to Athens and founds Lyceum.**
335	**Demosthenes incites Greek rebellion against Macedonian rule. Alexander subdues rebellions in Thrace, Illyria and Greece; destroys Thebes.**
334	Macedonian victory over Persians at battle of Granicus. Macedonian capture of Ionian coastal cities from Persia. **Alexander invades Persia.**
333	Macedonian victory over Persians at battle of Issus. **Alexander cuts Gordian Knot.**
332	Sieges of Gaza and Tyre.
332/1	**Alexander crowned pharaoh at Memphis and worshipped as son of Amun-Ra.**
331	Foundation of Alexandria. Macedonian victory over Persians at battle of Gaugamela. Capture of Babylon and Susa. **Alexander at Oracle of Siwah.**
330	Sack of Persepolis. Darius III murdered. Conspiracy of Philotas uncovered; Parmenio executed. **Alexander proclaims himself Great King of Persia.**
329	Macedonian victory over Scythians. **Alexander crosses Hindu Kush and Oxus.**
328	**Alexander murders Cleitus.**
327	Capture of Soghdiana. 'Pages' Conspiracy'; execution of Callisthenes. Invasion of India. **Alexander marries Roxane.**
326	Capture of Aornos. Macedonian victory over Porus at battle of Hydaspes; death of Bucephalus. Mutiny of Macedonian army at Hyphasis; begins journey west down Hydaspes and Indus rivers. **Alexander badly wounded at Multan.**

325	March through Gedrosian desert. Purge of satraps.	298	Alliance between Ptolemy I and Demetrius the Besieger. Pyrrhus goes to Ptolemy I as 'hostage' and marries his stepdaughter Antigone.
324	Mass marriage of Macedonians and Persians at Susa. Death of Hephaestion. Harpalus flees to Athens. Mainland Greek rebellion against Macedon. **Alexander proclaimed a deity at Olympic Games.**	297	Death of Cassander. **Demetrius of Phalerum settles in Alexandria. Ptolemy I helps to restore Pyrrhus to throne of Epirus.**
323	**Death of Alexander III in Babylon. Aristotle's self-imposed exile on Euboea.** Succession of Alexander IV and Arrhidaeus as joint kings of Macedon. Perdiccas appointed regent. **Demosthenes imprisoned for embezzlement; escapes and flees Athens.**	?c. 295	**Death of Apelles.**
		295	**Death of Pyrrhus' wife Antigone.**
		294	Demetrius the Besieger seizes throne of Macedon.
		293	Mainland poleis revolt against Demetrius the Besieger.
322	Defeat of Athens and allied Greeks by Antipater at battle of Crannon. **Death of Aristotle. Suicide of Demosthenes.**	291	Cumae and rest of Campania assimilated by Rome. **Menander drowns at Piraeus.**
		288	**Pyrrhus seizes Macedon from Demetrius the Besieger, shares it with Lysimachus.**
321	**Ptolemy I takes Alexander's body to Egypt. First performance of Menander's debut play, *Orge*.**	c. 287	**Birth of Archimedes.**
		286	**Pyrrhus defeats Antigonus Gonatas and takes Thessaly.**
320	Perdiccas' unsuccessful invasion of Egypt and assassination.	285	**Ptolemy I abdicates in favour of his younger son, Ptolemy II. Demetrius of Phalerum placed under house arrest by Ptolemy II.**
319	Death of Antipater. **Birth of Pyrrhus.**		
318	Cassander secures control of mainland Greece.	285	Demetrius the Besieger captured by Seleucus I.
317	Olympias has Arrhidaeus murdered. **Demetrius of Phalerum appointed governor of Athens by Cassander.**	284	Pyrrhus' troops desert to Lysimachus. **Pyrrhus flees to Epirus.**
		c. 283	**Death of Demetrius of Phalerum.**
316	Cassander seizes Macedon and has Olympias condemned to death. **Pyrrhus in exile at court of Glaucias of Illyria. Menander wins first prize at Lenaea with *Dyskolos*.**	283	Death of Demetrius the Besieger in captivity. Lysimachus plunders Epirus. Roman alliance with Thurii, Locris, Croton and Rhegium against Lucanians brings Rome into conflict with Taras. **Death of Ptolemy I.**
313	**Alexandria becomes Ptolemy I's capital.**		
311	**Epicurus sets up school at Mytilene.**	281	Lysimachus defeated and killed at battle of Corypedium by Seleucus I. Seleucus I killed by Ptolemy the Thunderbolt, who becomes king of Macedon. **Taras seeks help from Pyrrhus against Rome.**
c. 310	Cassander has Roxane and Alexander IV murdered.		
310	**Epicurus sets up school at Lampsacus.**		
307	Demetrius the Besieger takes Athens. **Pyrrhus returned to throne of Epirus by Glaucias of Illyria. Demetrius of Phalerum ousted from power and exiled to Thebes.**	280	**Pyrrhic victory over Romans at battle of Heraclea. Roman peace terms rejected. Pyrrhus' army marches north to Rome, then withdraws. Pyrrhus crosses to Italy.**
306	Demetrius the Besieger defeats Ptolemy I in sea battle off Rhodes. **Epicurus sets up school at Athens.**	279	**Pyrrhic victory over Romans at battle of Asculum.** Gauls kill Ptolemy the Thunderbolt in Macedon.
304	Demetrius the Besieger besieges Rhodes.	278	**Carthaginian siege of Syracuse raised by Pyrrhus. Pyrrhus crosses to Sicily.**
303	**Demetrius the Besieger marries Pyrrhus' sister Deidameia.**	277	**Majority of Sicily taken back from Carthaginian control by Pyrrhus.**
302	**Pyrrhus ousted from Epirus; flees to Demetrius the Besieger.**	276	**Pyrrhus returns to Italy.**
301	Defeat of Antigonus the One-Eyed and Demetrius the Besieger by Lysimachus and Seleucus I at battle of Ipsus. Death of Antigonus. Philetaerus begins rule in Pergamum. **Pyrrhus fights on losing side at battle of Ipsus.**	275	**Stalemate between Rome and Pyrrhus at battle of Beneventum.** Hieron II appointed commander in Syracuse. **Pyrrhus returns to Epirus.**
c. 300	Zeno of Citium begins teaching in Stoa Poikile in Athens.	274	**Most of Macedonia and Thessaly overrun by Pyrrhus.**

272	Sparta repels Pyrrhus' invasion. Pyrrhus killed in battle for Argos.	201	Victory of Philip V over Attalus I in sea battle near Erythrae. Philip V attacks Pergamum. **Philopoemen and Achaean League defeat Nabis of Sparta.**
270	Rome completes annexation of Greek cities of southern Italy. Hieron II becomes tyrannos of Syracuse. **Death of Epicurus.**	200	Philip V attacks Athens. Rome declares war on Macedon and demands Pergamene aid. **Attalus I given hero's welcome in Athens. Birth of Polybius.**
269	**Birth of Attalus I.**		
263	Hieron II concludes treaty with Rome. Death of Philetaerus of Pergamum and accession of Eumenes I.	199	**Philopoemen returns to Crete as mercenary captain.**
253	**Birth of Philopoemen.**	198	**Attalus I persuades Achaean League to abandon Philip V.**
241	Death of Eumenes I of Pergamum. **Attalus I becomes ruler of Pergamum. Victory of Attalus over Gauls at River Caicus.**	197	Roman victory over Macedon at battle of Cynoscephalae; Philip V forced to become ally of Rome. Eumenes II becomes king of Pergamum. **Death of Attalus I.**
238	**Attalus I takes title of king.**		
?235	**Death of Apollonius of Rhodes.**	193	Achaean League resumes hostilities against Sparta, but Rome imposes peace. **Philopoemen re-elected strategos of Achaean League.**
235	**Eratosthenes succeeds Apollonius of Rhodes as head of the Library at Alexandria.**		
		192	Murder of Nabis and occupation of Sparta by Aetolian League.
228	**Attalus I defeats Antiochus I to extend Pergamene control over western Asia Minor.**	191	Victory of Romans over Antiochus III at Thermopylae.
223	Cleomenes III of Sparta occupies Megalopolis. **Philopoemen conducts evacuation of Megalopolis.**	188	**Sparta is defeated and its constitution annulled by Philopoemen.** Antiochus III defeated and cedes much of western Asia Minor to Rome.
222	Victory of Achaean League and Macedon over Sparta at battle of Sellasia. **Philopoemen wounded at Sellasia.**	183	Rebellion of Messene against Achaean League. **Philopoemen captured by Messene and forced to drink hemlock. Polybius bears Philopoemen's ashes to Megalopolis.**
221	**Philopoemen goes to Crete as mercenary captain.**		
217	Defeat of Ateolian League by Philip V of Macedon.	180	**Polybius on embassy to Alexandria.**
215	Death of Hieron II of Syracuse; Hieronymus briefly succeeds as tyrannos. Syracuse and Macedon ally with Carthage in its war against Rome.	171	Outbreak of war between Rome and Macedon.
		170	**Polybius appointed second-in-command of Achaean League.**
214	Roman siege of Syracuse begins.	168	Roman victory over Macedon at battle of Pydna. Macedon partitioned and Perseus V taken as captive to Rome.
213	**Pergamene territory ceded to Seleucid empire in treaty between Attalus I and Seleucus III.**		
212	Roman capture of Syracuse. Sicily becomes a Roman province. **Archimedes killed by Roman soldiers.**	167	Rome captures Epirus. **Polybius goes to Rome as hostage.**
		146	Rome sacks Carthage and Corinth. Greece becomes Roman province. **Polybius witnesses falls of Carthage and Corinth.**
211	Aetolian League allies with Rome. **Attalus I elected strategos of Aetolian League.**		
210	**Capture of Aegina by Aetolian League and Attalus I.**	144	**Polybius leaves Greece to begin research for his Universal History.**
209	Achaean League and Macedon defeat Aetolian League at battle of Larissus River. **Philopoemen fights at battle of Larissus River.**	133	Attalus III bequeaths Pergamum to Rome.
		118	**Death of Polybius.**
		87	Rebellion of Roman provinces of Asia and Greece.
207	Victory of Achaean League over Sparta at battle of Mantinea. **Philopoemen kills Spartan king Machanidas in single combat at Mantinea.**		
		86	Greek rebellion crushed and Athens sacked.
		31	Victory of Octavian over Cleopatra VII and Mark Antony at battle of Actium.
205	End of hostilities between Achaean League and Macedon and Aetolian League and Sparta.	30	Death of Cleopatra VII, ruler of last independent Greek kingdom. Roman annexation of Egypt.
205/4	**Attalus I introduces goddess Cybele as Magna Mater to Rome.**		

Who's Who

Subjects of the fifty lives appear in **bold**, mythological characters or gods in *italics*.

Achilles Greek hero of the Trojan War, central character of the *Iliad*

Aeschines 389–314, Athenian pro-Macedonian politician

Aeschylus 525/4–456/5, Athenian tragic playwright

Agamemnon king of Mycenae, leader of legendary expedition against Troy

Agariste (1) *fl.* 560, daughter of Cleisthenes (1), wife of Megacles (2)

Agariste (2) *fl.* 495, Athenian aristocrat, mother of Pericles

Agathe Tyche see Tyche

Agathocles 361–298, tyrannos of Syracuse

Agesilaus II 444–360, king of Sparta, friend of Xenophon

Agis II r. 427–401, king of Sparta, half-brother of Agesilaus II

Alcibiades (1) (Alcibiades the Elder) *fl.* first half of fifth century, Athenian aristocrat, grandfather of Alcibiades (2)

Alcibiades (2) 450–404, Athenian politician and general

Alexander III 356–323, king of Macedon, called 'the Great'

Alexander IV 323–309, son of Alexander III and Roxane, nominal joint king of Macedon with Arrhidaeus

Amasis II r. 570–526, Egyptian pharaoh

Anacreon 582–485, lyric poet from Teos

Anaxagoras *c.* 510–428, Ionian astronomer and rationalist philosopher

Antigone (1) daughter of Oedipus

Antigone (2) *c.* 317–295, stepdaughter of Ptolemy I, wife of Pyrrhus

Antigonus the One-Eyed 382–301, general under Alexander III, subsequently ruler and self-declared king of west Asia, father of Demetrius the Besieger

Antigonus Gonatas 319–239, king of Macedon, son of Demetrius the Besieger

Antigonus III Doson 263–221, king of Macedon, grandson of Demetrius the Besieger and great-grandson of Ptolemy I

Antiochus *fl.* 410, helmsman of Alcibiades (2)

Antiochus the Hawk d. 226, rebel leader within Seleucid empire, bane of Attalus I

Antiochus III *c.* 241–187, ruler of the Seleucid empire, called 'the Great'

Antipater *c.* 397–319, general under Alexander III, subsequently regent in Macedon, father of Cassander

Apelles pre 360–?*c.* 295, court artist to Alexander III

Aphrodite goddess of sex

Apollo god of music, the arts, health, light and prophecy

Apollonius of Rhodes pre 270–?235, scholar and poet, head of the Library at Alexandria

Appian *c.* AD 95–c. AD 165, Alexandrian author of Roman history

Archelaus I r. 413–399, king of Macedon, patron of Euripides and Zeuxis

Archimedes *c.* 287–212, Syracusan mathematician and inventor

Aristagoras *fl.* 500, tyrannos of Miletus, nephew and son-in-law of Histiaeus, leader of the Ionian Revolt

Aristarchus *c.* 310–*c.* 230, Alexandrian mathematician and astronomer, first proponent of a heliocentric universe

Aristeides 530–468, Athenian politician and general, called 'the Just'

Aristogeiton d. 514, one of the 'Tyrannicides', assassin of Hipparchus

Aristophanes *c.* 446–*c.* 386, Athenian comic playwright

Aristotle 385/4–322, philosopher and polymath, tutor of Alexander III

Arrhidaeus 359–317, son of Philip II, nominal successor to Alexander III, joint king of Macedon with

Alexander IV (also known as Philip III)

Arrian *c.* AD 86–*c.* AD 160, Greek historian, polymath and politician from Bithynia

Artaphernes *fl.* 497, Persian satrap, brother of Darius I

Artaxerxes I r. 465–424, Persian Great King

Artaxerxes II r. 404–358, Persian Great King

Artemis goddess of nature, hunting and childbirth

Asclepius god of healing and medicine

Aspasia *c.* 470–*c.* 400, Milesian intellectual, ? wife of Pericles (1), mother of Pericles (2)

Athene goddess of wisdom, patron goddess of Athens

Atossa 550–475, queen of Persia, wife of Darius I, mother of Xerxes I

Attalus I 269–197, first king of Pergamum

Attalus III *c.* 170–133, king of Pergamum, bequeathed kingdom to Rome

Bacchylides *fl.* first half of fifth century, lyric and epinicean poet, nephew of Simonides

Bessus d. 329, Persian satrap, assassin of Darius III

Brasidas d. 422, Spartan general

Bucephalus d. 322, Thessalian horse of Alexander III

Caesar *see* Julius Caesar

Callias (1) *fl.* first half of fifth century, wealthy Athenian, brother-in-law of Cimon

Callias (2) *fl.* second half of fifth century, wealthy Athenian, grandson of Callias (1)

Callisthenes *c.* 360–327, Macedonian historian to Alexander III, executed for conspiracy, nephew of Aristotle

Cassander *c.* 350–297, general and king of Macedon, son of Antipater

Chaerephon *fl.* second half of fifth century, friend and follower of Socrates

Cicero (Marcus Tullius Cicero) 106–43, Roman politician, philosopher and writer

Cimon *c.* 510–450, Athenian general and politician, son of Miltiades

Cineas *fl.* 280, advisor and ambassador for Pyrrhus

Cleisthenes (1) r. *c.* 600–560, tyrannos of Sicyon, grandfather of Cleisthenes (2)

Cleisthenes (2) 570–?507, Athenian democratic reformer

Cleitus d. 328, general under Alexander III, by whom he was murdered (also known as Cleitus the Black)

Cleomenes I d. *c.* 490, king of Sparta, father-in-law of Leonidas

Cleomenes d. 322, administrator of Egypt for Alexander III

Cleomenes III 260–222, king of Sparta

Cleon ?–422, Athenian politician and general

Cleon of Halicarnassus *fl.* 400, speech-writer

Cleopatra (1) d. 336, wife of Philip II of Macedon

Cleopatra (2) (Cleopatra VII) 69–30, Ptolemaic queen of Egypt

Clinias d. 447, Athenian politician, father of Alcibiades

Codrus legendary king of Athens

Cratinus 519–422, Athenian comic dramatist

Critias 460–403, leader of the Thirty Tyrannoi in Athens, uncle of Plato

Croesus 595–*c.* 547, wealthy Lydian king defeated by Cyrus (1)

Cybele Asiatic mother goddess

Cylon (1) *fl.* mid-seventh century, Olympic victor and aspirant tyrannos of Athens in failed coup of 632

Cylon (2) *fl.* late sixth–early fifth centuries, leader of pro-democratic faction in Croton

Cyrus (1) (Cyrus II) d. 530, founder of the Persian empire, known as 'the Great', subject of Xenophon's *Education of Cyrus*

Cyrus (2) (Cyrus the Younger) d. 401, son of Darius II, pretender to the Persian throne

Damarete *fl.* mid-fifth century, wife of Gelon of Syracuse

Darius I r. 522–486, Persian Great King, known as 'the Great', invader of mainland Greece

Darius II r. 423–404, Persian Great King

Darius III r. 336–330, Persian Great King

Demaratus (1) r. *c.* 515–491, king of Sparta, co-ruler with Cleomenes I

Demaratus (2) (Demaratus of Corinth) d. 330, Macedonian courtier

Demeter Greek goddess of the earth's fertility

Demetrius of Phalerum *c.* 347–*c.* 283, governor of Athens and scholar

Demetrius the Besieger 337–283, Macedonian general and king, son of Antigonus the One-Eyed

Democritus *c.* 460–*c.* 370, philosopher and atomic scientist from Abdera

Demodeces *fl.* sixth century, itinerant doctor from Croton, physician to Polycrates and Darius I, son-in-law of Milo

Demosthenes (1) d. 413, Athenian general

Demosthenes (2) 384–322, Athenian orator and politician

Diodorus (1) *fl.* fourth century, twin son of Xenophon

Diodorus (2) *fl.* first century, historian from Sicily (also known as Diodorus Siculus)

Diogenes Laertius *fl.* third century AD, biographer of philosophers

Dion 408–354, pupil of Plato, tyrannos of Syracuse

Dionysius I *c.* 432–367, tyrannos of Syracuse, patron of Plato

Dionysius II *c.* 397–343, tyrannos of Syracuse, patron of Plato

Dionysus god of wine and drama

Dioscorides *fl.* late third century, Alexandrian lyric poet

Dorieus d. 510, Spartan prince, brother of Leonidas

Elpinice *fl.* fifth century, sister of Cimon, wife of Callias

Empedocles *c.* 495–?, Sicilian philosopher and mystic

Epaminondas *c.* 418–362, Theban general

Epicurus 341–270, Athenian philosopher

Epizelus *fl.* early fifth century, Athenian hoplite at Marathon

Eratosthenes (1) *fl.* 404, member of the Thirty Tyrannoi in Athens, prosecuted by Lysias

Eratosthenes (2) *c.* 276–*c.* 195, polymath, head of the Library at Alexandria, nicknamed 'Beta'

Eros god of lust, son of Aphrodite

Eumenes *c.* 361–316, secretary and historian of Alexander III (also known as Eumenes of Cardia)

Eumenes I r. 263–241, ruler of Pergamum, succeeded by his nephew Attalus I

Eumenes II r. 197–159, king of Pergamum, son and successor of Attalus I

Euphorion (1) *fl.* sixth century, wealthy Athenian, father of Aeschylus

Euphorion (2) *fl.* mid-fifth century, Athenian tragic playwright, son of Aeschylus

Euripides *c.* 485–406, Athenian tragic playwright

Gelon ?–478, tyrannos of Syracuse, brother of Hieron I

Glycera *fl.* late fourth century, mistress of Harpalus and Menander

Gorgias 485–380, philosopher and rhetorician from Leontini

Gryllus d. 362, twin son of Xenophon

Gylippus *fl.* late fifth century, Spartan mothax and general, who helped to defeat Athens' Sicilian Expedition

Hades god of the dead and, by extension, his realm

Hannibal 247–183/2, Carthaginian general

Harmodius d. 514, one of the 'Tyrannicides', assassin of Hipparchus

Harpalus d. 323, errant treasurer of Alexander III

Hecataeus *c.* 550–*c.* 476, innovative Milesian historian and geographer

Helen queen of Sparta, cause of the Trojan War

Hera goddess of marriage, wife of Zeus

Heracles semi-divine hero, known for his strength

Hermes god of travel and communications, conductor of souls to Hades

Hermias d. 342, eunuch pupil of Plato, ruler of Assos, friend and relative by marriage of Aristotle

Herodotus *c.* 484–?420s, historian from Halicarnassus

Hesiod ? *fl.* late eighth century, epic poet

Hieron I ?–467, tyrannos of Syracuse, brother of Gelon

Hieron II r. 270–215, tyrannos of Syracuse, patron of Archimedes

Hipparchus d. 514, Athenian, son of Peisistratus, brother of Hippias

Hippias ?–490, tyrannos of Athens, son of Peisistratus

Hippocrates (1) *fl.* late seventh century, Athenian aristocrat, father of Peisistratus

Hippocrates (2) d. 491, tyrannos of Gela, succeeded by Gelon

Hippocrates (3) (Hippocrates of Cos) *c.* 460–*c.* 370, doctor and medical writer

Histiaeus ?–?494, tyrannos of Miletus

Homer ? *fl.* late eighth century, epic poet

Horace (Quintus Horatius Flaccus) 65–8, Roman poet

Ibycus (Ibycus of Rhegium) *fl.* late sixth century, lyric poet

Inarus d. 454, Libyan king

Iphigenia daughter of Agamemnon

Jason leader of the Argonauts, consort of Medea

Jason of Pherae d. 370, general and king of Pherae in Thessaly

Julius Caesar (Gaius Julius Caesar) 100–44, Roman general and politician

Lamachus d. 414, Athenian general, one of the leaders of the Sicilian Expedition

Leonidas I *c.* 540–480, king of Sparta

Leonidas *fl.* mid-fourth century, kinsman of Olympias, tutor of Alexander III

Leotychidas *fl.* early fourth century, Spartan prince, son of Agis II (or Alcibiades)

Lucian *fl.* mid-second century AD, humorous essayist and raconteur from Samosata

Lucretius (Titus Lucretius Carus) *c.* 94–?55, Roman Epicurean epic poet

Lygdamis r. 545–524, ally of Hippias and tyrannos of Naxos

Lysander ?–395, Spartan general

Lysias 445–380, Athenian orator and speech-writer

Lysimachus (1) *fl.* first half of fifth century, son of Aristeides

Lysimachus (2) *c.* 355–281, Macedonian general and king, ruler of Thrace

Lysimachus (3) third–second century author of *The Education of Attalus I*

Megacles (1) *fl.* late seventh century, Athenian politician, grandfather of Megacles (2)

Megacles (2) *fl.* sixth century, Athenian politician, rival of Peisistratus, father of Cleisthenes (2), grandfather of Pericles

Memnon (1) Ethiopian hero at Troy, killed by Achilles

Memnon (2) (Memnon of Rhodes) 380–333, mercenary general fighting for Darius III

Menander 342–291, Athenian comic playwright

Milo *c.* 555–?, wrestler and general from Croton

Miltiades (1) (Miltiades the Elder) d. *c.* 524, Athenian politician, tyrannos of Chersonese, uncle of Miltiades (2)

Miltiades (2) *c.* 554–489, tyrannos of Chersonese and Athenian general, father of Cimon

Nabis r. 207–192, king of Sparta

Nausiphenes *fl.* second half of fourth century, philosopher from Teos, tutor of Epicurus

Neoptolemus (1) son of Achilles, also known as Pyrrhus

Neoptolemus (2) *fl.* fourth century, king of Epirus, father of Olympias

Nicias *c.* 470–413, Athenian mining mogul and general, one of the leaders of the Sicilian Expedition

Nicomachus (1) *fl.* early fourth century, doctor to the Macedonian court, father of Aristotle

Nicomachus (2) *fl.* late fourth century, philosopher, son of Aristotle

Odysseus king of Ithaca, central character of the *Odyssey*

Oedipus king of Thebes

Olorus (1) *fl.* late sixth century, Thracian king, father-in-law of Miltiades (2)

Olorus (2) *fl.* fifth century, Athenian, father of Thucydides

Olympias 375–316, Epirote princess, mother of Alexander III

Orestes hero, son of Agamemnon

Oroetes r. *c.* 530–*c.* 520, Persian satrap, killer of Polycrates

Orpheus semi-divine musician and mystic

Ovid (Publius Ovidius Naso) 43–AD 17, Roman poet

Palamedes Greek hero of the Trojan War, executed following malicious accusations by Odysseus

Pamphilus *fl.* fourth century, artist from Amphipolis, tutor of Apelles

Pan god of the countryside, sower of panic

Paralus d. 429, Athenian, son of Pericles

Paris prince of Troy, abductor of Helen, also known as Alexander

Parmenio *c.* 400–330, Macedonian general, executed for conspiracy by Alexander III

Patroclus Greek hero of the Trojan War, companion of Achilles

Paul (Saul) *c.* AD 5–67, Christian apostle and saint

Pausanias (1) d. 470, Spartan regent and general

Pausanias (2) r. 409–395, king of Sparta

Pausanias (3) *c.* AD 110–180, traveller, geographer and author from Magnesia

Peisistratus ?*c.* 605–528, tyrannos of Athens

Pelopidas d. 364, Theban general, friend of Epaminondas

Pericles (1) 495–429, Athenian statesman and general

Pericles (2) d. 406, Athenian general, son of Pericles (1) and Aspasia

Persephone goddess of the underworld, daughter of Demeter, consort of Hades

Pheidias (1) *c.* 480–*c.* 430, Athenian sculptor

Pheidias (2) *fl.* early third century, Syracusan astronomer, father of Archimedes

Philip II 382–336, king of Macedon, father of Alexander III

Philip V 221–179, king of Macedon

Philo of Byzantium *c.* 280–*c.* 220, engineer and writer

Philopoemen 253–183, Megalopolitan general and statesman

Philotas d. 330, Macedonian general, son of Parmenio, executed for conspiracy by Alexander III

Phrynichus (1) *fl.* late sixth–early fifth centuries, Athenian tragic dramatist

Phrynichus (2) *fl.* second half of fifth century, Athenian comic dramatist

Phya *fl.* mid-sixth century, Attic woman, confederate of Peisistratus

Pindar *c.* 522–*c.* 442, Theban lyric poet

Plato *c.* 427–348/7, Athenian philosopher

Pliny the Elder (Gaius Plinius Secundus) AD 23–79, Roman polymath and admiral

Plutarch *c.* AD 46–*c.* 120, polymath and biographer from Chaeronea

Polemarchus d. 404, brother of Lysias

Polybius 200–118, Megalopolitan politician and historian

Polycleitus *fl. c.* 460–*c.* 410, sculptor from Argos

Polycrates ?–522, tyrannos of Samos

Polyperchon *fl.* late fourth century, Macedonian general, successor to Antipater

Poseidon god of earthquakes, horses and the sea

Protagoras 490–420, philosopher from Abdera

Ptolemy I 367–283, Macedonian general and dynast

Ptolemy the Thunderbolt d. 279, son of Ptolemy I, king of Macedon

Ptolemy 295–272, son of Pyrrhus

Ptolemy II Philadelphus 309–246, son of Ptolemy I, king of Egypt

Ptolemy III r. 246–222, son of Ptolemy II, king of Egypt

Pyrrhus (1) *see* Neoptolemus (1)

Pyrrhus (2) (Pyrrhus of Epirus) 319–272, king of Epirus and general

Pythagoras *c.* 570–*c.* 485, Samian philosopher and mystic

Pythias *fl.* first half of fourth century, niece of Hermias, wife of Aristotle

Quintilian (Marcus Fabius Quintilianus) *c.* AD 36–*c.* 100, Roman rhetorician

Romulus legendary founder and first king of Rome

Roxane *c.* 343–*c.* 310, Soghdian princess, wife of Alexander III

Sappho post 630–*c.* 570, lyric poet from Lesbos

Scipio Aemilianus (Publius Cornelius Scipio Aemilianus Africanus) 185–129, Roman general, conqueror of Carthage, friend of Polybius

Seleucus (Seleucus I) *c.* 358–281, Macedonian general and king, ruler of eastern Asia

Serapis Graeco-Egyptian god, whose worship promoted by Ptolemy I

Simonides *c.* 556–468, lyric poet from Ceos

Socrates ?469–399, Athenian philosopher

Solon *c.* 638–558, Athenian poet, politician and lawgiver

Sophocles 497/6–405, Athenian tragic playwright and politician

Sulla (Lucius Cornelius Sulla Felix) *c.* 138–78, Roman politician and general, sacker of Athens

Themistocles 524–459, Athenian politician and general

Theocritus 315–260, Syracusan lyric, epic and bucolic poet

Theophrastus *c.* 371–*c.* 287, philosopher and scientist from Lesbos, author of *Characters*

Theron r. 488–472, tyrannos of Acragas

Theseus legendary king of Athens

Thrasydeus r. 472, son of Theron, briefly tyrannos of Acragas

Thucydides (1) *fl.* 442, son of Melesias, Athenian politician, opponent of Pericles

Thucydides (2) *c.* 455–*c.* 395, son of Olorus, Athenian general and historian

Timon of Phlius *c.* 320–*c.* 230, playwright, comic poet and Sceptic

Tissaphernes d. 395, Persian satrap

Tyche goddess of fortune, as *Agathe Tyche* (Good Fortune), worshipped increasingly after mid-fourth century

Xanthippus (1) *fl.* early fifth century, Athenian general, father of Pericles

Xanthippus (2) d. 429, Athenian, son of Pericles

Xenophon *c.* 430–*c.* 354, Athenian general, historian and literary innovator

Xerxes r. 486–465, Persian Great King, invader of mainland Greece

Zeno (1) (Zeno of Elea) *fl.* first half of fifth century, mathematician and philosopher

Zeno (2) (Zeno of Citum) 333–264, philosopher, founder of Stoicism

Zeus supreme god of the Greek pantheon

Zeus Ammon conflation of supreme Greek and Egyptian gods, possessor of an influential oracular shrine

Zeuxis ?460–?, Heraclean artist

Further Reading

The following list is by no means exhaustive, but is intended to provide suggestions for further reading from the general to the specialist. The main primary sources are most readily available in English translation in the editions specified below. In addition, the Loeb Classical Library contains texts of works in the original language with parallel translations, and many works are now accessible online both in translation and in the original languages.

GENERAL

Primary Sources

Ancient Greece: Social and Historical Documents from Archaic Times to the Death of Socrates, ed. M. Dillon and L. Garland, New York, 2000

Early Greek Philosophy, trans. J. Barnes, London, 2002

The First Philosophers: The Presocratics and Sophists, trans. R. A. H. Waterfield, Oxford, 2009

Greek Lyric Poetry: The Poems and Fragments of the Greek Iambic, Elegiac, and Melic Poets (Excluding Pindar and Bacchylides) down to 450 BC, trans. M. L. West, Oxford, 2008

Pausanias, *Guide to Greece*, trans. P. Levi, 2 vols, London, 1979

Plutarch, *The Age of Alexander*, trans. T. Duff and I. Scott-Kilvert, London, 2012

——, *Greek Lives: Lycurgus, Pericles, Solon, Nicias, Themistocles, Alcibiades, Cimon, Agesilaus, Alexander*, trans. P. Stadter and R. A. H. Waterfield, Oxford, 2008

——, *On Sparta*, trans. R. Talbert, London, 2005

——, *The Rise and Fall of Athens*, trans. I. Scott-Kilvert, London, 1973

Translated Documents of Greece & Rome: Archaic Times to the End of the Peloponnesian War, ed. C. W. Fornara, Cambridge, 1983

Overviews

Aubet, M. E., *The Phoenicians and the West: Politics, Colonies and Trade*, Cambridge, 2001

Boardman, J., J. Griffin and O. Murray (eds), *The Oxford History of the Classical World*, Oxford, 1986

Boys-Stones, G., B. Graziosi and P. Vasunia (eds), *The Oxford Handbook of Hellenic Studies*, Oxford, 2009

Cartledge, P., *Ancient Greece: A History in Eleven Cities*, Oxford, 2009

——, *The Greeks: A Portrait of Self and Others*, London, 2002

——, *The Spartans: An Epic History*, London, 2013

Ehrenberg, V., *From Solon to Socrates*, London, 1968

Fine, J. V. A., *The Ancient Greeks: A Critical History*, Cambridge, MA, 1983

Finley, M. I., *The Ancient Greeks*, London, 1963

Hornblower, S., and A. Spawforth (eds), *The Oxford Companion to Classical Civilization*, Oxford, 2004

Hornblower, S., A. Spawforth and E. Eidinow (eds), *The Oxford Classical Dictionary*, Oxford, 2012

McEvedy, C., *Cities of the Classical World*, London, 2011

Pomeroy, S. B., *Ancient Greece: A Political, Social, and Cultural History*, New York, 1999

Political and Military

Bury, J. B., and R. Meiggs, *A History of Greece*, London, 1975

Campbell, B., and L. A. Tritle (eds), *The Oxford Handbook of Warfare in the Classical World*, Oxford, 2013

Garlan, Y., *War in the Ancient World: A Social History*, London, 1975

Hammond, N. G. L., *A History of Greece to 322 BC*, Oxford, 1959

Lazenby, J. F., *The Defence of Greece*, Warminster, 1993

Salkever, S., (ed.), *The Cambridge Companion to Ancient Greek Political Thought*, Cambridge, 2009

Shipley, G., *A History of Samos, 800–188 BC*, London, 1987

Social and Cultural

Beye, C. R., *Ancient Epic Poetry: Homer, Apollonius, Virgil*, Ithaca, NY, 1993

Budelmann, F., (ed.), *The Cambridge Companion to Greek Lyric*, Cambridge, 2009

Easterling, P. E., *The Cambridge Companion to Greek Tragedy*, Cambridge, 1997

Easterling, P. E., and B. M. W. Knox, *The Cambridge History of Classical Literature*, Cambridge, 1985

Fantham, E., *Women in the Ancient World*, Oxford, 1954

Gagarin, M., and D. Cohen (eds), *The Cambridge Companion to Ancient Greek Law*, Cambridge, 2005

Garland, R., *The Greek Way of Life*, Bristol, 1996

Gerber, D. E., *A Companion to the Greek Lyric Poets*, Boston, MA, 1997

Graziosi, B., *Inventing Homer: The Early Reception of Epic*, Cambridge, 2002

Habinek, T. N., *Ancient Rhetoric and Oratory*, Oxford, 2004

Hornblower, S., *Thucydides and Pindar: Historical Narrative and the World of Epinikian Poetry*, Oxford, 2004

Howatson, M. C., *The Oxford Companion to Classical Literature*, Oxford, 2013

Jenkins, I., *Greek Architecture and Its Sculptures*, London, 2006

Lesky, A., *Greek Tragedy*, London, 1979

Luce, J. V., *An Introduction to Greek Philosophy*, London, 1992

Luce, T. J., *The Greek Historians*, London, 1997

McDonald, M., and M. Walton (eds), *The Cambridge Companion to Greek and Roman Theatre*, Cambridge, 2007

Neer, R. T., *Art and Archaeology of the Greek World*, London, 2012

Page, D., *Sappho and Alcaeus: An Introduction to the Study of Ancient Lesbian Poetry*, Oxford, 1979

Parker, R., *Athenian Religion: A History*, Oxford, 1996

Revermann, M., (ed.), *The Cambridge Companion to Greek Comedy*, Cambridge, 2014

Rowe, C. R., *An Introduction to Greek Ethics*, London, 1976

Sedley, D., (ed.), *The Cambridge Companion to Greek and Roman Philosophy*, Cambridge, 2003

Sommerstein, A. H., *Greek Drama and Dramatists*, London, 2002

Woodford, S., *The Art of Greece and Rome*, Cambridge, 1982

FROM HOMER TO THE BIRTH OF DEMOCRACY
(CHAPTERS 1–3)
....

Primary Sources

Aeschylus, *Oresteia*, trans. C. Collard, Oxford, 2008

———, *Persians and Other Plays*, trans. C. Collard, Oxford, 2009

Hesiod, *Theogony and Works and Days*, trans. M. L. West, Oxford, 2008

Homer, *The Iliad*, trans. B. Graziosi and A. Verity, Oxford, 2012

———, *The Odyssey*, trans. G. S. Kirk and W. Shewring, Oxford, 2008

Pindar, *The Complete Odes*, trans. S. Instone and A. Verity, Oxford, 2008

Sappho, *Stung with Love: Poems and Fragments of Sappho*, trans. A. Poochigian, London, 2009

General

Andrewes, A., *The Greek Tyrants*, London, 1956

Boardman, J., *The Greeks Overseas: Their Early Colonies and Trade*, London, 1999

Murray, O., *Early Greece*, London, 1993

Shapiro, H. A., (ed.), *The Cambridge Companion to Archaic Greece*, Cambridge, 2007

Snodgrass, A., *Archaic Greece: The Age of Experiment*, Berkeley, CA, 1992

Political and Military

Dunbabin, T. J., *The Western Greeks: The History of Sicily and South Italy from the Foundation of the Greek Colonies to 480 BC*, Oxford, 1948

Lavelle, B. M., *Fame, Money and Power: The Rise of Peisistratos and Democratic Tyranny at Athens*, Ann Arbor, MI, 2004

McGlew, J. F., *Tyranny and Political Culture in Ancient Greece*, Ithaca, NY, 1993

Osborne, R., *Greece in the Making, 1200–479 BC*, London, 1996

Podlecki, A. J., *The Political Background of Aeschylean Tragedy*, Ann Arbor, MI, 1966

Social and Cultural

Burkert, W., *Lore and Science in Ancient Pythagoreanism*, Cambridge, MA, 1972

Fisher, N. R. E., *Social Values in Classical Athens*, London, 1976

Guthrie, W. K. C., *The Greek Philosophers: From Thales to Aristotle*, London, 1960

———, *A History of Greek Philosophy*: Vol. 1, *The Earlier Presocratics and the Pythagoreans*, Cambridge, 1979

———, *A History of Greek Philosophy*: Vol. 2, *The Presocratic Tradition from Parmenides to Democritus*, Cambridge, 1979

Hall, J. M., *A History of the Archaic Greek World, ca. 1200–479 BCE*, New York, 2013

Long, A. A., (ed.), *The Cambridge Companion to Early Greek Philosophy*, Cambridge, 1999

Rosenmeyer, T. G., *The Art of Aeschylus*, Berkeley, CA, 1982

Sommerstein, A. H., *Aeschylean Tragedy*, London, 2010

West, M. L., *Early Greek Philosophy and the Orient*, Oxford, 1971

Lives

Bowra, C. M., *Pindar*, Oxford, 1964

duBois, P., *Sappho Is Burning*, Berkeley, CA, 1995

Greene, E., *Reading Sappho: Contemporary Approaches*, Berkeley, CA, 1996

Kahn, C. H., *Pythagoras and the Pythagoreans*, Indianapolis, IN, 2001

Kurke, L., *The Traffic in Praise: Pindar and the Poetics of Social Economy*, Berkeley, CA, 1991

Murray, G., *Aeschylus: The Creator of Tragedy*, Oxford, 1978

Reidwig, C., and S. Rendall, *Pythagoras*, Ithaca, NY, 2005

Primary Sources

Aristophanes, *Birds and Other Plays*, trans. S. Halliwell, Oxford, 2008

——, *Frogs and Other Plays*, trans. D. Barrett, London, 2007

——, *Lysistrata and Other Plays*, trans. A. H. Sommerstein, London, 2003

Aristotle, *The Art of Rhetoric*, trans. H. Lawson-Tancred, London, 1991

——, *The Athenian Constitution*, trans. P. Rhodes, London, 1984

——, *The Eudemian Ethics*, trans. A. Kenny, Oxford, 2011

——, *The Metaphysics*, trans. H. Lawson-Tancred, London, 1998

——, *The Nicomachean Ethics*, trans. L. Brown and D. Ross, Oxford, 2009

——, *Physics*, trans. D. Bostock and R. A. H. Waterfield, Oxford, 2008

——, *Poetics*, trans. A. Kenny, Oxford, 2013

——, *The Politics*, trans. R. F. Stalley and E. Barker, Oxford, 2009

Demosthenes, *Selected Speeches*, trans. C. Carey and R. A. H. Waterfield, Oxford, 2014

Demosthenes and Aeschines, trans. A. N. W. Saunders, London, 1975

Euripides, *The Bacchae and Other Plays*, trans. J. Davie, London, 2006

——, *Bacchae and Other Plays*, trans. E. Hall and J. Morwood, Oxford, 2008

——, *Electra and Other Plays*, trans. P.E. Easterling and D. Raeburn, London, 2008

——, *Heracles and Other Plays*, trans. J. Davie, London, 2002

——, *Medea and Other Plays*, trans. E. Hall and J. Morwood, Oxford, 2008

——, *Orestes and Other Plays*, trans. J. Morwood, E. Hall and R. A. H. Waterfield, Oxford, 2008

——, *Three Plays: Alcestis, Hippolytus, Iphigeneia in Tauris*, trans. P. Vellacott, London, 1972

——, *The Trojan Women and Other Plays*, trans. E. Hall and J. Morwood, Oxford, 2008

Greek Political Oratory, trans. A. N. W. Saunders, London, 1970

Herodotus, *The Histories*, trans. T. Holland, London, 2013

——, *The Landmark Herodotus*, trans. Andrea L. Purvis, London, 2007

Plato, *Early Socratic Dialogues*, trans. C. Emlyn-Jones and T. Saunders, London, 2005

——, *Gorgias*, trans. R. A. H. Waterfield, Oxford, 2008

——, *The Last Days of Socrates*, trans. H. Tarrant and C. Rowe, London, 2010

——, *The Laws*, trans. T. Saunders, London, 2005

——, *Meno and Other Dialogues*, trans. R. A. H. Waterfield, Oxford, 2009

——, *Phaedrus*, trans. R. A. H. Waterfield, Oxford, 2009

——, *Protagoras*, trans. C. C. W. Taylor, Oxford, 2009

——, *The Republic*, trans. M. Lane and D. Lee, London, 2007

——, *Republic*, trans. C. Rowe, London, 2012

——, *Symposium*, trans. R. A. H. Waterfield, Oxford, 2008

——, *Theaetetus*, trans. L. Brown and J. McDowell, Oxford, 2014

——, *Timaeus and Critias*, trans. A. Gregory, and R. A. H. Waterfield, Oxford, 2008

Sophocles, *Antigone, Oedipus the King, Electra*, trans. E. Hall and H. D. F. Kitto, Oxford, 2008

——, *The Three Theban Plays*, trans R. Fagles, London, 1984

——, *Electra and Other Plays*, trans. P. E. Easterling and D. Raeburn, London, 2008

Thucydides, *The Landmark Thucydides*, trans. Richard Crawley, London, 1998

——, *The Peloponnesian War*, trans. P. J. Rhodes and M. Hammond, Oxford, 2009

Xenophon, *Conversations of Socrates*, trans. H. Tredennick, London, 1990

——, *Hiero the Tyrant and Other Treatises*, trans. R. A. H. Waterfield, London, 2006

——, *A History of My Time (Hellenica)*, trans. R. Warner, London, 1979

——, *The Landmark Xenophon's Hellenika*, trans. John Marincola, London, 2011

——, *The Persian Expedition*, trans. R. Warner, London, 2004

General

Burn, A. R., *Pericles and Athens*, London, 1948

Hale, J. R., *Lords of the Sea: The Triumph and Tragedy of Ancient Athens*, London, 2010

Miller, M., *Athens and Persia in the Fifth Century BC*, Cambridge, 1997

Samsons, L. J., (ed.), *The Cambridge Companion to the Age of Pericles*, Cambridge, 2007

Tritle, L. A., *The Greek World in the Fourth Century*, London, 1997

Political and Military

Anderson, J. K., *Military Theory and Practice in the Age of Xenophon*, Berkeley, CA, 1970

Cartledge, P., *After Thermopylae: The Oath of Plataea and the End of the Graeco-Persian Wars*, Oxford, 2013

de Ste Croix, G. E. M., *The Origins of the Peloponnesian War*, London, 1972

Hansen, M. H., *The Athenian Democracy in the Age of Demosthenes*, Norman, OK, 1999

Jones, A. H. M., *Athenian Democracy*, Oxford, 1957

Kagan, D., *The Fall of the Athenian Empire*, Ithaca, NY, 1987

————, *The Outbreak of the Peloponnesian War*, Ithaca, NY, 1969

————, *The Peace of Nicias and the Sicilian Expedition*, Ithaca, NY, 1981

————, *The Peloponnesian War: Athens and Sparta in Savage Conflict, 431–404 BC*, New York, 2003

————, *Pericles of Athens and the Birth of Democracy*, New York, 1991

McGregor, M. F., *The Athenians and Their Empire*, Vancouver, 1987

Meiggs, R., *The Athenian Empire*, Oxford, 1972

Mossé, C., *Athens in Decline*, London, 1973

Phillips, D., *Athenian Political Oratory*, London, 2004

Rhodes, P. J., *The Athenian Empire*, Oxford, 1985

————, *A History of the Classical Greek World, 478–323 BC*, New York, 2010

Strauss, B. S., *Athens After the Peloponnesian War*, Ithaca, NY, 1986

Vidal-Naquet, P., and P. Leveque, *Cleisthenes the Athenian: An Essay on the Representation of Space and Time in Greek Political Thought from the End of the Sixth Century to the Death of Plato*, Atlantic Highlands, NJ, 1996

Social and Cultural

Barnes, J., *The Presocratic Philosophers*, London, 1982

Boardman, J., *Greek Sculpture: The Classical Period*, London, 1985

————, (ed.), *The Oxford History of Classical Art*, Oxford, 1977

Dewald, C., and J. Marincola (eds), *The Cambridge Companion to Herodotus*, Cambridge, 2006

Dover, K. J., *Aristophanic Comedy*, Berkeley, CA, 1992

————, *Greek Popular Morality in the Time of Plato and Aristotle*, Berkeley, CA, 1974

Guthrie, W. K. C., *A History of Greek Philosophy*: Vol. 3, *The Fifth Century Enlightenment*, Cambridge, 1969

————, *A History of Greek Philosophy*: Vol. 4, *Plato: The Man and his Dialogues: Earlier Period:*, Cambridge, 1986

————, *A History of Greek Philosophy*: Vol. 5, *The Later Plato and the Academy*, Cambridge, 1986

————, *A History of Greek Philosophy*: Vol. 6, *Aristotle: An Encounter*, Cambridge, 1990

Hermann, G., *Morality and Behaviour in Democratic Athens*, Cambridge, 2006

Kerferd, G. B., *The Sophistic Movement*, Cambridge, 1981

Kirk, G. S., J. E. Raven and M. Schofield, *The Presocratic Philosophers*, Cambridge, 1983

Kraut, R., (ed.), *The Cambridge Companion to Plato*, Cambridge, 1992

MacDowell, D. M., *Aristophanes and Athens: An Introduction to the Plays*, Oxford, 1995

Morrison, D. R., (ed.), *The Cambridge Companion to Socrates*, Cambridge, 2010

Neils, J., (ed.), *The Parthenon from Antiquity to the Present*, Cambridge, 2005

Pickard-Cambridge, A., *The Dramatic Festivals of Athens*, Oxford, 1988

Rist, J. M., *Epicurus: An Introduction*, Cambridge, 1972

————, (ed.), *The Stoics*, Berkeley, CA, 1978

Stuttard, D. A., *Parthenon: Power and Politics on the Acropolis*, London, 2013

————, *Power Games: Ritual and Rivalry at the Greek Olympics*, London, 2012

Thomas, R., *Herodotus in Context*, Cambridge, 2000

Wardy, R., *The Birth of Rhetoric: Gorgias, Plato and Their Successors*, New York, 1996

Warren, J., (ed.), *The Cambridge Companion to Epicureanism*, Cambridge, 2009

Webster, T. B. L., *The Tragedies of Euripides*, London, 1967

Lives

Adcock, F. E., *Thucydides and His History*, Cambridge, 1963

Anderson, J. K., *Xenophon*, London, 2001

Cartledge, P., *Aristophanes and His Theatre of the Absurd*, Bristol, 1991

Dillery, J., *Xenophon and the History of His Times*, London, 1995

Dover, K. J., *Thucydides*, Oxford, 1973

Ehrenberg, V., *Sophocles and Pericles*, Oxford, 1954

Ellis, W. M., *Alcibiades*, London, 1989

Henry, M. M., *Prisoner of History: Aspasia of Miletus and Her Biographical Tradition*, Oxford, 1995

Herington, C. J., *Aeschylus*, New Haven, CT, 1986

Kagan, D., *Thucydides: The Reinvention of History*, London, 2010

Podlecki, A., *Pericles and His Circle*, London, 1998

Rhodes, P. J., *Alcibiades*, Barnsley, 2011

Taylor, C. C. W., *Socrates: A Very Short Introduction*, Oxford, 2001

Tracy, S. V., (ed.), *Pericles: A Sourcebook and Reader*, Berkeley, CA, 2009

Vlastos, G., *Socrates, Ironist and Moral Philosopher*, Ithaca, NY, 1991

THE HELLENISTIC AGE AND ROME
(CHAPTERS 7–9)

Primary Sources

Apollonius, *Jason and the Golden Fleece*, trans. R. Hunter, Oxford, 2009

Arrian, *Alexander the Great: The Anabasis and the Indica*, trans. J. Atkinson and M. Hammond, Oxford, 2013

———, *The Campaigns of Alexander*, trans. A. de Selincourt, London, 1971

———, *The Landmark Arrian: The Campaigns of Alexander the Great*, trans. P. Mensch, New York, 2012

Curtius Rufus, *The History of Alexander*, trans. J. Yardley, London, 1984

Epicurus, *The Art of Happiness*, trans. J. K. Strodach, London, 2013

Greek Pastoral Poetry, trans. A. Holden, London, 1973

Menander, *The Plays and Fragments*, trans. P. Brown and M. Balme, Oxford, 2008

Polybius, *The Histories*, trans. B. McGing and R. A. H. Waterfield, Oxford, 2010

Theocritus, *Idylls*, trans. R. Hunter and A. Verity, Oxford, 2008

General

Austin, M. M., *The Hellenistic World from Alexander to the Roman Conquest*, Cambridge, 1981

Bugh, G. R., (ed.), *The Cambridge Companion to the Hellenistic World*, Cambridge, 2006

Burn, A. R., *Alexander the Great and the Hellenistic World*, New York, 1962

Cary, M., *A History of the Greek World from 323 to 146 BC*, London, 1963

Erskine, A., (ed.), *A Companion to the Hellenistic World*, Oxford, 2003

Green, P., *Alexander the Great and the Hellenistic Age*, London, 2007

———, *Alexander to Actium: The Historic Evolution of the Hellenistic Age*, London, 1990

Shipley, G., *The Greek World After Alexander 323–30 BC*, London, 2000

Walbank, F. W., *The Hellenistic World*, London, 1992

Political and Military

Allen, R. E., *The Attalid Kingdom: A Constitutional History*, Oxford, 1983

Beck, H., *Central Greece and the Politics of Power in the Fourth Century BC*, Cambridge, 2008

Goldsworthy, A., *The Punic Wars*, London, 2000

Grimal, P., *Hellenism and the Rise of Rome*, London, 1968

Walbank, F. W., *Polybius, Rome and the Hellenistic World: Essays and Reflections*, Cambridge, 2002

Waterfield, R. A. H., *Dividing the Spoils: The War for Alexander the Great's Empire*, Oxford, 2012

———, *Xenophon's Retreat*, London, 2006

Wood, M., *In the Footsteps of Alexander the Great*, Berkeley, CA, 1997

Social and Cultural

Algra, K., J. Mansfeld and M. Schofield (eds), *The Cambridge History of Hellenistic Philosophy*, Cambridge, 1999

Bett, R., *The Cambridge Companion to Ancient Scepticism*, Cambridge, 2010

Clauss, J. J., and M. Cuypers (eds), *A Companion to Hellenistic Literature*, Oxford, 2010

Feldherr, A., (ed.), *The Cambridge Companion to the Roman Historians*, Cambridge, 2009

Hadas, M., *Hellenistic Culture: Fusion and Diffusion*, New York, 1959

Lewis, N., *Greeks in Ptolemaic Egypt: Case Studies in the Social History of the Hellenistic World*, Oxford, 1986

Martin, L. H., *Hellenistic Religions*, Oxford, 1987

Lives

Cartledge, P., *Alexander the Great: The Truth Behind the Myth*, London, 2013

Champion, J., *Pyrrhus of Epirus*, Barnsley, 2009

Ellis, W. M., *Ptolemy of Egypt*, London, 1993

Garoufalias, P., *Pyrrhus, King of Epirus*, London, 1979

Green, P., *Alexander of Macedon, 356–323 B.C.: A Historical Biography*, Berkeley, CA, 1991

Hammond, N. G. L., *Alexander the Great*, London, 1981

Lane Fox, R., *Alexander the Great*, London, 1973

Stoneman, R., *Alexander the Great*, London, 2004

Sources of Illustrations

2 Musei Vaticani, Rome; 11 British Museum, London; 12 Musei Capitolini, Rome; 15 Metropolitan Museum of Art, New York. Rogers Fund, 1947; 19 British Museum, London; 21 I Musei Capitolini, Rome; 22 National Archaeological Museum, Athens; 29 Acropolis Museum, Athens; 30 Metropolitan Museum of Art, New York. Classical Purchase Fund, 1978; 33 Prisma Archivo/Alamy; 35 Zoonar GmbH/Alamy; 36 Interfoto/Alamy; 39 Walters Art Museum, Baltimore; 43 Photo Art Archive/Alamy; 47 akg-images/Erich Lessing; 51 Museo Archeologico Nazionale, Naples; 54–55 Heidi Grassley © Thames & Hudson Ltd, London; 59 Museo Archeologico Nazionale, Naples; 60 Images & Stories/Alamy; 63 National Museums of Scotland, Edinburgh; 64 Archaeological Museum, Olympia; 65 Photo Scala, Florence; 69 The Art Archive/Museo Archeologico Nazionale Naples/Gianni Dagli Orti; 70 Erin Babnik/Alamy; 74 D.A.I., Rome; 77 Ancient Art & Architecture Collection Ltd/Alamy; 78 akg-images/Nimatallah; 81 Archaeological Museum, Sparta; 86 The Art Archive/Manuel Cohen; 88 Archaeological Museum, Delphi; 91 Heritage Image Partnership Ltd/Alamy; 95 The Art Archive/De Agostini Picture Library; 97 Hemis/Alamy; 99 Photo Scala, Florence; 104 akg-images/Nimatallah; 109 Musée du Louvre, Paris; 112 Musei Vaticani, Rome; 121 Erin Babnik/Alamy; 122 Birmingham Museums & Art Gallery; 125 Musei Vaticani, Rome; 129 Ancient Art & Architecture Collection Ltd/Alamy; 136 Antikensammlung, Staatliche Museen zu Berlin; 140 bpk/Antikensammlung, Staatliche Museen zu Berlin; 142 J. Paul Getty Museum, Malibu; 147 Photo Scala, Florence; 153 Archaeological Museum, Ephesus; 155 GL Archive/Alamy; 158–59 British Museum, London; 163 Archaeological Museum, Pella; 168 British Museum, London; 174 Rijksmuseum, Amsterdam; 176 akg-images/De Agostini Picture Library; 181 North Wind Picture Archives/Alamy; 184–85 Photo Scala, Florence – courtesy of the Ministero Beni e Att. Culturali; 189 Palazzo Altemps, Rome; 192 Photo Scala, Florence; 197 Acropolis Museum, Athens; 200–1 Museo Archeologico Nazionale, Naples; 205 Archaeological Museum, Istanbul; 208 British Museum, London; 211 J. Paul Getty Museum, Malibu; 213 Museo Archeologico, Florence; 214 Mary Evans Picture Library/Alamy; 218 The Art Archive/Collection Dagli Orti; 221 Galleria degli Uffizi, Florence; 223 Musei Capitolini, Rome; 227 Museo Archeologico Nazionale, Naples; 233 The Art Archive/Musée du Louvre, Paris/Gianni Dagli Orti; 241 akg-images/Erich Lessing; 245 The Art Archive/Museo Nazionale Palazzo Altemps Rome/Gianni Dagli Orti; 247 Musée du Louvre, Paris; 253 The Art Archive/De Agostini Picture Library; 256 Ara Pacis, Rome; 258 Musei Vaticani, Rome

Acknowledgments

The idea for this book – a history of ancient Greece told through the lives of some of its most outstanding sons and daughters – came from Colin Ridler, commissioning editor for Thames and Hudson. I consider it a great honour that he entrusted me with its execution, and am profoundly grateful to him for setting me such a wonderfully exhilarating challenge. I hope he feels that I have risen to it. I am hugely grateful, too, to Alice Reid, Associate Editor at T&H, who has guided me on my way so patiently and whose unstinting encouragement and unerring insights have made the writing process seem significantly less onerous than it might otherwise have been.

I should like also to thank Kit Shepherd, a colossus among editors, who not only (with laser-like intensity) exposed many a shortcoming in the text, but communicated his concerns with charm and humour. Thanks, too, to Kate Slotover, by dint of whose design the book is a thing of such beauty, to Sally Nicholls, who has ensured that the illustrations complement the text so perfectly, to Martin Lubikowski for his elegant and clear maps, to Celia Falconer, who has overseen the production with such efficiency and to Rosalie Macfarlane, who has promoted the book with her usual, if extraordinary finesse.

Although tremendously enjoyable, the process has been arduous, and has seen me plunged into long spells of purdah as I researched and wrote. So, I would like to pay especial tribute to the tolerance and support of my friends and family, and especially my wife Emily Jane, a tower of strength, without whom this book could never have been written, and to whom in gratitude for everything it is dedicated. Lastly, I must acknowledge the vital role played by our two cats, Stanley and Oliver, who were never far away when there was work to be done and who (usually) helped to put things in perspective.

Index